NATIONAL HEALTH INSURANCE: CAN WE LEARN FROM CANADA?

Edited by

Spyros Andreopoulos

Foreword by

Philip R. Lee, M.D.

A volume on current health care issues from

The Sun Valley Forum on National Health, Inc.

A WILEY BIOMEDICAL-HEALTH PUBLICATION

JOHN WILEY & SONS

New York • London • Sydney • Toronto

Library of Congress Cataloging in Publication Data

Sun Valley Forum on National Health.
National health insurance.

(A Wiley-biomedical health publication)
Proceedings of the Forum's 1974 symposium.
"A volume on current health care issues.
Includes index.
1. Insurance, Health—Canada—Congresses. 2. Medical economics—Canada—Congresses. I. Andreopoulos, Spyros, 1929- ed. II. Title. [DNLM: 1. Insurance, Health—Canada—Congresses. 2. Insurance, Health—U. S. —Congresses. 3. State medicine—Canada—Congresses. 4. State medicine—U.S.—Congresses. W275 DC2 N21 1974]
HD7102.C2S85 1975 368.4'2'00971 75-2348

ISBN 0-471-02925-4

Printed in the United States of America

10 9 8 7 6 5 4 3 2 1

CONTENTS

Page

CONTENTS

LIST OF FIGURES AND TABLES

Chapter One

ABOUT THE AUTHORS AND CONTRIBUTORS

Stuart H. Altman, Ph.D. is deputy assistant secretary for planning and evaluation/health in the Department of Health, Education and Welfare, Washington, D.C. . . . Chairman of the Royal Commission of Enquiry on Health and Social Welfare from 1966 to 1970, **Claude Castonguay** was elected to the national assembly in Quebec and entered the cabinet as minister of the Department of Social Affairs during the crucial period of the implementation of Medicare. He returned to private life in 1973 as a partner in the firm of Castonguay, Pouliot, Guérard et Associés, Inc., actuaries and counselors in social affairs in Quebec . . . **Maurice LeClair, M.D.** is deputy minister of Health and Welfare of Canada. Before that he served as chairman of the department of medicine at the University of Sherbrooke, as director of its clinical sciences division and as dean of the school of medicine . . . British born and Harvard trained, **Robert G. Evans, Ph.D.** wrote *Efficiency Incentives in Hospital Reimbursement* and went on to become an authority on health economics. He is an associate professor in the department of economics at the University of British Columbia in Vancouver and also serves as consultant to a number of committees and projects dealing with hospital, health insurance and medical matters . . . **Horace Kreever, Q.C.** is a distinguished professor of law at the University of Toronto. He teaches civil procedure, law and health care, and legal medicine. He served on the Federal Community Health Center Project (The Hastings Committee) and was a key figure in the enactment of the Human Tissue Gift Act of 1971 . . . **Theodore R. Marmor, Ph.D.**, a political scientist at the University of Chicago, has authored *Politics of Medicare* (Routledge and Aldine, 1970, 1973) and edited *Poverty Policy* (Aldine, 1971). He was a special assistant to former HEW undersecretary Wilbur Cohen at the beginning of the Medicare debate. His chief interests are in health, social security and welfare issues . . . A former HEW assistant secretary for health and scientific affairs and chancellor at the University of California, San Francisco, **Philip Lee, M.D.** is co-author with Milton Silverman of *Pills, Profits and Politics* (University of California Press, 1974). Lee directs the Health Policy Program at UCSF . . . **Spyros Andreopoulos** is information officer of the Stanford University Medical Center and editor of Stanford M.D. magazine. He edited two books, *Medical Cure and Medical Care* (Milbank Memorial Fund, 1973) and *Primary Care: Where Medicine Fails* (John Wiley & Sons, 1974). Andreopoulos is a member of the National Association of

Science Writers and the American Medical Writers Association, and is active on several advisory groups dealing with health education matters.

Participants

Stuart H. Altman, Ph.D.
Deputy Assistant Secretary for Planning and Evaluation/Health, Department of Health, Education and Welfare, Office of the Secretary, Washington, D.C.

Odin Anderson, Ph.D.
Director, Center for Health Administration Studies, University of Chicago

William O. Bailey
Executive Vice President, Aetna Life & Casualty Company, Hartford, Connecticut

Peter J. Banks, M.D.
Past President, the Canadian Medical Association, Ottawa, Ontario

Richard Berman
Assistant Dean and Associate Hospital Director for Ambulatory Care Services, New York, Cornell Medical Center, New York, New York

Robert Blendon, Ph.D.
Vice President, The Robert Wood Johnson Foundation, Princeton, New Jersey

Howard Bowen, Ph.D.
Chancellor, Claremont University Center, Claremont, California

Phillip Caper, M.D.
Staff Professional, Senate Health Subcommittee, Committee on Labor and Public Welfare, The United States Senate, Washington, D.C.

Claude Castonguay
Pouliot, Guérard, Castonguay & Associates Inc., Actuaries and Counselors in Social Affairs, Quebec, Canada

Matthew Clark
Newsweek, Rye, New York

Jay B. Constantine
Professional Staff Member, Committee on Finance, United States Senate, Washington, D.C.

Lloyd C. Elam, M.D.
President, Meharry Medical College, Nashville, Tennessee

John I. Evans, M.D.
President, The University of Toronto, Canada

Robert G. Evans, Ph.D.
Associate Professor, Department of Economics, University of British Columbia, Vancouver, B.C., Canada

Melvin A. Glasser
Director, Social Security Department, United Automobile Workers, Solidarity House, Detroit, Michigan

Arthur E. Hess
Deputy Commissioner, Social Security Administration, Department of Health, Education and Welfare, Baltimore, Maryland

John R. Hogness, M.D.
President, The University of Washington, Seattle, Washington

Joan Hollobon
Medical Reporter, *The Globe and Mail,* Toronto, Ontario, Canada

Lee Hyde, M.D.
Professional Staff Member, Interstate and Foreign Commerce Committee, U.S. House of Representatives, Washington, D.C.

Horace Kreever, Q.C.
University of Toronto, Toronto, Canada

Maurice LeClair, M.D.
Deputy Minister of Health and Welfare, Canada, Ottawa, Canada

Philip R. Lee, M.D.
Director, Health Policy Program, School of Medicine, University of California in San Francisco

Robert G. Lindee
Vice President, the Henry J. Kaiser Family Foundation, Palo Alto, California

Gordon McLachlan
The Nuffield Provincial Hospitals Trust, London, England

Florence Mahoney
Washington, D.C.

Margaret Mahoney
Vice President, the Robert Wood Johnson Foundation, Inc., Princeton, New Jersey

Bayless Manning
President, Council on Foreign Relations, Inc., New York, New York

Theodore R. Marmor, Ph.D.
Associate Professor of Policy, School of Social Services Administration, University of Chicago

Judith K. Miller
Director, Health Staff Seminar, The George Washington University, Washington, D.C.

The Hon. Richard B. Ogilvie
Isham, Lincoln & Beale, Counselors at Law, Chicago, Illinois

Don K. Price
Dean, John Fitzgerald Kennedy School of Government, Harvard University, Cambridge, Massachusetts

Judith Randall
Washington Star-News, Washington, D.C.

Jean Rochon, M.D.
Chairman, Department of Health and Community Medicine, Laval University, Quebec, P.W., Canada

Robert M. Sigmond
Executive Vice-President, Albert Einstein Medical Center, Philadelphia, Pennsylvania

Mitchell Spellman, M.D.
Dean, Drew Postgraduate Medical School, Los Angeles, California

John G. Veneman
Veneman Associates, San Francisco, California

Kerr L. White, M.D.
Professor, Department of Medical Care and Hospitals, School of Hygiene and Public Health, The Johns Hopkins University, Baltimore, Maryland

Dwight L. Wilbur, M.D.
Practicing Physician, former President, American Medical Association, San Francisco, California

Editor:

Spyros Andreopoulos
Information Officer, Stanford University Medical Center, Stanford, California

Staff:

Judith Gustafson
Council on Foreign Relations, New York, New York

Judy Spates Housel
Sun Valley Forum on National Health, Inc., Sun Valley, Idaho

FOREWORD • PHILIP R. LEE

The year 1974 has seen national health insurance move to the top of the domestic policy agenda in the United States. In the debates on the many national health insurance proposals before the Congress, some basic questions repeatedly surface: Who will be covered? What services will be included? How will physicians, hospitals and other providers be paid? Who will pay and how? What will be the role of private insurance companies in the administration of the program? How will costs be controlled? And how can the goals of equity and access to care be reconciled with the goal of cost control?

These and other questions lay behind the decision to focus on the Canadian experience with national health insurance at the 1974 symposium of the Sun Valley Forum on National Health. The Canadian experience was felt to represent the foreign model most relevant to the United States. Rather than examining the experiences of several countries with national health insurance programs, it was felt that an indepth examination of the health care system most similar to that in the United States would be most productive.

The Sun Valley Forum on National Health was organized in 1970 to consider issues related to health care in the United States. The purpose of the forum has been to identify and clarify key problems, to discuss alternatives and, when possible, to advance solutions. The areas covered in previous forum meetings have been the financing of medical care, the organization of medical care, and primary medical care.

In considering the possible implications for the United States of the Canadian experience with national health insurance, the forum examined issues and alternatives relevant to the specifics of national health insurance, but also looked at the broader issues of equity and access as well as the cost of health care.

The characteristics shared by the United States and Canada that make it particularly important to understand the Canadian experience include:

- the medical profession is independent and self regulating and physicians are paid largely on a fee-for-service basis;
- the hospitals are locally controlled as nonprofit, charitable organizations;
- the cost of physicians' services, hospital services and other health care services has been rising rapidly for more than a decade;
- the quality of medical care has been difficult to define and even more difficult to regulate; and
- the geographic and specialty maldistribution of physicians has created serious problems of access to primary medical care.

Policy makers in both countries are greatly concerned about the rising costs of medical care. And there is concern about access to care, quality of care and efficient use of resources.

Although these and other similarities exist, it became apparent that there are also major differences in the way the two nations approach public policy and the role of government. A major factor is that Canadians appear to have more trust in government officials and the government in general than do Americans.

Social programs in Canada have tended to provide universal benefits, rather than being restricted to a specific group, such as the poor or the aged. The latter categorical approach has been followed in the United States. The result of the Canadian approach has been a program that provided first hospital and then physicians' services to the entire population. In the United States, there has been a variety of categorical programs such as Medicaid for the poor and Medicare for the aged. As the Medicare program has been extended by Congress, the traditional pattern has been followed, adding specific groups, such as the disabled and those with end-stage renal disease, rather than providing universal coverage for a benefit such as hospital care.

Important differences

There are also important differences in the American and Canadian views of the public interest. Americans tend to conceive of the public interest as coming after the resolution or compromise of the various vested interests. The policy making process provides the means, usually through the adversary system, to evolve a public policy. That these policies are not always in the best interests of the public is obvious, but the system is so well entrenched that periodic efforts to modify it have had little impact.

In Canada the strength of the vested interests appears to be somewhat muted by the concepts of public service and by the expectations Canadians have for their civil servants and elected officials. More than Americans, Canadians expect their officials to be concerned about and to reflect the broad public interest, as opposed to the variety of private interests on any major issue.

Royal commissions have also played an important role in Canada. Far more than the host of Presidential commissions in the United States, the Royal commissions have been able to focus on the broad principles involved, to reach agreement on them, and to separate the question of whether to adopt a program from the question of how to carry it out. The Royal Commission on Health Services, established in 1961, performed just such a task with respect to national health insurance. In the United States the debates have inextricably mixed the questions of whether a program should be adopted and what the basic policies should be with the question of how the program should be carried out. The Canadians through their policy processes seem to have been able to clarify key issues and define the values they consider most important in relation to major policies like national health insurance, without mixing and confusing these with how the program is to be carried out.

In both countries special interest groups remain active and important. They seem to exert a greater influence on health in the United States because of the new patterns of federalism that have emerged. This development has been described and analyzed by Douglass Cater, former Special Assistant to President Johnson:

> In the politics of modern America, a new form of federalism has emerged, more relevant to the distribution of power than the old. The federalism which ordered power according to geographic hegemonies–national, state, and local–no longer adequately describes the governing arrangement. New subgovernmental arrangements have grown up, by which more of the pressing domestic business is ordered.*

He points out that health has become such a subgovernmental arrangement consisting of five groups:

1. political executives;
2. career bureaucrats at all levels of government;
3. key committeemen in Congress, but not in state legislatures;
4. interest group professionals; and
5. public interest elites.

The development of subgovernments in the United States has had a profound effect on public policy. The role of the states has been seriously weakened, the role of the federal government enhanced and the power of vested interests has increased.

In Canada the geographic hegemonies, particularly provincial governments, remain strong because of the limited role assigned to the national government by the British North American Act (BNA). In the health field the limits are clear:

> The BNA Act allocates for the federal parliament jurisdiction over quarantine and the establishment and maintenance of marine hospitals, and to the provincial legislatures jurisdiction over the

---

*Douglass Cater and Philip R. Lee, Politics of Health (Medcom Press, 1972), p. 4.

establishment, maintenance and management of hospitals, asylums, charities, and other charitable institutions in and for the province, other than marine hospitals.

More than 100 years after enactment these basic constitutional arrangements in Canada are still intact. Provincial governments retain primary responsibility with respect to health matters.

The role of the subgovernmental arrangements in health will have significant impact on whatever national health insurance program is adopted in the United States. Because of the power of the various elements in the subgovernment of health, it is unlikely that the United States will develop a national health insurance program that provides a major role for the state governments in its administration, analogous to that of the Canadian provinces. It is more likely that a federal government agency (e.g., the Social Security Administration) or the private sector will be chosen to administer the program. If the latter route is chosen, a major role for commercial and nonprofit health insurance companies in the collection of premiums, in reimbursement of providers and in utilization review and cost control will be likely. It is no surprise that this latter approach has the support of private groups such as the hospital associations, organized medicine and the drug industries–all important members of the subgovernment of health.

The planning and staging of the legislative enactments and administrative arrangements for national health insurance in Canada and the United States have had similarities and dissimilarities. Both countries focused initially on the supply side, providing funds particularly for the construction of hospitals and other health care facilities. Both began with a modest federal role in financing which was initially limited to the poor.

Beginning in the period immediately after World War II, Canada established a federally funded program to build or expand hospitals in areas of need. After some provincial experiments with hospital insurance, a national program was adopted by all of the provinces and the federal government to provide financing for acute general hospital care for all Canadians. The federal government bore about 50 percent of the total cost of the program. After this program was well established, the Royal Commission on Health Services issued its reports which recommended the basic policies later adopted for the program of national health insurance. Benefits were extended in the late 1960's to include physicians' services and related medical care services provided to ambulatory patients. The program has now been implemented in all of the provinces.

The role of national government

This staging process was based on a solid partnership between the provincial and the national governments. The principal role of the national government was the development of uniform standards for the scope of benefits and in the financing of the program. The administration of the programs was largely at the provincial level. After some early experience there proved to be no place for private insurance companies in the administration of the program.

The national health insurance program in Canada is based on the established policy that every citizen has the right to adequate health care and it is the government's responsibility to assure that right. The four basic principles of the program are:

1. universal coverage;
2. comprehensive benefits;
3. portability of benefits; and
4. public administration and accountability.

The pattern followed by the United States as it moves toward national health insurance has been far less clear cut than the pattern in Canada; in fact, no articulated policy has been established. Although the federal government has been a provider of medical and hospital care to a limited number of beneficiaries, such as members of the armed forces and the merchant marine since the founding of the republic, it was not until enactment of the Social Security Act in 1935 that its contemporary role began to emerge.

The Social Security Act not only created a new role for the federal government in old age, survivors and disability insurance, it also initiated a pattern of federal-state relations in health and welfare programs that prevails to this day. The pattern of federal grants for public health, maternal and child health and crippled children's services initiated in 1935 was gradually expanded to include virtually every conceivable disease category, health care facility and environmental health program. Similar principles, applying mainly to universities, colleges and research institutes, evolved for the support of biomedical research and health manpower development.

The pattern of federal-state-local government relations, federal-university relations, federal-investigator relations, federal-hospital and private health insurance relations and the host of other federal-institutional relationships that make up our health care system pose formidable obstacles to the development of broad national goals in health care that can be translated into effective services. The current proliferation of categories, the fragmentation of services and the lack of public accountability confuse and perplex even the most sophisticated public administrator.

Implications for the United States

In spite of the fragmented and confusing pattern in the United States, and in spite of the differences between the two countries, there is much to learn from the Canadian experience with national health insurance. We can learn what problems have been solved by national health insurance and what problems remain. And we can learn what has really happened in regard to such problems as cost control. The Canadian participants were flatteringly frank about the problems they encountered.

This book provides the best single source of information on the Canadian experience with national health insurance, particularly with respect to the implications for the United States. Dr. Theodore R. Marmor, who discusses these implications in detail in the book, has several observations. I found the following to be of particular interest:

1. The movement of medical care prices, use and expenditures is similar in the United States and Canada, particularly for hospital care, and the proportion of national resources or personal income being spent on medical care is almost identical.

2. Hospital costs, but not utilization have risen sharply in Canada. Copayments designed to reduce costs by directing incentives to patients, had little effect on utilization; they redistributed the cost to the ill and did not restrain increasing hospital costs.

3. After more than a decade of experience with detailed budgets and incentive reimbursement experiments for hospitals, Canadian officials have adopted a strategy to limit the future establishment of hospital beds as the best means of cost control.

4. Any fee-for-service system of reimbursing physicians, even if combined with fee schedules and peer review, is likely to be associated with continuing cost increases because the tendency toward multiplying units of care in a fee-for-service system is very hard to control.

5. A strategy, based on increasing the supply of physicians to improve their geographic distribution and to restrain cost increases through competition among fee-for-service physicians, is likely to fail on both counts.

6. We should expect relatively modest changes in overall utilization of medical services on the basis of the Canadian experience. Changes that do occur are likely to improve access for the poor and others in greatest need of medical care.

Each of these implications is discussed at length and a variety of views are expressed. My views and those of Professor Marmor are by no means universally shared. Although different conclusions may be drawn from the book, it represents a milestone in the attempt to place the debate on national health insurance in the United States on a more rational basis. It is important reading for all who are concerned with the major issues of national health insurance, such as what benefits should be provided, who will pay, and how the program will be administered. It will also give Americans some thought as to "Why national health insurance?"

INTRODUCTION • SPYROS ANDREOPOULOS

The Health of Canadians

There are many reasons Americans should look at Canada for lessons about their health care system. At present everyone in Canada is covered by health insurance. Canadian health programs protect the public from crippling medical bills. They provide capital and support the many essential components of the health system–hospitals, outpatient clinics, and medical and nursing schools. Canadian programs seem to have achieved their goal of a satisfactory level of medical services in all provinces. The Canadian people accomplished all this because their central government set certain basic conditions. The provinces had to meet these before the federal government would share the cost of their programs.

Constitutionally, in Canada the 10 provinces have autonomy in the health field. As a result there are 10 separate provincial plans of government-financed health care. This arrangement gives Canadians 10 separate administrative approaches for solving problems. Like the United States, Canada is a big country. The differences in local needs are profound and so are the local resources to meet those needs.

The Canadian experience with government-financed health care spans some 25 years. During this time various plans were phased in. First, came hospital construction in 1948. It was followed by hospital insurance in 1958 and health manpower development in 1965. Finally, medical care insurance was started in 1968 to cover physician costs. This completed the developmental phase of the Canadian national health system.

In providing universal coverage, Canadians were motivated mainly by human concerns rather than organizational objectives. The purpose of their national program was to remove barriers to health care. They decided that coverage had to be comprehensive, meaning it would pay for all medically needed services rendered by the doctor or hospital, without limit. They agreed that coverage would be available to all eligible residents on uniform terms and conditions. They required that benefits had to be portable when a person moved from one province to another, and would be covered if he became ill while visiting another country. And they determined that health insurance had to be operated on a nonprofit basis and run by public agencies accountable to the people.

The Canadians have accomplished many of their goals as can be seen in the following table. It shows how Canada compares with other countries in terms of three overall indicators of the level of health services. These are the ratio of the health professions to the total population, the extent of prepaid coverage, and the ratio of treatment facilities to the population. Canada in 1971 spent 7.1 percent of its gross national product for health. The per capita annual expenditure was $306.11. For the part that comprised personal health care* only, the per capita cost was $271.72, or about $1,100 for a family of four. By comparison, the average family in the United States spends about $500 per year for each man, woman and child for medical care.

Country	% covered by Medical and Hospital Insurance	No. of Hosp. beds per 10,000 Population	No. of Physicians per 10,000 Population	No. of Nurses per 10,000 Population
Australia	79% (hosp.) 75% (Med.)	117.4	11.8	66.6
Canada	Almost 100%	102.3	15.7	57.3
Denmark	96.7%	89.4	14.5	53.4
Sweden	Almost 100%	145.8	12.4	43.7
United Kingdom	Almost 100%	111.4	12.5	35.1
United States	85% (Hosp.) 65% (Reg. Med.) 35% (Maj. Med.)	82.7	15.3	49.2

Source: Lalonde, Marc, *A New Perspective on the Health of Canadians,* a working document, Government of Canada, Ottawa, April 1974, p. 27.

It is clear that in hospital and medical insurance coverage Canada equals the best of the five countries chosen for comparison; it leads in terms of physicians, is in the middle rank with respect to hospital beds, and is second only to Australia in nurses. Since the countries chosen are among those believed

*Personal health care refers to services received by individuals and provided by hospitals, physicians, nurses, dentists, pharmacists, etc.

to have the best health services in the world, Canada, judged by the four measures used in the table, ranks among the world leaders.

Canadians did not wait until all the information was in to start their programs. When it became apparent that high costs were a deterrent to hospital care for many Canadians, they established hospital insurance. They moved on to the next steps through a process of evolution. This gave them time to develop the necessary administrative machinery in the provinces and in the central government to handle the new programs; it allowed doctors and patients to familiarize themselves with the system; finally, it began to clarify through experience the long-term implications of a national system.

Canadians did not find it necessary to nationalize their voluntary hospitals. They retained fee-for-service as a method of paying doctor bills. Patients have free choice of physician and free choice of hospital without losing their benefits. The insurance plans are tax supported. In some provinces the plans are funded by premiums but even those plans are subsidized heavily. There are no deductibles and out-of-pocket payments or if they exist they are nominal.

The Canadian health plans took no steps to control the type, quantity, and quality of hospital services, and made no attempt to determine the number and types of doctors that would be needed to care for the population. Consequently, Canada today has too many specialists and not enough primary doctors.

Because in Canada hospital insurance was started first, doctors were given an incentive to hospitalize patients whether they needed it or not. Every town and city was encouraged to build hospitals and to gain economically and socially from funds supplied by the federal and provincial treasuries. With federal construction funds available and 50 percent of hospital costs guaranteed under hospital insurance, Canadian communities built more acute and general hospitals than they actually needed.

While on balance the Canadian health system has achieved its original goals, new problems are now facing those with responsibility for providing health services. The annual rate of cost escalation has been between 12 and 16 percent, which is far in excess of the economic growth of the country. In fact, the Economic Council of Canada has forecast that if health services and higher education are added at the same rate as in recent years, these services could equal the gross national product by the year 2000. As mentioned earlier the past 20 years have seen an emphasis on the construction of hospitals and not enough on other needed facilities. Canada now finds itself with an excess of expensive acute care beds, coupled with a shortage of alternative treatment such as convalescent and custodial care facilities. Medical services are not yet equally accessible to all segments of the population because doctors prefer to practice in cities, and it is difficult to attract them to rural or isolated locations. Dental services are not equally accessible to all segments of the population, mainly because of the cost to the patient of dental care, a shortage of dentists and a poor distribution of dental manpower.

In addition, Canadians have found that present cost-sharing arrangements between the federal and provincial governments tend to encourage use of physicians and acute treatment hospitals, even for services that could be provided through less costly means. They, therefore, seek alternatives such as improved ambulatory health centers, with round-the-clock comprehensive outpatient care.

Conflicting goals

These developments are indicative of the concerns of many Canadians which have given rise to reexamination of the principles on which a nationwide system of health insurance is based.

In his document *A New Perspective on the Health of Canadians,* Marc Lalonde, Canadian minister of National Health and Welfare, believes the problems of providing and financing health care within reasonable limits arise from attempts to meet conflicting goals.

There is a goal to make doctors equally accessible to everyone, but it is also a goal to permit them to practice medicine where they wish. The result is that physicians are maldistributed.

There is a goal to try to control costs while removing all incentives to patients, physicians and hospitals to do so. A generous supply of beds and physicians makes it easier for patients to seek care even for minor conditions and for physicians to hospitalize more patients, especially when they are no financial barriers. Hence, the desire of ready access to health services conflicts with the goal of controlling costs.

There is a goal to provide a balanced supply of the various medical specialties while permitting physicians to select their fields of special training.

There is a goal to have services provided by staff trained only to the level of skill needed for the task performed. Yet the present licensing patterns for health professionals, the fee-for-service system and the notion that the doctor alone bears responsibility for the patient, encourages physicians to do tasks which could be done by others.

"Finally, there is the paradox," concludes Lalonde, "of everyone agreeing to the importance of research and prevention, yet continuing to increase disproportionately the amount of money spent on treating existing illness. Public demand for treatment services assures these services of financial resources. No such public demand exists for research and preventive measures." As a result resources allocated for this purpose are generally insufficient.

When the demand for health services exceeds what a nation can afford, the government promising the services must apply rationing. If the consumer is not prepared to accept some individual responsibility for health care, controls are inevitable. Canadian authorities have attempted to reduce consumer demand by levying patient deterrent fees in some instances. These are believed to have been successful in reducing physician visits and waiting lists for hospital beds. But they became a political issue and were subsequently reduced or dropped in those provinces that had started them. The next step was to introduce controls on the providers of health services. Because Canada had ample acute beds to service the population, the federal government phased out its construction grants for hospitals. In Quebec 1,500 acute care beds were taken out of service and plans are to drop more in the future. In several provinces, the number of private laboratories that can offer services has been limited, and the licensing of private hospitals, nursing homes and so on has been tightened.

Health services affect the market forces of supply and demand quite differently from other sectors of the economy. If payment for care is guaranteed by the government without limits, then any doctor who sets up practice anywhere in Canada is guaranteed a respectable income as well as a hospital system that will respond to his demand for care for his patients. One Canadian, Lloyd F. Detwiller, administrator of the Health Sciences Center at the University of British Columbia in Vancouver, estimates that on the average, for every new physician, the system incurs expenses of about $50,000 for his services and costs plus another $100,000 for inpatient hospital care, laboratory, special nursing, etc. If 100 doctors are added to the complement of any province, about $15 million would be added to the cost of the plan in a year.

Consequently, some provinces now have considered curtailing the doctors' freedom to practice in any one province.

"Until recently," Detwiller wrote in an article in *Hospital Progress,* "the situation has been akin to guaranteeing service station operators customers who are encouraged to drive their cars continuously and whose gasoline bills are paid by the government, with no limit being placed on the number of service stations that can be opened in a province, and no limit to the number of cars that can be driven or miles that can be travelled. Little wonder that operators of such service stations would make a handsome income each year."

Canadian governments have also begun to analyze the major problem areas in the health field, particularly patient and physician contacts from the point of view of demand, productivity, and cost benefit. They are developing jointly with the appropriate physician organizations, doctor profiles to analyze patterns of practice and measure them against certain standard criteria. These are expected to lead to measures concerning the actual organization and delivery of health care.

But in the final analysis, controls can succeed only if they are acceptable to the physicians, hospitals and consumers. The problem of achieving consensus on this score is exceedingly difficult in societies where the rights of the individual are considered paramount and the freedom of professional groups and societies is considered essential, Detwiller observes.

In the United States presently a consensus is emerging that Congress will pass some form of health legislation in the next year or so—perhaps even before the end of 1975. Such a passage would revolutionize the financing of health care for 220 million Americans now benefiting from private health insurance and the

50 million people now covered by Medicare and Medicaid programs. But there are many questions raised of side effects: what impact would national health insurance have on medical practice, medical research and the average taxpayer's pocketbook? Some fear the side effects of a national plan might be highly undesirable. And so instead of humane and egalitarian concerns, the current debate in the United States seems to be preoccupied with names—providers, insurers, beneficiaries, deductibles, economists and big budget makers. Can we have a health policy if it tries to relate only with doctors, hospitals, insurance companies, medical schools, and economists? In the final analysis no expert in the economics of health care can say with certainty how national health insurance will affect costs or skew the future availability of health services.

An excellent laboratory

Canada provides an excellent laboratory in which many of the basic issues of health care delivery and finance are being worked out. There are many similarities in the health systems of the United States and Canada as well as differences. Canadian experience with health programs should be studied carefully, but should not be emulated without question. The United States can learn a great deal from neighboring Canada, and some of the lessons of the Canadian experience are discussed in detail elsewhere in this book. But there are two lessons which stand out:

- The main objective of a national health insurance program is *not* to control costs, but to remove barriers to health care.
- If doctors and health services are badly organized, national health insurance will only reveal the magnitude of the problem, and lead to a determination to do something about it. This catalytic process now seems fully under way in Canada under joint efforts of the profession, the hospitals, and governmental authorities. Perhaps without going through such an experience once, it is unrealistic to expect professionals, providers, and politicians to agree on methods and goals.

Canada is now looking beyond the problems of organization of health services—to find ways to a healthier country. In this respect Canadians are perhaps 20 years ahead of the United States. Canadian policy makers are exploring the issues of sickness and death from three broad perspectives: *human biology*—the diseases which are part of the inheritance or organic makeup of the individual; *environmental issues,* and *lifestyle*—personal decisions and habits that are bad, from a health standpoint, and create self-imposed risks. These are the threats to health that an organized health system can do little more than serve as a catchment net for its victims.

Initiatives in this area, of course, will depend on availability of funds and will be carefully paced in relation to the ability of the Canadian economy to absorb them. But as Lalonde states, "there will be a much clearer picture of the options available. In the end—by individuals, by society and by governments—choices must be made."

FOOTNOTES

Lalonde, Marc, *A New Perspective on the Health of Canadians,* a working document, Government of Canada, Ottawa, April 1974.

Shapley, Deborah, National Health Insurance, Will It Promote Costly Technology? *Science,* 186: 423-25, Nov. 1, 1974.

Detwiller, Lloyd F., National Health Insurance: Can the U.S. Learn from Canada? *Hospital Progress,* Sept. 1974, pp. 48-53 and 80.

Rodgers, P. A., Putting medical care issues into focus, *San Francisco Examiner,* Nov. 14, 1974, p. 37.

ACKNOWLEDGMENTS

It appears possible that within the coming year the U.S. Congress will enact some form of national health insurance. The Sun Valley Forum on National Health, Inc. felt that a conference to discuss the issues could make a contribution to defining problems expected to arise and to incorporate measures to prevent or alleviate them. The Canadian health care system is as good as any found elsewhere and we felt it should be examined by any nation considering a similar approach to health care.

The general format of the conference was determined by Margaret Mahoney, Bayless Manning, and John Evans, president of the University of Toronto, who made the initial contact with the four key Canadian authors. The initial idea to look at the Canadian system came from Melvin Glasser and we are indebted to him for suggesting it.

The Sun Valley Forum symposium was held in Sun Valley, Idaho in August, 1974. There were 39 participants–individuals who have thought a great deal about these issues–and there was ample opportunity during the six-day session not only for the speakers but also the participants to have a full discussion on the Canadian experience and its implications for the United States.

However, it was recognized that there would be many people who would welcome the opportunity to study the material more intensively. The papers and discussion have, therefore, been edited to make this book. Discussants were asked to contribute their commentaries if they wished and many did. For reasons of space, the discussions have been slightly pruned; also I have rearranged contributions to group those on related topics. I have not attempted to impose any extensive uniformity of style on the manuscripts and, in most instances, I have done no more than edit and minimize overlap. They are diverse not only in content but also in approach and attitude. And they are, I felt, as interesting from the point of view of attitudes they indicate in people in a wide range of positions, as from what they actually say. One chapter by Stuart Altman, an American commentator, was not actually a part of the commissioned papers. But I have included it as such because of the important lessons he sees from the cross-country comparison of the U.S. and Canadian systems. After all that's what the book is all about.

In addition to the great debt we owe the authors and participants, we wish to thank those who have generously supported the 1974 symposium: The Branta Foundation, Inc., the Janss Foundation, the Robert Wood Johnson Foundation, Aetna Life and Casualty Company, Boise Cascade Corporation, the Johns-Manville Company, the Times-Mirror Company, and the U.S. Department of Health, Education and Welfare, Contract #N01-MB-44151. Our gratitude also goes to the Mary W. Harriman Trust for a sustaining grant used to supplement support of Forum activities.

Finally, I should record my debt to Robert Lindee for very effective administrative support, and Judy Spates Housel and Judith Gustafson for their help during the conference. For this aspect I must also record a considerable debt to my wife, Christiane, for her assistance in proofreading and preparation of the index.

S.A.

I HISTORICAL PERSPECTIVE

CHAPTER 1 • MAURICE LECLAIR

The Canadian Health Care System

It was 16 years ago that Canada decided to launch its National Health Insurance Program. The gestational period was long, the program was installed gradually. Much controversy surrounded its planning and implementation, and at times the debate was very bitter. Yet at this moment, it is unanimously accepted by both consumers and providers of health care and there is absolutely no turning back. It is now an acceptable fact of life welcomed and enjoyed by all.

When the national health scheme started, Canada had a system of health care delivery almost identical to that of the United States. Canadian standard of living and many of the social attitudes and expectations are very close to those of the United States. The similarities extend to the system of hospitals, and to the physicians and nurses in terms of training and outlook. Most Canadian hospitals and the majority of medical specialists do belong to their sister associations. They read the same journals, attend the same meetings, prescribe the same drugs as doctors do in the United States. Canada started from a health care delivery system which, for the most part, was private, with very few controls. Within the space of a decade Canada developed an approach that has increasingly involved government particularly with regard to the financing and provision of basic hospital and physician services.

HISTORY

Constitutional background

When the fathers of Confederation met to draft Canada's fundamental constitutional document, the British North America Act of 1867, governmental involvement in health care services was minimal. For the most part, the individual was compelled to rely on his own resources and those of his family, and hospitals were administered and financed by private charities and religious organizations.

Since the role of the state was so modest, the subject of health could not be expected to claim an important place in the discussions leading up to Confederation nor in the British North America Act of 1867.* The Fathers of Confederation could not have foreseen the pervasive growth and range of health care needs of a large industrialized urban society, advances in medical science, nor the public expenditures required to maintain high quality health care.

The only specific references to health matters in the distribution of legislative powers under the British North America Act are to allocate to the Federal Parliament jurisdiction over quarantine and the establishment and maintenance of marine hospitals, and to provincial legislatures jurisdiction over "the establishment, maintenance and management of hospitals, asylums, charities and eleemosynary (charitable) institutions in and for the province, other than marine hospitals." In the context of the circumstances existing in 1867, this latter reference probably was meant to cover most health care services. Furthermore, since the provinces were assigned jurisdiction over "generally all matters of a merely local or private nature in the province," it is probable that this power was deemed to cover health care, while the provincial power over "municipal institutions" provided a convenient means for dealing with such matters. The provision of health care services has, therefore, traditionally been acknowledged as primarily a provincial responsibility.

Although Canada like the United States has a federal structure, the division of powers is different as far as health and education are concerned. In Canada, each province has the primary constitutional responsibility for all health and hospital services, for health science education and for the regulation of the health professions. The federal government, however, has major residual responsibilities in health and some of these are: "quarantine and immigration, Indians and Eskimos, the delivery of health care in the Yukon and Northwest Territories in cooperation with the local authorities, health of the military services, the penitentiaries, the Royal Canadian Mounted Police and some aspect of the health of federal public service employees." The federal government is also involved in the international aspects of health, statistics, food and drug quality and hazards, environmental quality and hazards, health surveillance, drug, alcohol and tobacco abuse, fitness and recreation, nutrition, emergency health services, prosthetic services, the fields of biomedical and public health research and many other endeavors in the general field of health education and prevention. In addition, it takes part in any joint effort which the provinces agree to undertake in cooperation with the federal government. Health insurance in Canada functions largely at the provincial level but planning, development and finance are subject to national influence.

*This fundamental constitutional document, unlike the United States Constitution, does not contain an exhaustive summary of constitutional law; there are other statutes, both of the British Parliament and Canadian statutes, which, together with the British North America Act, form Canada's written constitution.

This constitutional arrangement has brought the administration of health care much closer to those served and consequently reduced the sense of remoteness and anonymity of governmental involvement. It has also permitted the evolution of programs in relation to the needs and political philosophy of the individual provinces. As a result, changes have been introduced early and with less difficulty than if a single nationwide policy had been required as a first step. Hospital insurance and medical care insurance, for example, were introduced in certain provinces several years before they were accepted as national programs.

In 1935, the Federal Parliament passed the Employment and Social Insurance Act. This statute envisaged the establishment of a federal program providing certain social security benefits, including health benefits. This was to be financed by premiums levied on the population by the federal government. A question of jurisdiction was raised and this was finally carried to the highest court in the land. It ruled this Act to be ultra vires since the power to levy a direct premium on provincial residents was a matter pertaining to health and welfare and came within the jurisdiction of the provinces; it was made clear that if Canada was to establish programs for the health and welfare of its citizens, it could only be done through programs administered by the provinces or by constitutional amendment.

Canada started its two major health insurance programs (the Hospital Insurance Program first and the Medical Care Program second), ten years apart but because of the nature of the Constitution, the federal government does not actually administer the individual provincial plans. Each province is responsible for implementing and administering its own plan but in order to receive the federal contributions in respect of its plan, it has to meet certain requirements to be referred to later.

Early provincial experiences

Immediately after World War II, many provinces started piecemeal to establish universal insurance schemes; some of these were quite selective such as for the treatment of tuberculosis or mental illness, but there was a ferment evident in most provinces toward universal schemes. Saskatchewan was a leader and in 1946 passed the Saskatchewan Hospitalization Act, which resulted in the implementation in 1947 of a universal compulsory hospital program covering virtually all residents of that province. Also in 1946, a Health Services Act was passed in Saskatchewan which provided for the integration of municipal doctor plans into broader health region programs. In July 1946, all municipal doctor plans in Swift Current Health Region No. 1 were integrated into a regional medical care program, financed by personal and property taxes and supported by the provincial government.

Hospital insurance

On the federal scene, the first step was the National Health Grant Program.

It was started in 1948 by the federal government which viewed these grants as "being fundamental prerequisites of a nationwide system of health insurance. The grants inaugurated at that time were in the fields of hospital construction, health surveys, professional training, public health research, general public health, mental health, tuberculosis control, cancer control, venereal disease control and crippled children. Other grants including one for rehabilitation were added subsequently. This paved the way for the second step by leading to a standard accounting and reporting system for Canadian hospitals, an upgrading of the diagnostic services and through the hospital construction grant, an upgrading of the physical facilities.

By the middle sixties the grants available totalled more than $60,000,000 annually. In December 1967, the government announced its intention of reducing the national health grants as the provinces began to participate in the federal government's plan for financial assistance for a nationwide medical care program. With the exception of the Professional Training Grant and the Public Health Research Grant, all others were phased out by March 31, 1972. From 1948 to March 31, 1970 when the Hospital Construction Grant was terminated, federal assistance had been approved toward the cost of space for more than 130,000 hospital beds (Canada now has approximately 150,000 general and allied special beds) and 15,000 bassinets in newborn nurseries. In addition, federal construction grants made possible more than 24,000 beds in nurses' residences, 900 beds in interns' residences and more than 7,000,000 sq. feet for public health hospital laboratories, community health centers, teaching areas in hospitals and diagnostic and treatment areas available to inpatients and outpatients. The Professional Training Grants to date have provided more than 30,000 bursaries to health personnel and an equal number have benefited from assistance for short courses.

In the middle fifties, interest in health insurance had grown and many provinces were pressing the federal government for some action in this field. The provincial governments were finding it very difficult to raise the necessary revenues to meet the escalating costs of providing hospital services. Many Canadian hospitals were in financial trouble, especially the smaller and rural ones. Technology was beginning to burst forth and also unionization of hospital workers had become a fact. While hospital workers had previously been the poor cousins of the labor force, with increasing militancy the unions were insisting that the wage gap be closed and eventually eliminated between the hospital workers and the rest of the working force. The hospitals were finding it extremely difficult to finance their operations and keep up their standards because less than 40 percent of the population at that time had some hospital insurance coverage and much of it was not adequate. The entry of the federal and provincial governments into the hospital insurance field was generally welcomed by the public, by the medical profession and by other levels of government as well. It was in April 1957 that the Federal Parliament passed the

Hospital Insurance and Diagnostic Services Act. Prior to the introduction of the Bill, there had been very considerable federal-provincial consultations at the technical level, many intergovernmental meetings and a permanent Federal-Provincial Advisory Committee had been established. The federal government would contribute to the programs administered by the provinces which included institutional care in general hospitals and related hospitals, and diagnostic services. Mental and tuberculosis hospitals were excluded primarily on the grounds that care in such hospitals was already provided by the provinces, virtually without cost to provincial residents. Rather than providing fiscal assistance after the fact of illness and hospitalization, the program provided the necessary service benefit on a prepaid basis. The federal legislation defined the institutions and services for which cost would be shared and established the formula for determining the federal contributions that would be paid to the provinces toward such cost. This formula provided for a lower percentage of federal contribution in those provinces where hospital services were highest and conversely where costs were lower, the federal contribution would be proportionally higher.

The Act provided that no federal contributions would be paid until at least six provinces containing one half of the population of the country had entered into agreements with the federal government. Only five provinces were ready to start in 1958, so a change of government and an amendment to the relevant section of the law made it possible for the hospital insurance program to start rolling. On July 1, 1958, five provinces started the program and the last province joined the program on January 1, 1961.

Medicare

In the early 1960's, a Royal Commission on Health Services (the Hall Commission) was established by the federal government. After carefully conducting the most thorough and complete survey of the health situation ever done in Canada up to that time, the Commission came out strongly in favor of a parallel shared-cost program to the Hospital Insurance program, in other words, a universal and government operated program for medical services.

Prior to the implementation of the Canadian Medicare program, approximately one Canadian in every five did not have *any* form of protection against the rapidly rising costs of medical and surgical care. The remaining 80 percent had varying degrees of protection, some of which was quite inadequate, in a variety of private plans and public arrangements. The Commission considered that a third of all the private medical insurance coverage was totally inadequate. Physicians often had to read the fine print in a patient's policy to know what the patient was entitled to because many insurance companies had a great range of benefits. Under such circumstances, and with nearly 100 percent of the population covered by hospital insurance, it is not surprising that many were in favor of financing the costs of physicians' services on the same prepaid basis as for hospital costs to which they were now accustomed. Apart from those who, for one reason or another, could not obtain prepaid medical care insurance coverage, and the varying benefits provided by the different carriers, there was marked variation in the premiums charged for private insurance coverage. Group rates tended to be lower than individual rates and there were marked differences in the rates charged according to the province of residence. Wide variations existed in the cost-benefit ratios of the schemes offered by the commercial insurance carriers. For example, 1965-67 data indicate that insurance company premium collections per dollar of benefits paid varied from about $1.16 for the large insurance groups of industrialized Ontario to about $1.89 for nongroup coverage in Prince Edward Island. The cost-benefit ratio for the coverage of the virtually universal Saskatchewan plan was about $1.06 per dollar of benefits paid as the nonprofit government plan built no retention factor other than the cost of administration into its collection structure. The experience of the commercial insurance industry and of the governmental plan in Saskatchewan clearly indicated definite economies of scale and of uniformity of coverage in a nonprofit type of operation.

In most Canadian provinces there were fee schedules established by the medical profession prior to Medicare and in all provinces but one, the most popular type of insurance coverage was of the first dollar type with no deductibles, cocharges or upper limits. Most Canadians favored the service-type of insurance coverage in which the service was insured rather than a fixed dollar amount. The Canadian Medicare program has evolved from the prevailing pattern.

Shortly after the establishment of the Hall Commission, a number of provincial government initiatives took place. Saskatchewan, again the pioneer, established its program in 1962; in 1963, the next-door province of Alberta, which was strongly in favor of free enterprise, attempted to provide universal coverage through commercial insurance carriers. Its approach was that any company wishing to sell health insurance in Alberta had to provide as a minimum a certain standard of benefits. The government, in fact, had to approve the maximum premium which could be charged and the insurers had to guarantee a renewability of the contracts so that an individual could not be dropped the minute he had a severe illness. The government also made available premium subsidies for those who could not pay the full premium. In spite of all this, not much more than 70 percent of the population was covered after several years and Alberta eventually abandoned this program. It is interesting to note that in Australia, which also has had fairly free available coverage through nonprofit private carriers, a similar percentage was covered. As you know, Australia is now proposing a universal program. Other provinces had begun schemes with governmental involvement but not uniformly. At the Federal-Provincial Meeting in July 1965, the then prime minister announced the intention of his government to introduce a new shared-cost program to cover the professional services of physicians. The Act was introduced in July 1966, and proclaimed in December 1966. It was called the Medical Care Act; it created a great commotion for some time, and there was a five-month parliamentary debate on the proposed Act, but only two members of Parliament voted against it when it came to final vote. As we will see later, the approach taken in this Act was rather simpler than that under the Hospital Insurance Act, reflecting the greater experience of both the private and public sectors over the previous 10 years.

The Saskatchewan episode

Saskatchewan in 1946 had established its universal compulsory hospital insurance program and this being firmly in operation, the province began to think of the universal medicare plan. In moving second reading of the Saskatchewan Hospitalization Act in March 1946, the premier had given notice that a medical care plan was in contemplation, describing the hospital bill as "the first milestone on the road to complete socialized health services."

In 1952, a Committee of Health Professionals, including physicians, dentists and others as well as lay members, recommended that "a comprehensive insurance program should be undertaken in Saskatchewan at the earliest possible date." Nothing significant happened until Premier Douglas proceeded to implement his medical care insurance plan in 1962. The medical profession reacted vigorously in opposing the introduction of the scheme. While maintaining that they favored health insurance, the physicians opposed the principle of a universal compulsory scheme to be administered by a board responsible to the provincial government. This stand by the medical profession was a distinct break with the position taken in 1943. In January of that year, the General Council of the Canadian Medical Association unanimously approved and made public a declaration favoring the principle of universal health insurance under a state insurance fund with the elimination of other carriers. Extended negotiations between the government of Saskatchewan and the Saskatchewan College of Physicians and Surgeons had resulted in the appointment, in April 1960, of the Advisory Planning Committee on Medical Care. A provincial election was called before the committee could act and the dominant issue during the campaign was that of a medical insurance care scheme which the premier said would be implemented if his party were re-elected. Many physicians campaigned against the government. A special voluntary levy plus a contribution of $35,000 from the Canadian Medical Association provided an election fund of $95,000 to oppose the incumbents. The government won and the following day, the general secretary of the Canadian Medical Association offered to cooperate in setting up the best possible plan. He said: "This is democracy. The CMA accepts the decision in this light. Our efforts will be bent on avoiding the defects we see in government plans elsewhere." This, however, was repudiated by the president of the Saskatchewan College of Physicians and Surgeons who said the

College remained unalterably opposed. A few days later, at the annual CMA convention, it became clear that the general secretary was not speaking for the members and the association formally declared that it believed, "A tax supported comprehensive program compulsory for all is neither necessary nor desirable."

The Advisory Planning Committee had recommended in favor of a comprehensive scheme to be administered by a public commission. It favored that the scheme be universal and all persons should pay a premium low enough to be met by all self-supporting persons. Physicians' services would be paid on a fee-for-service basis, with the patient responsible at the time of the service for a small part of the fee. Legislation followed closely the majority recommendations of the committee and it was introduced in October of 1961, with the important exception that no utilization or deterrent fee was provided for. The College and the physicians continued their opposition; government was determined to go ahead with its plan; the parties were on a collision course. The Bill became law on November 17, 1961, and was to become effective April 1, 1962; the government then set about appointing the Medical Care Insurance Commission and the College of Physicians and Surgeons refused to name or consent to any of its members serving on the commission. The government postponed implementation to July 1, 1962, and even though there were amendments made to the Act, the physicians did not agree to cooperate. At the beginning of May 1962, a meeting attended by 600 of the province's 900 doctors sent an ultimatum to the government saying, "Repeal the Act or face a withdrawal of services except emergency services." In the interim, the public took sides. Pressure groups for and against the plan came into existence, public meetings were held, the news media were involved in the controversy and finally the College of Physicians and Surgeons rejected all changes proposed by the government. On July 1, there was an almost complete withdrawal of services, the first physicians' strike in North America. Public opinion began to move against the striking physicians and some of them resumed practice and their number was growing; the College asked for renewed negotiations and eventually on July 23, the parties signed a document which became known as the Saskatoon Agreement. After the Saskatoon Agreement, the program settled down as most of the anticipated fears did not materialize. The profession re-established itself in the public's esteem and continued to give medical care of the high quality that the province had been accustomed to having. Some physicians left the province but it is interesting to record that by July 1, 1964, two years after the plan came into being, there were 124 more doctors in the province than there were on July 1, 1962.

The role of organized medicine

The Canadian Medical Association like the American Medical Association has always put the same emphasis on free choice, the sanctity of the doctor-patient relationship, fee-for-service and independence from third party involvement in the practice of medicine. However, as was pointed out many years ago by Malcolm G. Taylor, "The CMA has more readily acknowledged the changes in both medicine and society that seem to require an organized approach to the economic problem resulting from unpredictable illness."

As early as 1934, the CMA's Committee on Economics submitted a report on health insurance applying principles reaffirmed in 1938 and serving as the basis for major policy statements such as the one in 1943, recommending that the plan be "compulsory for persons having an annual income below a level which proves to be insufficient to meet the cost of adequate medical care" and that "payment of the premium should be made by the employee, employer and government." This was reaffirmed in 1944, but a shift of position began to be evident by 1947, when the potentialities of voluntary health insurance were known. In 1949, the Association issued a policy statement proposing the extension of voluntary prepaid medical care plans with governmental subsidies to pay premiums totally or in part for low-income persons. The major themes coming from the Medical Association's six statements on health between 1943 and 1965, are clearly related to the central anxieties facing the medical profession: the control by third parties, particularly public medical care insurance commissions or agencies over the conditions of work of the physicians. Secondly, freedom; this was also one of Canada's major social values and adopting it as a theme tended to justify an ideological claim in the eyes of the community as well as those of the physicians. Emphasizing freedom as a value for both consumer and the provider of medical services, the medical profession was trying to legitimize its status as a free autonomous self-governing profession where the entrepreneur's spirit was quite evident. A patient also should be free to choose his own physician. Thirdly, quality of medical care was also frequently stressed in the official statements of the medical profession concerning health and medical care insurance. According to the profession, high quality care was not really available to all, a recognition that the demand for such care exceeded the ability of the profession to meet it. The Canadian Medical Association linked and still does link high quality of medical care with fee-for-service.

After the 1959-1962 critical years in Saskatchewan, there was for the medical profession the added shock of the report of the Royal Commission on Health Services in 1964. That commission had been appointed in part because of the pressure by the Canadian Medical Association on the government to set up just such a study.

Explicitly the reason for the move was the plethora of political party proposals and consumer demands which the profession feared might result in action adverse to its interest. Implicitly, it seemed that the association felt that its "supplement don't supplant" approach was so sound that any reasonable commission would endorse it. The CMA was encouraged in this view by the support of the insurance industry and later on by the actions of the governments of Alberta, Ontario and British Columbia, in setting up provincial medical insurance plans that provided just that: subsidies geared to income tax exemption thresholds for anyone who purchased policies from insurance companies or profession-sponsored plans.

The report of the Royal Commission released in June 1964, completely rejected the CMA-insurance industry's approach. It recommended strongly ten provincial government programs subsidized by matching federal funds, paralleling the national Hospital Insurance Program. The CMA and the insurance industry had based their estimates of those needing subsidies on only the premiums for medical services. The commission, on the other hand, looked at the total package of health services, which in 1962, averaged approximately $350 for a family. Assuming that 5 percent was the maximum that a consumer could reasonably allocate to health services, then all below an income of $7,000 a year would be entitled to subsidy. This would require "means-testing" half or more of the population in 1962, an administrative task not worth the effort. It was clearly much simpler to subsidize the then insurance funds than millions of individuals. Chief Justice Hall, the chairman of the commission, reported: "We determined that the fee-for-service method was a practical one to recommend for Canada. The capitation method which was reasonably successful in England was virtually unknown to medical practice in North America. If the program was to be successful it had to have much cooperation from and acceptance by the medical profession as was possible to obtain. In the aftermath of the Saskatchewan strike we discerned a growing support for a medicare program from many doctors, particularly among the younger practitioners and in the teaching hospitals."

The consternation in the medical profession and in the insurance industry was intense and their opposition vociferous. The medical profession never thought that the Hall Commission would recommend a universal and government-operated program. The profession had hoped that the commission would decide that all government should do would be to supplement the existing insurance arrangements and pay the premium for those who could not pay. In June 1965, the Canadian Medical Association, although agreeing that such insurance should be available to all Canadians, stated that alternative types of insurance must be maintained, that every physician must be free to participate or not, that the subscriber who consults a non-participating physician must not be obliged to relinquish any benefits, that the profession should be satisfactorily represented in a non-political administered structure, and enough financial assistance to persons in need to enable them to purchase insurance must be assured.

Organized medicine at that time waged a major campaign to try to influence the government into accepting its proposition for inclusion in the impending Medical Care Bill. The public and particularly physicians, were submitted to a barrage of representations. The CMA joined with the insurance industry to persuade both federal and provincial governments that a national plan was unnecessary.

When the Bill was introduced in July of 1966, the CMA urged redrafting to eliminate "rigid requirements for universality of coverage" and proposed that public funds should be used not to "subsidize the self-sufficient," but to "assist the lower-income groups to purchase insurance." The Medical Care Act became law in December of 1966, and the CMA charged that approval of the Act showed the "inflexible attitude which government leaders have demonstrated during our discussions with them." In reviewing the history of the Bill, the CMA said that "opting out" appeared to be possible under the legislation but that "in every other respect the Bill set out a point of view completely opposed to recommendations which the CMA has made." In 1966, Dr. R. O. Jones, CMA president, speaking at the 99th meeting of the Association, reported that Medicare would be "a serious threat to the quality of medical care in this country . . . the patient would become a sort of background on which the hostilities of government and doctor are worked out." By 1969, the CMA in its review of Medicare negotiations reported: "We pointed out that the federal government's insistence on an all or nothing program meant that needy persons would be deprived of medical insurance benefits. We are greatly concerned about the insistence on universality." However, in fairness to the CMA, it urged acceptance of the Bill as the law of the land and affirmed that "as physicians we will accept the role of trying to provide the best quality medical services for our patients with the limitations which this Act will impose."

It must be remembered that in 1962, the College of Physicians and Surgeons of Saskatchewan had probably misjudged the ultimate public reaction to a doctors' strike; the medical profession in other parts of Canada as well as the United States by encouragement and some financial assistance (promised but not that forthcoming) had probably misled the College into thinking that it could count on the loyalty of the general public. Certainly, the ultimate result of this strike had a major deterrent effect on the Canadian Medical Association in 1966, to even mention that possibility as a negotiating tool. All of this opposition by the medical profession to universal medicare is now water under the bridge. The Canadian Medical Association has accepted Medicare and has worked to the best of its ability to provide under the Act the best available care for Canadians. The marriage has not been one of love but it has been one of reason and for this, credit must be given to the medical profession. True, it is evident, as we will see later, that physicians never had it so good. Governments have not interfered in the practice of medicine and have respected their end of the bargain. Nowadays we tend to forget all of this and the partnership between the medical profession and the government at least at the federal level is one which we are grateful for and proud of. It is interesting to see how we have really forgotten the past; recently a leading member of the medical profession in a publication to be distributed in the United States wrote: "Although the United States seems to be inching its way in the same direction, many of my American colleagues are somewhat stunned to learn that health care in Canada is not completely socialized; and astonishingly enough at least to Americans that it came about with no real opposition from our physicians." The man who wrote this is quite knowledgeable about the past history and perhaps as it should be, is looking to the future rather than to the past. The things that the medical profession really wanted were incorporated in the plan; there was opting out (although later one province did not grant its physicians this opportunity), this opting out was without penalty to the physician or the patient, the patient-physician relationship was protected, there was continuation of the selection of a physician by a patient rather than by a panel system, a physician could choose his patients and there was really no interference by a third party in the direct delivery of this service even though the third party did provide the payment.

Why hospital insurance first and Medicare later?

In theory it might have been better to bring in the medical program first so as to encourage outpatient care and then later to phase in the hospital insurance program. This was not done, however, for many reasons: a) In the latter 1950's many hospitals were in financial trouble and only a minority of the population had adequate hospital insurance coverage. Unionization and technology were beginning to cause marked increases in hospital rates and the situation was obviously going to get worse in the absence of adequate insurance coverage for the population. The provinces felt obliged to help in the hospitals' financial position since Canadian hospitals had largely been built as community projects and operated essentially on a nonprofit basis. In fact, two provinces had substantial stakes in supporting hospitals for the care of indigents and pressed for federal financial support. b) The Canadian Medical Association and the Canadian Hospital Association if not 100 percent in favor were not opposed and did not mount a lobby against the incoming Bill. c) The National Health Grant Program of 1948, through the Hospital Construction Grant had encouraged hospital construction and led to an emphasis on hospital care and diagnostic services rather than alternative forms of care. d) It was not until after it had achieved rather complete hospital insurance coverage that the Canadian public began to demand and purchase medical insurance to a significant degree outside of heavily industrialized and unionized areas where medical care insurance was frequently a fringe benefit.

Commercial carriers and Medicare (experience in Ontario)

When the Province of Ontario became a participant in the National Medical Care program on October 1, 1969, there were more than 200 separate insuring agencies, each with its own administration and its own premium collection system operating a variety of policies, some of which gave quite inadequate protection.

While the Federal Medical Care Act prohibited any carrier from offering benefits which could duplicate those under the provincial plan, there was provision for the provincial authority to utilize the services of designated agencies provided the designation did not extend to include the assessment and approval of accounts or to determine the monies to be paid in respect thereof.

Conformity to the above provisions could not be accepted by a number of nonprofit carriers. In response to a forceful lobby on behalf of a number of the larger private carriers, the government entered into agreement, with a consortium composed of 30 of the largest carriers. Inherent to this agreement was the reiteration of the legislative controls by the provincial authority in respect of the assessment and payment of claims. Accordingly, under the aegis of one of the largest carriers which assumed responsibility for the performance of the consortium, the government of Ontario employed each of the carriers, on a cost-plus basis, to process and pay the claims incurred by the subscribers already enrolled by the individual carriers. It was also agreed between the government and the insurance consortium that there would be a so-called "standard basic benefit package" representing all medically required services rendered by physicians on equal terms and conditions to all insured persons in the province.

This arrangement permitted the government to literally enroll all groups previously insured by the commercial carriers. It also provided the insurance carriers with an opportunity to cover services not insured under the national program, i.e. life, income indemnity, etc. This coverage was to be extended to the groups already organized and enrolled, with the overhead, in effect, at the expense of the government which included these extra benefits with the basic governmental package.

For two and a half years, this consortium administered the coverage for approximately 2.5 million Ontario residents. During this time, the central provincial government insuring agency proceeded to enroll as subscribers under the Ontario plan, various categories of individuals who for one reason or another, i.e. poor health risk, not in labor force, etc., had not been covered previously.

With many carriers involved it was very difficult for physicians and the public alike to direct their billings to the proper carrier, particularly since patients with group coverage through payroll deduction often were unaware of the name and address of their insurer. Each carrier processed only claims for its own groups. The commercial carriers had little interest in forwarding claims to other agents. Similarly, the various carriers had little interest in arranging for the transfer of coverage. Likewise, when changing coverage, management did not go out of its way to prevent lapses in coverage.

Commercial carriers traditionally only kept on record the most minimal statistical data sufficient to maintain actuarial solvency. Even within the consortium there were no compatible statistics which could provide a common data base. As a result, no comprehensive data base was produced on a province-wide basis, so that Ontario was the last province to have available the necessary statistical data for utilization and fiscal control.

Effective April 1972, the Ontario government amalgamated the medical and hospital insurance plans, having previously phased out all nongovernmental carriers, and replaced them with eight district offices of the provincial plan. While the consortium claimed to be operating with an overhead of approximately 5 percent of premiums collected, it was well recognized that by using one public authority, it would simplify the use of forms and records and provide for a realistic approach to obtaining a comprehensive health data base for all residents of the province. In addition, such an arrangement should lend itself to cost-benefit advantages through economies of scale. As well, through a single authority, there would be more uniformity in terms of processing procedures.

The present arrangement appears to be achieving many of these benefits, especially in terms of economy, uniformity, etc., through an arrangement which now allows the province to build up a universal, comprehensive data base enabling it to control its operations.

Since the federal government does not share the cost of provincial administration of the programs, each province is free to determine such matters as methods of administration, financing, and so on. Any decision to use or not to use agents would be a provincial decision. However, both Canadian Federal Acts require provincial plans to be accountable to a provincial legislature as a condition for receiving the very sizeable federal contributions.

No province made use of commercial or private, nonprofit carriers in relation to its hospital insurance program except to collect premiums and disseminate information. However, four provinces did involve such carriers as agents in their medicare plans at the outset, but most of these have been or are in the process of being phased out.

The Health Resources Fund

In keeping with the recommendation of the Royal Commission on the Health Services, the Health Resources Fund Act (established in 1965) provides for assistance in the planning, acquisition, construction, renovation and equipping of health training facilities.

The appropriation under the Act is $500 million, to be applied to costs incurred between January 1, 1966 and December 31, 1980, a fifteen-year period. The $500 million Fund was divided under the Act into three parts: $300 million was allocated to the provinces on a per capita basis; $25 million was allocated to the four Atlantic provinces for joint projects; and $175 million was to be allocated by the Governor in Council (Cabinet). Contributions, approved by the minister, are payable to the provinces in amounts up to 50 percent of the reasonable cost. To be eligible, projects must be included in a provincial five-year plan for the development of health training facilities.

On May 25, 1971, the $175-million unallocated portion of the Health Resources Fund was divided on the following basis:

(a) $100 million to the provinces on a per capita basis according to the

1966 census; and,

(b) $75 million for support of health training and research projects of national significance.

During the first seven and a half years of the program, contributions toward 176 projects were approved, amounting to over $306.5 million.

As an example of the use of this Fund, the number of medical schools in Canada has increased from 12 to 16. Besides 50 percent participation from the Fund in the planning, construction and equipping of the four new schools, the existing 12 were assisted for projects to extend and improve their facilities. In teaching facilities, there is a high research element with the ratio of approximately 70 percent teaching to 30 percent research support. The new and the improved facilities have caused the number of medical graduates to increase from 881 graduating in 1966, to 1,292 in 1972. The expectation is that 1,742 medical students will be graduating each year by 1978. This is almost a 100 percent increase in 12 years.

Most of the nine schools of dentistry have received financial assistance toward new construction/renovation and equipment costs and a new dental school was supported.

A large number of projects supported by the Health Resources Fund were devoted to nursing training facilities. These ranked from assistants, to diploma nurses (Registered Nurses), to university-trained nurses. As a result of the new and renovated teaching facilities, the actual output of nurses (Baccalaureate plus Diploma Nurses) shown as 7,387 in 1966 increased to 10,083 in 1972. This figure could rise to 11,000 by 1978. For the same years the number of nursing assistants who graduated went from 3,898 to 4,395 and is expected to reach 4,962 in 1978.

Other manpower groups that will benefit from increased and improved facilities for health teaching and health research include optometrists, pharmacists, physiotherapists, dental hygienists and various types of technicians. New, extended and improved facilities for these latter groups have been provided in many centers across Canada.

DESCRIPTION OF THE NATIONAL PROGRAMS

General description and comparison with other countries

The Canadian approach to national health insurance is quite different from most other countries in the world and this is for a variety of reasons, one of which is constitutional. Thus, instead of having a national plan as in most countries, we have national programs that are achieved through interlocking provincial plans, all of which share certain common features. This means in practice that the implementation of any one of these programs in Canada is spread over a period of several years rather than brought in all at once as is possible in a unitary state or in a country where the federal government itself operates the programs. As was mentioned before, the programs have been implemented in three main stages, spaced 10 years apart: the National Health Grants in 1948, Hospital Insurance in 1958 and Medicare in 1968.

Before describing the programs in detail, I should emphasize the ways in which the Canadian programs differ from those of other countries because they do differ from every other national health program, though not necessarily in the same ways.

First, the Canadian approach to health insurance is that the programs are almost entirely prepaid. In other words, the approach differs completely from the reimbursement schemes in some countries or from the liability schemes that exist in other countries. Following World War II, there were quite progressive developments in the Swift Current Region of Saskatchewan and the Saskatchewan and British Columbia Hospital Insurance Plans were introduced. All of these innovations involved the prepaid approach and other governmental initiatives since that time have also been in the direction of prepayment.

Another Canadian characteristic is the preference for "service plans" rather than liability plans. In other words, the level of payment is intended deliberately to leave little or nothing to the patient to pay at the time of illness or in direct relation to the illness. His benefit is a needed service as opposed to the liability approach which tends to pay according to a relatively fixed scale which may or may not cover the full bill. Again, unlike the schemes in a number of countries, there are no limits on the benefits payable subject only to medical need. There are no limits on the number of days of hospital care which will be covered. There are no limits on the number of visits to the doctor or the number of dollars which will be paid to hospitals and doctors provided that the patient needs the benefit on medical grounds.

The Canadian plans are universal rather than occupation, age- or income-oriented. As you know, in many European countries the plans are occupation-oriented. An individual who does not belong to one of the main occupation groups may not be able to obtain coverage. There are no disease exclusions as is characteristic of categorical programs.

Our plans are very heavily tax supported rather than being financed through direct contributions. Even where there are premiums (and some plans do have premiums) there is still a very heavy element of tax subsidy in the system.

Canadian plans operate on a pay-as-you-go basis rather than on a funded basis. This means that coverage can be provided to a resident of Canada from the first day of taking up residence. He does not have to pay into the scheme for x years or x months before he becomes entitled to benefits.

Another distinction between the Canadian approach to health insurance and that of some other countries is that there was no substantial interference with the ownership or operation of hospitals at the time of implementation of the Hospital Plan or with the private practice of medicine when the Medical Care

Plan was brought in. By contrast, in a number of countries the hospitals were nationalized. And private practice, in its pre-existing form, was markedly changed when national health insurance plans were introduced.

The Canadian Hospital and Medical Care Insurance plans provide for portability of benefits when the beneficiary is temporarily absent from Canada. The plans of quite a few other countries do not provide benefits outside their own borders and the National Health Service in Britain is a prime example of this. However, some of these countries do arrange trade-offs with another country. They agree to provide benefits for visitors from the other country in return for somewhat similar privileges for their own, but they do not, on their own account, provide the portability which is built into most Canadian programs.

Canadians covered under our schemes have free choice of physician and free choice of hospital without losing their benefits. There is a very minor exception to this in Quebec where the services of some doctors are not covered (other than in emergency) because the physicians (very few) have chosen to practice completely outside the scheme.

Both Canadian programs are universal with the state being the insurer. Within the scope of the coverage, benefits are intended to be virtually complete except where the beneficiary desires preferred accommodations, chooses to consult a nonparticipating physician or electively seeks care outside Canada. There are no deductibles and cocharges (where they exist) are nominal. The basic benefits, therefore, of all provincial plans are identical. That means there is complete coverage for all necessary hospital and physicians' care subject only to medical need in each province. Most provinces offer varying supplementary benefits for services such as optometry, which would be portable only where the worker moved between two provinces where the same supplementary benefits were offered. Surgical-dental services requiring a hospital for their performance are covered at both the professional and hospital end. Otherwise dental services are not covered under the national program at the present time. Vision care by ophthalmologists is covered in all provinces. Vision care by optometrists is not a benefit under the national program but is provided by six provinces as an extra benefit. Pharmacare is beginning to be covered in some provinces for categories of residents (indigents, the aged, etc.).

The Hospital Insurance Program–definitions

The Act setting out the universal hospital insurance program is called "The Hospital Insurance and Diagnostic Services Act" (HIDS).

Hospital is defined as a hospital or other facility providing inpatient or outpatient services but excludes:

1) a tuberculosis hospital or sanatorium,
2) a hospital or institution for the mentally ill,
3) a nursing home, a home for the aged, an infirmary or other institution,

the purpose of which is the provision of *custodial care.*

The hospitals must be approved by the province and meet the standards established by provincial law, including such matters as supervision, licensing and inspection of such facilities.

Residence as such is not defined and federal health insurance legislation only refers to a "resident" in terms of a person lawfully entitled to be or to remain in Canada, who makes his home and is ordinarily present. It excludes tourists, transients or visitors. Most provincial plans have legislated an identical definition but varying interpretations vis-à-vis eligibility have been made by the different plans in their related regulations. The decision as to whether or not a person is, in fact, a bona fide resident of the province, rests with the appropriate provincial health authorities. Differences in the interpretation of the expressions "makes his home" and "ordinarily present" and in what constitutes temporary absence could and did result in lack of uniformity of entitlement to coverage. But the situation has been greatly improved as a result of an inter-provincial agreement on eligibility and portability which was concluded in 1972.

Outpatient services are defined as all or any of the services required to be provided to inpatients that are provided on an outpatient basis, and specified in the Hospital Insurance Agreement with the province. Outpatient diagnostic services are not defined separately.

Terms of the agreement

Under HIDS, it is necessary for each province to enter into an agreement with the federal government. These agreements must:

a) specify the insured services to be provided,
b) specify the amount of authorized charges, if any,
c) include a schedule of hospitals in the province, and
d) set out the scheme for administration of the provincial law.

Under each agreement, the provinces undertake to provide insured services to insured residents, and the federal government undertakes to share in the cost of the provincial administration costs. The provinces agree to set up collection procedures to recover the hospital costs where the insured services were provided because of the wrongful act of a third party.

Under the Medical Care Act, the basic criteria which qualify for federal financial contributions are known as "the Four Points." These were spelled out rather more explicitly under the Medical Care Act because of the experience under the Hospital Insurance Act where the same principles were present but in rather more flexible form.

For Hospital Insurance:

a) *Comprehensive coverage* was mandatory for inpatient care but optional for outpatient care.
b) *Universal coverage on uniform terms and conditions* was

mandatory.

c) *Portability* was provided for but not very explicitly. Provinces were able to limit rather arbitrarily the dollars per day which would be paid for hospitalization outside their borders. Gradually, all plans agreed to accept the full per-diem rate for necessary hospitalization *within Canada* but some still set unrealistic limits for hospitalization outside Canada. Coverage for persons moving from one province to another was mandatory but inadequate provision for travel time was made. This was remedied in 1972.

d) *Public administration* was not explicitly required but no province was interested in using fiscal intermediaries and none has used any.

In Canada, all general hospitals and the overwhelming majority of convalescent extended care and rehabilitation hospitals come under the public program. Provinces can deliberately not list facilities providing the generally accepted levels of care where it is to the provincial government's financial advantage. In practice, they could not ignore bona fide general hospitals, but for hospitals providing extended and chronic care, provinces have approached it rather differently. For example, British Columbia and Prince Edward Island, both of which have relatively high percentages of elderly residents, did not list a number of chronic hospitals thus allowing these facilities to charge those patients able to pay for their care. In the case of patients without financial resources, federal sharing could be obtained originally under the Unemployment Assistance Act and later the Canada Assistance Plan Act.

One of the requirements of the federal legislation was that provinces develop a scheme for inspecting and licensing hospitals to insure the quality of care provided. This was certainly necessary since in 1958, in many hospitals, especially the smaller ones, quality of care left much to be desired and many were understaffed and ill-equipped. Under the new program with mandatory inspection and regulation at the provincial level, hospitals were told what equipment they should add or replace and what the appropriate staffing should be. As a result, over the first few years of universal hospital insurance, the quality of hospital care had improved considerably.

The Canada Assistance Plan

The Canada Assistance Plan was enacted in 1966 as a comprehensive public assistance measure to complement other income security measures. It provides, under agreements with the provinces, for federal contributions of 50 percent of the cost of assistance to persons in need and of the cost of certain welfare services. The federal government is contributing half of the cost of health care services not covered by provincial hospital and medical care insurance plans which are available from provincial social assistance programs to those in need. The only eligibility requirement specified in the Canada Assistance Plan is that of need determined through an assessment of budgetary requirements as well as of income and resources. The onus for developing such plans remains, of course, with the individual provincial government and the service may include prescription drugs and other items associated with the provision of health care.

Inpatient services

To be eligible for contributions under the Hospital Insurance and Diagnostic Services Act, a province is required to provide without charge, except for any charge authorized in an agreement, inpatient services to its residents based on uniform terms and conditions. It is mandatory that the following inpatient services be provided:

a) Accommodation and meals at the standard or public ward level,
b) Necessary nursing service,
c) Laboratory, radiological and other diagnostic procedures together with the necessary interpretations for the purpose of maintaining health, preventing disease and assisting in the diagnosis and treatment of any injury, illness or disability,
d) Drugs, biologicals and related preparations as provided in an agreement when administered in the hospital,
e) Use of operating room, case room and anesthetic facilities, including necessary equipment and supplies,
f) Routine surgical supplies,
g) Use of radiotherapy facilities where available,
h) Use of physiotheraphy facilities where available,
i) Services rendered by persons who receive remuneration from the hospital, and
j) Such other services as are specified in an agreement.

Outpatient services

Under hospital insurance, laboratory, radiological and other diagnostic procedures together with the necessary interpretations to assist in the diagnosis and treatment of any injury or disability must be made available as an insured inpatient service by all hospitals listed in the agreement under the Act; and the federal government shares in the cost of these services to the extent the costs are approved by the provinces. The method of remuneration for pathologists and radiologists is a matter between the hospital and the specialist and is, of course, subject to approval of the province. They may be paid in different ways—some on straight salary, some on straight fee-for-service, some on fee-for-service up to a fixed maximum and some on fee-for-service declining with increased volume. Normally, payments for interpretations are limited to interpretations by a specialist and generally GP's are not paid for any interpretations.

Outpatient or ambulatory diagnostic services (x-ray or lab) may be cost-shared under either the HIDS or Medical Care Acts. In order to quality for sharing under HIDS, private clinics or facilities must be designated as "hospitals" by the province and listed as such in the federal-provincial agreement. The policy of the federal government is to list only private laboratories and x-ray facilities for payment under HIDS, that will accept referral work from any physician, and that are operated as a referral center and not as part of the office of any practicing physician or group of practicing physicians. In the non-institutional setting, it is becoming common practice to license private laboratories in accordance with their proven capability to satisfactorily perform certain procedures. Similarly, in all provinces, the paying agency on advice from the provincial College of Physicians and Surgeons recognizes only a "short list" of simple laboratory procedures when performed in the physician's office. In both Saskatchewan and Manitoba, the "short list" is included in the legislative regulations.

The Medical Care Act stipulates that to be insured, services must be rendered by or under the supervision of a physician. On the other hand, HIDS legislation allows for cost-sharing of services rendered by non-medical personnel (e.g. biochemists) if the facility is listed as a "hospital." Commonly, payments for outpatient laboratory services are per unit of service, and at the same rate whether performed in a hospital or a private facility.

Provision of insured outpatient services to insured residents is optional. Any of the required inpatient services *may* be provided on an outpatient basis as insured services, provided that: a) the services are given under uniform terms and conditions without a charge to the patient except for any authorized charge, and b) that the insured outpatient services are specified in the agreement.

The sharing formula

The sharing formula between the two levels of government is as follows:

For inpatient services, yearly the contribution is the aggregate of:

a) 25 percent of the national per capita cost–plus

b) 25 percent of the provincial per capita cost less the per capita amount of authorized charges, multiplied by the average for the year of the number of insured persons of the province at the end of each month of such year.

For outpatient services, the annual contribution under HIDS is the percentage that the inpatient contributions by Canada to a province bears to the inpatient costs of the province multiplied by the payments by the province for insured outpatient services in the year, e.g.

Provincial costs of inpatient services	$80,000,000
Inpatient contributions by Canada	42,000,000
% of contributions to inpatient costs	52.5%
Provincial payments in year for outpatient services	$6,000,000
Canada's contributions for outpatient services–52.5% of $6,000	
52.5% of $6,000	3,150,000

In relation to the funding of the program, in the 1950's private health insurers were rather conservative and the Hospital Insurance Program likewise started out in a fairly conservative way with detailed signed agreements between the two senior levels of government. These specified the institutions which would be covered and what optional services, if any, would be provided and under what conditions. The funding arrangements tended to be fairly traditional, with premiums being frequently used to finance the program at the provincial level and/or cocharges being charged to the patient. However, it turned out that the cost of premium collection in some provinces (especially those with scattered rural population, or populations largely self-employed or seasonally employed) was very high. In addition, millions of Canadians at that time were relatively unaccustomed to paying health insurance premiums and this meant that the cost of attempting to collect premiums in some provinces did not justify the effort. Within a few years the premium system was abandoned in many provinces. The program was financed by means of a sales tax or in other ways from general provincial revenues. The federal government finances its half of the cost of the programs nationally from general revenues (Table 1).

Authorized charges are those approved by a provincial plan to be charged in relation to the provision of insured services included in the province's agreement with the federal government. These charges are made directly to the recipient of the services by the provider. (Such charges are separate and apart from charges for premiums or other general charges to finance the program which are not related to a specific service.)

At the present time, the only authorized charges are in the provinces of Alberta and British Columbia and in the Northwest Territories. While an authorized charge can in theory be any amount, the policy at the federal level is not to accept an authorized charge that would be sufficiently high to act as a financial barrier to any person requiring insured hospital services. As an example, a daily charge for inpatient hospital services may be $1 or $2 per day in general hospitals, whereas the charge in longer term chronic hospitals may be $4 to $5 per day, provided arrangements are made for those patients who cannot afford such rates. Hospitals are permitted to charge the patients a differential charge for private or semi-private accommodation.

In 1966-67, a Hospital Insurance Supplementary Fund was established to pay hospital insurance claims for services incurred by a resident of Canada who, through no fault of his own, ceased to be eligible for and entitled to benefits

TABLE 1

METHOD OF FINANCING

HOSPITAL INSURANCE					
Province	Premiums	Federal Contribution	Consolidated Revenue Funds[1]	Authorized Charges	Interest on Investments
B.C.		x	x	x	
Alta.	(2)	x	x	x	
Sask.		x	x		
Man.		x	x		x
Ont.	x (3)	x	x		
Que.		x	x		
N.B.		x	x		
N.S.		x	x		
P.E.I.		x	x		
Nfld.		x	x		
Yukon		x	x		
N.W.T.		x	x	x	

(1) General provincial revenues (Consolidated Revenue Fund) in all cases include the proceeds of provincial income taxes and, in all provinces except Alberta, provincial sales taxes.

(2) While there are no separate premiums charged for the coverage of the provincial hospital insurance plan in Alberta, eligibility for hospital insurance coverage depends upon medical care insurance status.

The regular premiums charged for coverage by the provincial medicare plan are:

Single	$5.75
Family of 2 or more	11.50

(Note: premium-exemption is granted to the entire premium-unit if one member is 65 years of age or older.)

(3) In Ontario, there is a combined provincial hospital and medical care insurance plan. The regular premiums are:

Single	$11.00
Family of 2 or more	22.00

(Note: premium-exemption is granted to the entire premium-unit if one member is 65 years of age or older and has resided for at least the previous 12 months in the province.)

No provincial plan is financed exclusively by way of premiums. The regular premiums cited above are provided at monthly rates and are applicable to those persons who do not qualify for premium assistance on account of limited income. The provisions for assistance vary from province to province but in all premium-provinces premium-free coverage is available if the provincial criteria for assistance are met. Partial premium assistance may also be provided. It should also be noted that in many instances in Ontario and Alberta where premiums are levied for coverage, employers may be paying a portion or all of the premiums on behalf of their employees as a fringe benefit.

under the provincial hospital insurance plans. With the advent of the Medical Care Program the need arose to cover medical services on a similar basis and as of July 1, 1972, a new Health Insurance Supplementary Fund replacing the old Hospital Insurance Supplementary Fund was established. The new fund provides for the payment of claims for health services (hospital insurance and medical care services) covered for cost-sharing under the Hospital Insurance and Diagnostic Services and the Medical Care Acts for residents of Canada who have been unable to obtain coverage or have lost coverage through no fault of their own. From July 1, 1972, to the present only 51 claims were submitted while prior to this date 468 claims had been submitted.

Coverage

All residents of Canada are eligible for hospital insurance coverage with the exception of certain people who are covered under other legislation. The principal exceptions are persons covered by workmen's compensation (although they are insured persons for anything other than their occupational illnesses and injuries), serving members of the armed forces and the Mounted Police (although their dependents are covered) and inmates in federal penitentiaries.

Regarding hospitalization in a foreign country, such as the United States, the coverage would depend at the moment on what province the patient came from. For coverage outside Canada, the Canadian plans function as indemnity plans since there is no control over the charges submitted. In practice, except for U.S. charges, the rates paid would cover the full bill in most countries. In the case of Ontario, they would probably pay the full rate but some provinces have a daily maximum for out-of-Canada care. The provinces generally make a distinction between the person who goes outside the country for elective care that is available at home and a person who requires care through no fault of his own when he happens to be out of the country such as with an accident or sudden illness. There is currently a trend in favor of picking up the bill in full or very close to in full in the latter case and to limiting the amount paid in the former case so not to encourage people going to other countries for care that is available in Canada.

Two provinces have regulations governing the time limit for a hospital to appeal the provincial plan rate decision for that hospital; the other provinces have no special regulations, and appeals by hospitals can be made to the provincial authority at any time. With respect to rejected claims on behalf of patients who were not eligible at the time of service, such patients may appeal to the provincial authority at any time, and there is no formal system in effect for this.

Organization

Another basic principle which influenced the development of Canadian

Hospital Insurance was the belief that existing tradition should be maintained as far as possible and, therefore, the pattern of hospital care and ownership that existed before 1957 was retained and provincial autonomy in the matter of health care was not infringed upon. Today after 16 years of universal hospital insurance, 90 percent of Canadian hospitals with 94 percent of the beds are still owned and governed by private boards which is quite a contrast with the situation in some other countries.

In terms of organization, in six provinces the plans are organized under a department of government and in four provinces they are administered by special commissions reporting, except in one case, to the Ministry of Health. For all commissions, a fund is used rather than payments made directly from the provincial consolidated fund (as in New Brunswick) and the essential difference under a special commission is post audit only and somewhat more flexible payment arrangements such as timing, rules, etc.

Medicare

In 1965, when the Prime Minister first announced his intention to implement Medicare he stated: "This proposal does not require detailed agreements. It calls only for general federal-provincial understanding as to the nature of the health program which will make a federal fiscal contribution appropriate. The Federal Government believes that there are four criteria on which such an understanding should be based."

There were no detailed signed agreements between the two levels of government and because sharing was totally indirect, auditing procedures were greatly simplified.

The Medical Care Act provided that any province that had a medical care plan meeting four basic points would be eligible for the federal contribution. This was based on 50 percent of the national average per capita cost of the insured services of the national program times the average for the year of the number of insured persons in the province. These minimum criteria, which came to be called "the Four Points," are essentially similar to those under the Hospital Insurance Program except that they relate primarily to physicians' services.

The Four Points

The first point was that coverage had to be *comprehensive.* In the Canadian context, this means it would cover all medically required services rendered by a physician, without dollar limit or other restrictions provided there was medical need. Furthermore, the benefits had to be accessible to the patient in the sense that the plan had to be administered in such a way that there would be no financial impediment or preclusion to an insured person receiving necessary care. In other words, if there was a deterrent fee or utilization fee, it must not actually deter a person from getting necessary care. This requirement thus sets a limit in practice on the amount of co-charge which could be imposed and ruled out a deductible approach completely.

There was provision made in the Act to add other professional services as benefits. In fact, certain surgical-dental procedures carried out in hospital by dental surgeons were included from the beginning. However, the provinces were apprehensive that the federal government might unilaterally use this provision in the Act to expand the benefit coverage more rapidly than they were ready for it. The federal government promised it would not invoke this clause unless there was a provincial consensus in favor of such a move.

The comprehensive coverage requirement of the Medical Care Act forced the provinces, which did not provide diagnostic outpatient services under their hospital insurance plans, to include such services or to provide the services under their medicare plans. In a number of areas the provinces have exercised their discretionary judgment in determining what constitutes "medically required services"–e.g. family planning measures, plastic surgery–and which surgical-dental services will be recognized for plan benefits. Most provinces provide additional benefits beyond the cost-shared insured services of the national program.

The second requirement was that coverage must be available to all eligible residents on uniform terms and conditions. In other words, it had to be universally available and *universal* to the extent that it would not cover less than 95 percent of the population. This requirement was quite deliberate because in the context of the middle 1960's, if there was not a minimum percentage coverage, some provincial plans might deliberately not go out of their way to cover substantially the whole population and thus leave a wide opening for the private insurers. The experience had been that nonuniversal pre-Medicare governmental schemes operating in parallel with private carriers were the most expensive way to operate.

One hundred percent of the eligible population is now insured in Newfoundland, Prince Edward Island, Nova Scotia, New Brunswick, Quebec, Manitoba, Saskatchewan, the Northwest Territories and the Yukon Territory; virtually 100 percent in Alberta and British Columbia; and over 99 percent in Ontario.

The third requirement was that benefits had to be *portable* when the insured was temporarily absent and also when he was changing jobs, retiring or moving his place of residence from one province to another. Much of the private insurance coverage had been job related and if the individual left his job he commonly lost the coverage he had and would have to go through a waiting period to get coverage somewhere else. No longer was eligibility for coverage to be related to employment or nonemployment. It was to be based only upon the province of residence.

The mandatory portability requirement of the Medical Care Act exposed problems under hospital insurance which resulted in mobile Canadians losing coverage through no fault of their own when moving between plans and led to the inter-provincial agreement in 1972 which eliminated many of the anomalies.

There is nationwide portability of hospital and medical care insurance coverage. Prior to the implementation of the 1972 inter-provincial agreement on eligibility and portability, the difficulties had arisen primarily due to each province using its own interpretation of the term "resident."

The inter-provincial agreement has done much to resolve the problems. Basically, the agreement consists of a series of provisions and administrative interpretations on the way in which such mobile Canadians will be covered by the provincial plans in a coordinated manner. All provinces, except British Columbia, have accepted the agreement in full. British Columbia, nevertheless, accepted the most important provisions but declined to accept providing first day coverage for landed immigrants and to other new residents from abroad. Thus, the British Columbia reservation was in regard to eligibility rather than portability. All provinces, including British Columbia, provide up to three months coverage plus reasonable travelling time for persons moving to another province until the expiration of the waiting period in the new province of residence. British Columbia stipulated a maximum of three months travelling time but other provinces are considerably more generous.

Finally, the fourth requirement was that the plan had to be operated on a *nonprofit basis* and administered by a public agency *accountable* to the provincial government for its financial transactions, and this again pretty well cut out the private insurance industry, certainly as insurers.

This provision is not so restrictive, however, that a provincial plan is precluded from accumulating reserve funds to be applied against future costs, if the provincial government wishes this to be done. If this is done, the plan is still being operated on a nonprofit basis.

Coverage

Under Medicare all medically required services provided by physicians and a limited list of dental-surgical services provided by dentists in hospitals are covered. Payments are made to or on behalf of beneficiaries. Beneficiaries are persons residing in the province and lawfully entitled to be there. In premium-provinces generally, they must also have paid a premium unless they are exempt on account of limited income or age where such an exemption is granted. But in the Yukon, which has a compulsory premium plan, eligibility for coverage is not linked to payment of premiums. There are waiting periods for persons moving into the province but we have uniformity throughout Canada and no Canadian citizen is left "sitting between two provinces" so to speak, the former province covering until the new one takes over. Office-type dental services and prescription drugs remain outside the publicly financed and administered national program. Medical care is insured on a fee-for-service basis and over 90 percent of physicians adhere strictly to the benefit schedules which are negotiated between the Ministry of Health in the various provinces and the

Medical Association of that province.

Since all medically required services of a physician licensed to practice in the province are mandatory benefits, provinces can only exclude or limit coverage for borderline or optional services such as routine check-ups, refractions for spectacles, cosmetic surgery and immunizations for travel, etc. Even in Quebec where the patients of the very few physicians practicing totally outside the Plan are not normally reimbursed for medical expenses, exceptions are made in the case of emergency and urgently required services.

Auditing

An additional difference between the two Acts is that costs under the Medical Care Act are shared in relation to the fiscal year in which they are paid and final settlement is achieved within about six months after the fiscal year ends. On the other hand, under the Hospital Insurance and Diagnostic Services Act, shareable costs are related to the calendar year to which they refer. By virtue of retroactive pay increases, delays in hospital, provincial and federal audits, etc., settlement of any given year is normally delayed for about 27 months. For example, while by November, 1973, the Medicare costs for the fiscal year 1972-73 had been settled, final Hospital Insurance settlements and payments for 1971, were made at the end of April 1974. At that time, five provinces financed Medicare based on general revenue, four on premiums and one province on income tax surcharge. The federal share in 1971-72 ranged from a high of 81 percent (Newfoundland) down to 43 percent (Ontario) (Table 2).

Administration

In two provinces and the Territories the Plan is administered by a department of government and in the remaining provinces by a commission.

In three provinces physicians can appeal to the commission; six provinces have special committees to hear appeals and one province has a committee of the Medical Association for this purpose.

Extension of benefits

Through an Order in Council (a Cabinet decision), the federal government can permit cost-sharing of additional benefits without resorting to new legislation; this can be done by regulations under the existing legislation. However, any so-added benefit coverage must satisfy the requirements of the Medical Care Act, that is, it must be comprehensive, universal, portable and be administered publicly.

A further constraint is the political commitment made originally by the Prime Minister and then by successive health ministers, that there be a "consensus" among the provinces in favor of any such extension before the federal government would consider granting cost-sharing to these added benefits. To date the consensus in favor of optometry is the only one which has formally

TABLE 2

PROVINCIAL COSTS VS FEDERAL CONTRIBUTIONS UNDER THE HOSPITAL INSURANCE AND MEDICAL CARE PROGRAMS 1973-74

	HOSPITAL INSURANCE PROGRAM				MEDICAL CARE PROGRAM			
Province	Estimated Provincial Costs ($000)	Estimated Federal Contributions ($000)	Contributions of Provincial Costs ($000)	Balance of Provincial Costs (%)	Estimated Provincial Costs ($000)	Estimated Federal Contributions ($000)	Contributions of Provincial Costs (%)	Balance of Provincial Costs (%)
Newfoundland	58,824	33,866	57.6	42.4	20,434	16,657	81.5	18.5
Prince Edward Island	11,388	6,807	59.8	40.2	4,752	3,529	74.3	25.7
Nova Scotia	97,085	53,049	54.6	45.4	38,948	24,552	63.0	37.0
New Brunswick	85,108	43,631	51.3	48.7	26,539	20,093	75.7	24.3
Quebec	912,822	438,750	48.1	51.9	370,835	188,332	50.8	49.2
Ontario	1,072,851	530,230	49.4	50.6	550,442	246,351	44.8	55.2
Manitoba	133,608	70,944	53.1	46.9	54,030	31,703	58.7	41.3
Saskatchewan	115,481	61,280	53.1	46.9	46,997	28,189	60.0	40.0
Alberta	241,858	121,106	50.1	49.9	94,389	53,159	56.3	43.7
British Columbia	268,734	142,225	52.9	47.1	162,758	72,137	44.3	55.7
Yukon Territory	1,878	1,142	60.8	39.2	1,144	619	54.1	45.9
Northwest Territories	5,099	2,476	48.6	51.4	1,667	1,146	68.7	31.3
Canada	3,004,736	1,505,506	50.1	49.9	1,372,935	686,467	50.0	50.0

Notes: The federal contribution for the province of Quebec, under the hospital insurance program is paid through tax rebate under the Established Programs (Interim Arrangement) Acts, effective 1965-66.

The Provincial costs under the hospital insurance program are calculated on a "calendar year" basis, but have been "fiscalized" for comparison purpose with the medical care program. The last years for which actual audited costs are available is calendar year 1971 for hospital insurance and fiscal year 1972-73 for medical care.

developed but has not been acted on pending consideration of new financial proposals to be mentioned later.

Overbilling

On overbilling the Hall Commission had this to say:

"The emphasis on the freedom to practice should not obscure the fact that the physician is not only a professional person but also a citizen. He has moral and social obligations, as well as self-interest to do well in his profession. The notion held by some that the physician has an absolute right to fix his fees as he sees fit is incorrect and unrelated to the mores of our times. This nineteenth century laissez-faire concept has no validity in the twentieth century in its application to medicine, dentistry, law, or to any other profession, or, in fact, to any other organized group. Organized medicine is a statutory creation of legislatures and of Parliament. When the state grants a monopoly to an exclusive group to render an indispensable service it automatically becomes involved in whether those services are available and on what terms and conditions.

. . . The provision of and payment for services is to be the result of a negotiated contractual relationship based principally on the fee-for-service concept. The physician continues in private practice. He renders the service which, in his judgment, his diagnosis indicates. The state does not interfere in any way with his professional management of the patient's condition, nor with the confidential nature of the physician-patient relationship. 'Only the manner of receiving payment is altered.'

No one can seriously suggest that any one method of receiving payment is sacrosanct or that it has any therapeutic value. In fact, there is good reason to believe that eliminating the financial element at time of receiving services does have a salutary effect on the patient, and on the physician-patient relationship. Moreover, any physician is free to practice independently of the programme, either wholly or partially. There will undoubtedly be some patients who, though covered, will elect to make private financial arrangements to avail themselves of the services of such physicians. In such cases, the physician would look for payment only from the patient. Such arrangements would operate independently from the programme we have recommended and thus would not be contrary to the principle of extra billing rejected by us."

The Medical Care Act requires that the medical care insurance plans of participating provinces provide a reasonable level of payment for insured services. These payments are generally prorated at a percentage (e.g. 85 percent or 90 percent) of the provincial schedule of fees. Most doctors are willing to accept this level of payment as being payment in full due largely to the virtual elimination of bad debts. In addition, with one exception, provincial plans require physicians to notify patients in advance if they intend to charge more than will be paid by the provincial plan. In some provinces this is required in writing and the plan must be informed of the amount involved. This makes it possible for insured persons to make other arrangements if they do not wish to accept the additional charges.

In general, there is no overbilling made by a *participating* physician for insured general practice or *referred* specialist services and no province favors physicians charging more than the plan pays. However, in some provinces overbilling is permitted under certain circumstances where the patient has been informed and agreed in advance. In addition, some provinces pay specialists at GP rates for nonreferred work and permit the specialist to charge the difference between GP and specialist rates in such cases. Noninsured services to Canadian residents and services to foreign visitors are, of course, not under the control of the plans.

The theory behind the 85-90 percent proration practiced by most plans is based upon the philosophy of the physician-sponsored nonprofit prepaid plans which, beginning in the late 1930's, had in nine provinces the largest share of the private insurance coverage before the implementation of Medicare. The fees listed in professional fee schedules in those days contained an allowance for bad debts, repeated billings, bookkeeping costs and collection charges. Patients electing to *prepay* their physician's services automatically eliminated such considerations in the case of participating physicians who could be sure of being paid on one billing for their services to patients possessing such coverage. Accordingly the plans argued, and most physicians agreed, that by prepaying, the patient had already covered part of the physician's overhead and, unless the prepaid accounts were discounted appropriately, he would be paying this overhead component twice.

The profession, being anxious to foster this type of payment, covering office and home visits from the first dollar as opposed to commercial insurance which generally had deductibles and often co-insurance, strongly supported this plan. Most physicians found they were much better off to participate than to charge a higher fee and take their chances on collection. Participating physicians, with a few specified exceptions, had to participate for all their patients and to accept the plan's direct payment as payment in full.

When Medicare was implemented, the new plans, generally, retained the previous usual level of proration used by the nonprofit plans. In many provinces, the profession has resisted the plan's efforts to reduce the level of proration. This is for two reasons:

a) the profession feels it will get more public support in any conflict with government if it can say it is being paid *only* 85 or 90 percent, etc. of its fee schedule.
b) it gives some room for nonparticipating physicians to extra bill

without exceeding the schedule.

At a recent Ontario Medical Association Council, government overtures to provide an increase in payment level through reduction or elimination of proration were rejected. The Council, however, was firmly of the opinion that the profession needed a fee increase. Ultimately this was achieved by increasing the overall fee schedule but retaining the 90 percent proration.

RESULTS AND OTHER RELATED EFFECTS

Generally speaking

There is no doubt that universal hospital insurance and Medicare have been two of the most progressive changes in Canada in the last decades. In retrospect, governments, the public and the providers of services congratulate themselves for having taken those decisions; most of the rancor, debate, unpleasantness, etc. have been forgotten and most Canadians are satisfied that the situation is so much improved now compared to what it was before. There is really no regret; these plans are here to stay. This is not to say that they are perfect; there is dissatisfaction but slowly and gradually this is being ironed out in most provinces.

The greatest benefit has been the provision of financial accessibility to health care (this is discussed in greater detail in another chapter): no longer do people wait to seek care because they cannot afford it and a sudden illness or accident is not a financial catastrophe for an individual or a family. It is a fact though that the very poor are still not utilizing the system as much as they could for a variety of reasons: lack of a baby-sitter, taxi or bus fares, etc.

In the transition from a private more or less unregulated system to a National Insurance System, there were problems for some beneficiaries, some insurers, some administrators and some providers; but overall, many insurers and administrators and most beneficiaries and providers have benefited considerably albeit in vastly different ways. There was a period of mild to moderate confusion in adjustment lasting perhaps a year or so but with goodwill, most problems have been solved.

The Hospital Plan was implemented 10 years before the Medical Plan and this had some unfortunate side effects. Canadians had an incentive to be hospitalized, to get their drugs free, all their surgical supplies free, many had private insurance paying the physician at the hospital but not at the office, they were not a nuisance at home, etc. Furthermore, even the lowest levels of private insurance coverage that existed in those days, generally covered physicians' services in the hospital but not necessarily in the office so that the physician also had an incentive to hospitalize patients. The net result of this was that the system became even more oriented to the hospital than it had been before. Table 3 is informative on this point, showing that Canada has more hospital beds than the U.S. in every category and the same applies to patient days of care except very recently in tuberculosis. In theory, it might have been better to start with the medical program, so as to encourage outpatient care but in practice and in political reality, as we mentioned before, this was not possible. Thus, while a phased-in program may appear to cost less money in the short run, it may not necessarily do so in the long run. This obviously depends on how it is phased in, what parallel benefits are brought in simultaneously, etc.

Effects on health

When discussing the universal health programs, the first question is, what were the results of these programs, can it be said that such and such a measure has produced x results? It is very difficult to measure the impact of such a public program because methods of measuring the success or failure are not too precise, the factors are multiple, the situation is ever evolving and the cause-effect relationship is not always possible to prove.

The various mortality rates are used very commonly but these do not depend solely upon the adequacy of health care. Again costs can be looked at, but success from the standpoint of the public might be judged by the fact that the public has avoided personal costs at the time of need while from the standpoint of financial planners, such costs for the plan might not be looked upon as a success. It depends upon one's viewpoint.

But certainly in Canada we have had some marked changes in certain vital statistics. At the time our Hospital Insurance Program came in, our infant mortality rate was running approximately 40 percent higher than Australia's, 30 percent higher than that of England and Wales and about 5 percent higher than that of the United States. By the end of 1971, which was the first year that all provinces were in Medicare for the full year, our infant mortality rate was almost identical to that of Australia and England and Wales and 10 percent lower than that of the U.S. (Table 4). Yet our economic patterns and so on tend to follow those of the U.S. The major difference between what happened in the two countries in the interval was the implementation of our national health insurance programs. Our maternal mortality rate as it was on the eve of Medicare had dropped by a third again by the end of 1971 and it was noted in some of these pre- and post-Medicare studies that one of the effects of Medicare was that pregnant women were turning up a couple of months earlier for prenatal care than they had been doing before. It would be naive to try to suggest that this was entirely due to Medicare, but it seems almost impossible to conceive that the changed patterns of certain segments of the public in seeing physicians earlier did not play some major part.

Rates of utilization after Medicare

Throughout the world there is a tendency for utilization of medical services to increase at a modest rate from year to year because of technology, population shifts from rural to urban regions and so on. We are also experiencing that phenomenon in Canada. But after the first year, in each province for which

TABLE 3

COMPARATIVE RATES PER THOUSAND POPULATION FOR HOSPITAL ADMISSIONS AND PATIENT DAYS OF CARE BY TYPE OF HOSPITAL, CANADA AND THE UNITED STATES, 1966 TO 1972

	TYPE OF HOSPITAL (a)											
	General and Allied Special						Mental		Tuber-culosis		All Hospitals (c)	
Year	Short-Term (b)		Long-Term (b)		Total							
Admissions	Can.	U.S.	Can.	U.S.	Can.	U.S.	Can.	U.S.	Can.	U.S.	Can.	U.S.
1966	157.3	145.8	2.0	0.9	159.3	146.7	2.9	2.2	0.5	0.2	162.6	149.1
1967	156.2	144.8	2.1	1.0	158.3	145.8	2.8	2.8	0.5	0.1	161.6	148.7
1968	159.2	145.2	2.2	0.9	161.4	146.1	2.9	3.0	0.4	0.2	164.7	149.3
1969	159.6	148.0	1.9	1.7	161.5	149.7	2.8	2.7	0.4	0.2	164.6	152.6
1970	164.0	151.2	2.0	1.7	166.0	152.9	2.8	2.7	0.3	0.2	169.1	155.8
1971	167.5	154.3	2.1	1.1	169.6	155.4	2.6	2.8	0.2	0.2	172.4	158.4
1972	166.6	155.6	2.1	1.4	168.7	157.0	2.8	2.6	0.1	0.1	171.6	159.8
Patient Days of Care												
1966	1,685.3	1,289.5	324.1	126.5	2,009.3	1,416.0	1,189.0	1,154.0	64.5	40.0	3,262.8	2,610.0
1967	1,679.9	1,297.9	333.4	144.6	2,013.3	1,442.5	1,116.9	1,086.6	58.2	22.6	3,188.4	2,551.7
1968	1,703.6	1,325.2	342.1	116.6	2,045.7	1,441.9	1,053.4	1,061.4	50.0	26.8	3,149.1	2,530.1
1969	1,728.4	1,315.3	312.0	149.3	2,040.5	1,464.5	1,023.9	951.6	41.6	24.1	3,106.0	2,440.2
1970	1,734.0	1,329.6	324.4	133.7	2,058.4	1,463.3	960.2	838.6	31.9	22.1	3,050.6	2,324.0
1971	1,737.8	1,317.9	333.2	109.8	2,071.0	1,427.7	908.2	742.4	25.0	19.1	3,004.2	2,189.2
1972	1,684.2	1,290.2	336.8	118.0	2,021.0	1,408.2	836.9	702.8	13.7	13.8	2,871.6	2,124.8

(a) Distribution is by type of facility, not by type of care, e.g. psychiatric or tuberculosis care in units of general hospitals appears under "General and Allied Special" and not under "Mental" or "Tuberculosis."

(b) Undue emphasis should not be placed upon the distinction between short-and long-term care in general and allied special hospitals as the statistics are influenced by definition and the requirement to designate each facility under one category only. Many short-term hospitals provide some long-term care, whereas long-term facilities do not normally provide short-term care, and as a consequence the long-term data tend to be understated and the short-term data overstated.

(c) Components may not add to totals shown due to rounding.

DATA SOURCES:

United States

Admissions and Patient Days: Hospital Statistics, American Hospital Association, appropriate years, Table 2 for 1972 and corresponding tables for other years, adjusted to reclassify hospitals with an average patient stay of 30 days or less as short-term. Patient days calculated from average daily census.

Population: Statistical Abstract of the United States, 1973. Data used were for total resident population as of July 1 of each year.

Canada

Admissions and Patient Days: Hospital Statistics Volume 1 – Hospital Beds, Statistics Canada, Tables 9 and 11, for 1971 and prior years. Advance data for 1972. "Long-term hospitals" include chronic, convalescent and rehabilitation facilities.

Population: "Estimated Population of Canada by Province as of June 1, 1972," Statistics Canada. Data are for total resident population.

TABLE 4

INFANT AND GENERAL MORTALITY RATES IN DEVELOPED COUNTRIES

		General Mortality Rates per 1,000 Population		Infant Mortality Rates per 1,000 Live Births		
		1960	1970	1960	1970	1971
1)	Sweden	10.0	9.9	16.6	11.7	–
2)	Finland	9.0	9.5	21.0	12.5	–
3)	Netherlands	7.7	8.4	17.9	12.7	–
4)	Japan	7.6	6.9	30.7	13.1	–
5)	Norway	9.1	9.8	18.9	13.8	–
6)	Denmark	9.5	9.8	21.5	14.8	–
7)	France	11.4	10.6	27.4	15.1	–
8)	Switzerland	9.7	9.0	21.1	15.1	–
9)	New Zealand	8.8	8.8	22.6	16.7	16.5
10)	Australia	8.6	9.0	20.2	17.9	17.3
11)	England and Wales	11.5	11.7	21.8	17.9	17.4
12)	Canada	7.8	7.3	27.3	18.8	17.5
13)	German Democratic Republic	13.3	14.1	38.8	18.8	–
14)	Ireland (Republic)	11.5	11.5	29.3	19.2	–
15)	Scotland	11.9	12.3	26.4	19.6	–
16)	United States	9.5	9.4	26.0	19.8	19.2
17)	Belgium	12.4	12.4	31.2	20.5	–
18)	Czechoslovakia	9.2	11.4	23.5	22.1	–
19)	Northern Ireland	10.8	10.9	27.2	22.7	–
20)	Federal Republic of Germany	11.4	11.6	33.8	23.5	–
21)	Israel	5.7	7.0	31.0	23.6	–
22)	U.S.S.R.	7.1	8.2	35.0	24.4	–
23)	Luxembourg	11.8	12.2	31.5	24.9	–
24)	Austria	12.7	13.2	37.5	25.9	–
25)	Bulgaria	8.1	9.1	45.1	27.3	–
26)	Spain	8.8	8.6	43.7	27.8	–
27)	Malta	8.6	9.4	38.3	27.9	–
28)	Italy	9.7	9.7	43.9	29.2	–
29)	Poland	7.5	8.1	56.8	33.1	–
30)	Hungary	10.2	11.6	47.6	35.7	–
31)	South Africa	(c)	(c)	(c)	N/A	–
32)	Romania	8.7	9.6	75.7	49.5	–
33)	Yugoslavia	9.9	8.9	87.7	55.2	–
34)	Portugal	10.8	9.7	77.5	58.0	–

data are available, the initial spurt definitely levelled off and came down to a relatively predictable rate of increase. Table 5 shows rates of increase in the utilization of physicians' services in the first six provinces to implement Medicare plans after the initial plan year. You can see that while the number of services per thousand beneficiaries does creep up in most cases, the physician

TABLE 5
PERCENTAGE CHANGES IN UTILIZATION[1]
OF PHYSICIANS' SERVICES
SIX PROVINCES, 1970 OR 1970-71
TO 1971 OR 1971-72

	Percentage Changes		
	G.P.	Spec.	Total
Province 1			
Number of services per 1,000 beneficiaries	6.4	.9	4.2
Number of services per active physician	-1.5	-5.6	-3.0
Province 2			
Number of services per 1,000 beneficiaries	5.6	1.5	4.2
Number of services per active physician	1.5	-3.1	0.05
Province 3			
Number of services per 1,000 beneficiaries	2.4	4.9	3.4
Number of services per active physician	-2.5	1.1	-1.0
Province 4			
Number of services per 1,000 beneficiaries	4.6	7.3	5.2
Number of services per active physician	-2.6	4.8	0.2
Province 5			
Number of services per 1,000 beneficiaries	2.4	-1.9	0.87
Number of services per active physician	-5.4	-6.9	-5.7
Province 6			
Number of services per 1,000 beneficiaries	4.0	0.1	2.8
Number of services per active physician	1.5	-5.5	-1.1
Six Provinces			
Number of services per 1,000 beneficiaries	3.7	1.4	3.0
Number of services per active physician	-1.3	-3.7	-2.0

(1) Radiology and laboratory services excluded.

Source: Data submitted by the Medical Care Insurance Commissions of the six provinces.

supply has outpaced the growth of services with the result that on the average, the number of services per physician has been going down. In some provinces, this holds for both GP's and specialists and in others, just for one or the other. This table is now more than two years old and subsequent data show a continuation of this trend.

A number of pre- and post-Medicare studies show that there was not really any increase in the proportion of patients going to see physicians without reasonable cause. The rate of increase in medical costs since Medicare is now rather less than it was for physicians' services prior to Medicare. On an annual per capita basis, the rate of increase is currently running almost one third less than it was in the several years leading up to Medicare (Table 6).

Effect of deterrent fees or surcharge

Medical spokesmen had predicted that financial involvement of the patient at time of service should be a feature of the program to protect the physician and the public purse. Only Saskatchewan imposed a utilization fee on visits to the physician's office from 1968 to 1971.* Prior to 1968, Saskatchewan had the lowest rate of cost and utilization increase in Canada. After the utilization fee was started, there was a drop in utilization the first year, following which utilization began to increase again but at a higher rate than it ever had before. In other words, there was a rebound phenomenon.

Unfortunately, the decrease in utilization occurred in those who needed care most–the poor. It had a lesser effect on those who could easily afford the fee. Table 7 shows the effect resulting from the imposition of the $1.50 utilization fee. The poor here are those defined by the Economic Council of Canada as individuals who spend more than a certain percentage of their income on the basic necessities of food, shelter and clothing. There was an overall reduction in services to them of 18 percent and the table shows various breakdowns by type of service. The utilization fee was collected and retained by the provider of service (hospital or physician). The plan payments for insured services were reduced by the amount of the applicable utilization fees.

If a patient refused to pay the utilization fee, the provider of the service had the normal recourse through the courts to collect the debt. Physicians tended to collect the fee at the time that a service was provided and hospitals when a patient was discharged. The relatively small amount of the utilization fees per physician visit or for an average hospital stay would no doubt result in the majority of uncollected fees being written off as bad debts rather than subjected to court action.

Patients eligible for social assistance had the utilization fee paid on their

---

*The Saskatchewan utilization fees were:

a) *For hospital inpatients*–$2.50 for the first 30 days, $1.50 for the next 60 days;
b) *For physicians' services*–$1.50 for office visit, $2 per home or hospital outpatient visit;
c) *The maximum payable for hospital and physician utilization fees*–$180 per family per year.

behalf under the Saskatchewan Assistance Plan. The federal government paid the fees on behalf of those beneficiaries whose premiums were paid by the federal government (Treaty Indians and War Veterans Allowance recipients).

After the first year, there was an increase in utilization by young single males and females. Presumably these younger people found it easy to get an appointment when they were not competing with the elderly or with the lower-income people. These charges did not turn out to be popular and it was an important factor in the government defeat in 1971; the new government promptly abolished these surcharges.

Things that did not happen

One common prediction when Medicare came in was that Canada would cease to be an attractive country for physicians; that the immigration from abroad would dry up, that our physicians would emigrate to other countries in droves, and that the medical students would lose interest in going to medical schools because the practice of medicine would be so unattractive. In fact, what happened was that the immigration from abroad more than doubled–it went up from an average of around 600 a year to about 1,400 a year within several years of the passage of the Act. Emigration to other countries, particularly the United States, went down–way down from what it had been–and for the first time ever, universities could not accommodate all the well-qualified students who wished to enroll in medical school (Figure 1). Therefore, that prognosis did not turn out to be very accurate.

It was also alleged that without patient financial participation at the time of or in direct relation to the medical service, the physicians would simply be swamped and the quality of care would decrease. As was mentioned above, this did not happen.

The advent of universal hospital and medical care insurance programs did not quickly insure equitable access except for financial access. However, it is inevitable that when the government becomes the insurer (in our case the provincial governments), sooner or later it must become involved in correcting inadequacies in the infrastructure and organizational arrangements of the health service system. Mr. Claude Castonguay elsewhere in this volume elaborates on the experience of Quebec in this regard.

Concern has been expressed by medical educators at the possibility of finding themselves deprived of patients who would be available for teaching purposes since free care in the hospitals was to be eliminated. It is difficult to understand in retrospect why it should have been assumed that only poor people should be expected to make themselves available for teaching purposes; or that poor people should have been obligated to be available for teaching purposes simply on the grounds that they were receiving free hospital care. As it turned out, no problem was experienced and patients were as available for teaching purposes after the advent of hospital insurance and Medicare as prior to that

TABLE 6

PERCENTAGE CHANGES IN PER CAPITA COSTS OF PHYSICIANS' SERVICES, BY PROVINCE PRE- AND POST MEDICARE

	a) *Pre Medicare* % Change Over Preceding Year Calendar Years						b) *Medicare Program Costs* % Change Over Preceding Year Fiscal Years				
Province	1966	1967	1968	1969	1970	1971	1969-70	1970-71	1971-72	1972-73	1973-74
Newfoundland	8.3	11.6	27.4	xxx				7.6	3.9	6.6	18.7
Nova Scotia	12.0	4.7	20.1	xxx				9.0	7.6	8.9	6.3
Ontario	7.2	12.9	13.5	xxx				5.8	7.9	5.7	3.0
Manitoba	7.9	9.0	9.6	xxx				7.7	3.0	1.6	3.8
Saskatchewan	8.7	4.4	xxx*				10.7	14.1	16.6*	10.9	7.1
Alberta	9.9	21.8	25.6	xxx				7.4	2.9	5.6	-0.4
British Columbia	12.2	6.4	xxx				8.8	7.3	5.1	4.8	10.4
7 Provinces	8.8	11.7	14.3					7.1	7.1	5.8	4.5
Prince Edward Island	5.5	10.8	15.4	20.0	xxx				8.5	5.1	2.5
New Brunswick	3.8	19.9	9.3	11.8		xxx			7.0	12.4	8.8
Quebec	10.6	9.2	9.2	10.1	xxx				8.7	9.7	9.7
10 Provinces	9.1	11.3	13.0	—	—	—			7.6	7.0	6.0

xxx – Year of introduction of Medicare

* Utilization fees imposed April 15, 1968 and removed August 1, 1971

NOTES:

(i) % change figures are from previous calendar or fiscal year shown, e.g. in Newfoundland there was an 8.3% increase from 1965 to 1966.

(ii) First Medicare fiscal year in each province is annualized to give a hypothetical full-year's program costs so that comparison with subsequent years could be made.

(iii) These are per capita figures. Fee schedule revisions are reflected. No adjustments have been made for the steady and substantial increase in the physician to population ratio (e.g. in Newfoundland from 1969 to 1972 there was almost a one-third increase in the doctor supply relative to population), for the inflation factor (i.e. decreasing purchasing power of the dollar) or for utilization increases.

(iv) Adjustments have been made to compensate for switches in diagnostic services coverage from Medicare to Hospital Insurance in Ontario, Manitoba and Saskatchewan after originally being covered under Medicare. To preserve comparability these costs have been removed from all years—otherwise the rate of increase would have appeared much less after the "switch."

(v) The cost increase in the year of implementation over the previous year has been ignored in this table. It has been referred to in the text and in Table 1 for the country as a whole.

(vi) The figures for the pre-Medicare years are based upon per capita expenditures on physicians' services while figures for later years are based upon program costs. There are some minor differences, regarding the types of payments included in each, but it is believed that the rates of change would not be materially affected by this.

May 1974

TABLE 7

EFFECTS OF SASKATCHEWAN'S CO-CHARGE ($1.50 PER OFFICE VISIT) ON THE POOR (E.C.C. DEFINITION) BY TYPE OF SERVICE (AFTER BECK)

All Services	-18%
G.P. Services	-14%
Specialist Services	- 5%
Complete Examination	+13%
Regional Examination	-38%
Home and Emergency Calls	-27%
Hospital Visits	-16%
Laboratory Services	- 6%
Major Surgery	- 8%
Minor Surgery	-13%

time. In fact, the teaching material has never been better.

Some problems for the beneficiaries

The great majority of the public has greater benefits or greater potential insurance benefits under the new system than they had under the old. However, some people, who either had better than average private insurance coverage or whose financial circumstances were such that they were not particularly impeded from getting care under the pre-existing arrangements, find that they now have to compete with all their neighbors for medical attention on the basis of need.

Also, on the matter of cost, quite a large section of the public is paying less than before (particularly those people who were considered to be poor risks for whatever reason). It is, therefore, inherent to the national insurance program that there is a redistribution of cost of one sort or another over the population. Consequently, the healthy young prime risks (through premium or general taxation) who were in a very favorable category under private insurance arrangements, now find themselves picking up through this averaging process some of the costs for the older person. There are some people for whom the new program appears to provide fewer benefits; there were a number of individuals who luckily had a contract with very limited availability to the public such as in the case of a "loss-leader" that provided rather substantial benefits over and above the basic benefits. In Canada, a number of insurance companies simply backed out of the health area, they did not carry on the supplementary coverage

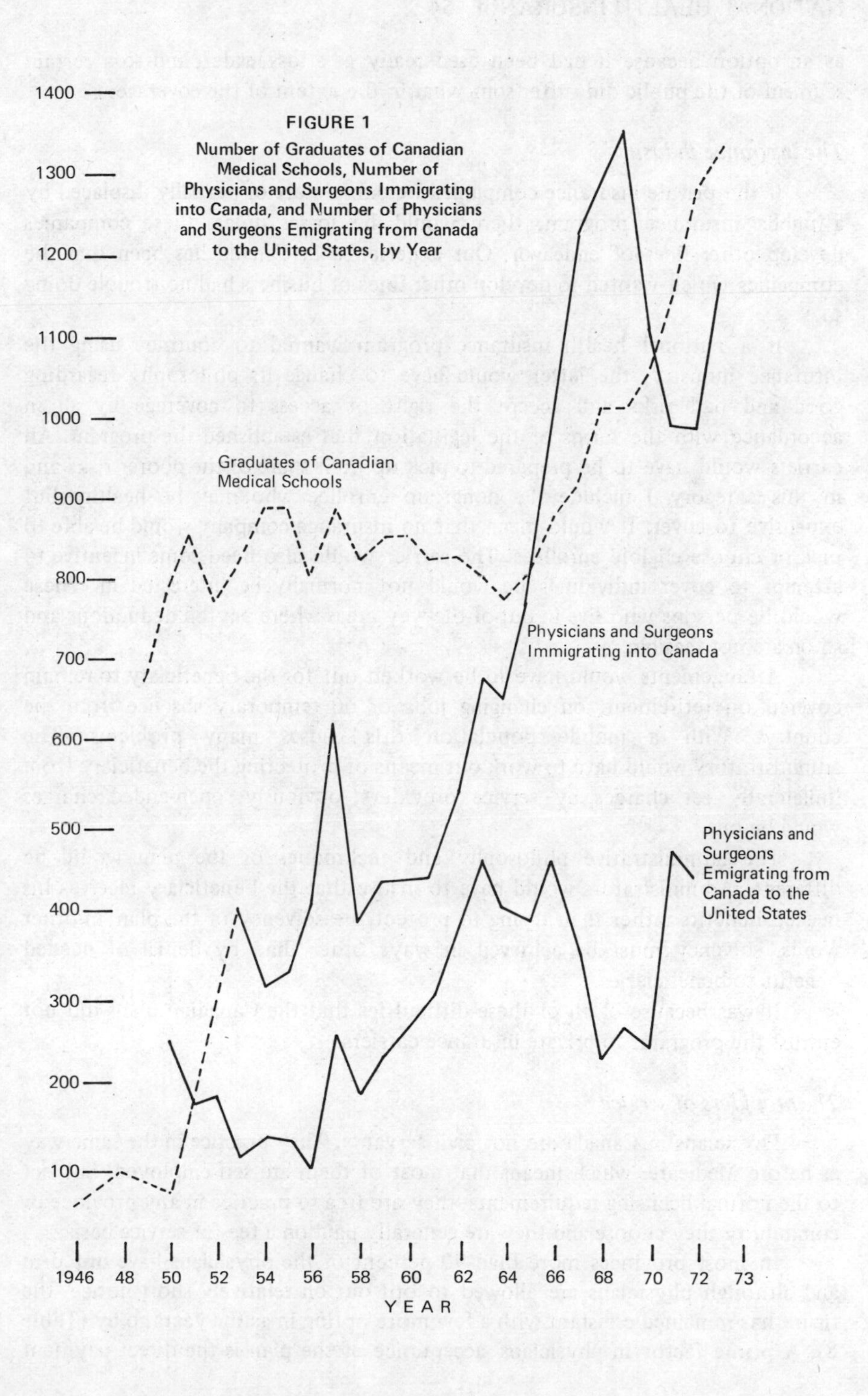

FIGURE 1
Number of Graduates of Canadian Medical Schools, Number of Physicians and Surgeons Immigrating into Canada, and Number of Physicians and Surgeons Emigrating from Canada to the United States, by Year

as an option because it had been used really as a loss-leader, and so a certain segment of the public did suffer somewhat in the extent of the coverage.

The insurance industry

If the private insurance companies are completely or partially displaced by a public insurance program, there would be losses unless these companies develop other lines of endeavor. Our experience in Canada has been that the companies which wanted to develop other lines of business had no trouble doing so.

If a national health insurance program wanted to continue using the insurance industry, the latter would have to change its philosophy regarding good and bad risks and accept the right of access to coverage by all in accordance with the terms of the legislation that established the program. All carriers would have to be prepared to pick up their share of the poorer risks and in this category I include the nongroup enrollee who may be healthy but expensive to cover. It would mean that no insurance company would be able to pick or choose eligible enrollees. The carrier would also need some incentive to attempt to cover individuals he would not normally be interested in. These would be persons who live in out-of-the-way areas where payroll deductions and so on are not feasible.

Arrangements would have to be worked out for the beneficiary to remain covered on retirement, on changing jobs or on temporary absence from the country. With a mobile population this causes many problems. The administrators would have to work out means of protecting the beneficiary from unilaterally set charges by service providers; obviously, open-ended charges would be out.

The administrative philosophy and techniques of the plan would be different. Administrators would have to insure that the beneficiary receives his needed benefits rather than trying to protect the solvency of the plan; in other words, solvency must be achieved in ways other than by denial of needed benefits to beneficiaries.

It was because of all of these difficulties that the Canadian plans did not entrust the programs to private insurance carriers.

The providers of service

Physicians in Canada are not civil servants. They practice in the same way as before Medicare, which means that most of them are self-employed. Subject to the normal licensing requirements, they are free to practice in any province or community they choose and they are generally paid on a fee-for-service basis.

In most provinces more than 90 percent of the physicians have opted in and although physicians are allowed to opt out on relatively short notice, the figure has remained constant with a few more opting in as the years go by (Table 8). A prime factor in physicians' acceptance of the plan is the direct payment

TABLE 8
CURRENT SITUATION RE OPTED-OUT PHYSICIANS

Province	Situation
Newfoundland	Four opted-out out of total of 500
Nova Scotia	Extra-Billing amounts to only 2.8% of plan payments
New Brunswick	Four opted-out
Prince Edward Island	None opted-out Extra-Billing less than ½ of 1%
Quebec	Seven specialists opted-out Three general practitioners opted-out (out of nearly 7,000 physicians)
Ontario	9% opted-out
Manitoba	5% opted-out
Saskatchewan	Approximately 3-4% opted-out
Alberta	None opted-out – can extra-bill under certain circumstances
British Columbia	None opted-out

mechanism. Obviously it is much simpler for each physician to send one statement to the government for all patients seen during the treatment period rather than to try to collect from hundreds of individual patients. Each physician participating in the provincial plan regularly receives a lump sum payment, seldom has a bad debt, and is paid for virtually everybody he sees, and does not have the added expense of collecting his fees from individual patients.

The service providers are now realizing that unilateral action on their part, collectively or individually, cannot be permitted to affect the overall solvency of the program or the adequacy of insurance coverage to the public. For example, if the insurance coverage is to be total and the amount of money provided for, say, professional services, is negotiated and agreed upon to be sufficient for an adequate level of remuneration to physicians in general, the profession cannot permit unilateral fee increases by one type of physician. If these fees were recognized by the plan, a reduction of the amount of money available to the other types of physicians would occur, thereby distorting the overall remuneration pattern which had been agreed upon. Similarly, individual hospitals cannot unrealistically raise their charges without having a similar effect upon the amount of money available for other hospitals. In other words, the providers of health services have to act in a coordinated way, which for many is a new experience.

The providers have appreciated that the public on the one hand and the elected representatives on the other, would not and could not permit the providers to frustrate the intention of the programs. In Canada, once the political decision had been made to implement the program, there was very little public support for either the private insurance industry or the medical profession in the few scattered efforts to harass or delay the program.

Distribution of physicians

During the 1950's and most of the 1960's, there was a marked emphasis on specialization in medicine. The appearance of the Hospital Insurance Program in 1958 accentuated this trend because salaries of interns and residents were covered under the program, thus making possible increased residency and internship positions in teaching hospitals to a degree theretofore financially impossible. Between 1958 (when Hospital Insurance began) and 1968 (when Medicare commenced), general practitioners, as a percentage of active civilian physicians, declined from 60 percent to 50 percent or conversely, specialists increased from 40 percent to 50 percent of the total physician supply. Actually, the effective change was somewhat greater than the numbers suggest because the general practitioner supply was aging relatively in comparison to the specialist contingent that was quite young.

The increased number and percentage of specialists effectively increased the concentration of physicians in larger urban centers because specialists by and large naturally gravitate to larger hospitals with special facilities and equipment. At the same time, physicians practicing in rural areas became older, reduced their activities or retired and were not being replaced proportionately.

Along with the increased trend to specialization was an increasing trend to restrict hospital privileges accorded general practitioners. In provinces with low levels of private insurance coverage, especially comprehensive coverage for services outside of hospital, the extension of hospital privileges acted as an additional incentive to young physicians to specialize.

With the implementation of Medicare, any community large enough to require a physician could support one financially and it was no longer necessary for physicians to specialize in order to have a reasonable opportunity for an adequate income. Medicare also provided a means for provinces to subsidize or otherwise encourage physicians to locate in underserviced areas. With the advent of universal health insurance, public expectations rose and hence provinces could no longer ignorc the problem of maldistribution of physician services, particularly as it affected rural areas.

The public's dissatisfaction with the relative difficulty in obtaining general practitioner services caused the provinces to put pressure on the medical schools to give much more emphasis to family practice than in the past. The relative oversupply in certain specialties in many communities plus a reasonable certainty of rapidly building up a remunerative family practice induced an increasing number of young graduates into general practice. Between 1968 and 1972, there was virtually no further decline in the proportion of general practitioners to specialists, although the specialists already in the training system at the start of Medicare had continued to swell the specialist ranks. The fact that the GP-specialist ratio remained virtually unchanged, indicates that a higher proportion of graduates are now turning to general practice.

Hospital Insurance doubtless contributed to the trend to specialization and indirectly to the concentration of physicians in urban as opposed to rural areas. It is too early to tell what the long term effect of Medicare might be, but in the comparatively short period since implementation, it appears to have stabilized the situation and halted the trend to ever-increasing specialization and urbanization of physicians. In fact, there is reason to hope that the trend may be reversing.

Hospital budgeting

In Canada, each hospital works on an approved budget basis. It is guaranteed that it will get enough money to meet its operating costs but it cannot add new services without getting them approved in advance. It cannot, for example, duplicate heart transplant facilities that other hospitals in the same community have, simply for prestige.

There are two ways of affecting budget allocation, line-by-line or global budgeting.

Line-by-line allocation

The line-by-line method of budget allocation is based on the concept that the individual amounts of each activity account must be assessed, and maximum amounts for each item of expense must be established. The paying authority does not normally approve costs in excess of these maxima. The totals of the amounts approved on an item-by-item basis constitute the total approved budget of each hospital.

The maximum allowable amounts are based on the average for a group of similarly sized hospitals. The amounts allowed in each hospital are usually based on the lesser of the hospital's actual cost experience or the maximum established for each cost category. Thus, under this system, any efficiency in one area is not transferred to other areas, and the hospital is penalized for its high cost areas, but not rewarded for its efficient cost areas; there is very little incentive to be efficient.

Generally, line-by-line budget approvals do not take sufficient cognizance of the individuality of the services and related costs of the individual hospital. As well, the system is time consuming and costly to administer. It focuses attention on the amounts deducted which creates friction between the paying agency and hospital officials, and hospitals are in a position to question (with some validity) the approval and allocation of costs as established by the central agency.

Global budget allocation

The global budget is a method of simplifying the allocation of funds to hospitals and is designed to distribute provincial funds more equitably than on a line-by-line basis. In addition, it achieves the following objectives which were not being met under the line-by-line method of budget assessment and allocation:

- It provides flexibility to hospital management in the administration of its responsibilities and makes management accountable for decisions.
- In the case of hospitals that overspend their approved budget, it limits additional payments to factors that are generally beyond the hospital to control, and would have been approved when the initial rate was established had the factors been known at that time.
- It rewards hospitals for providing an acceptable volume and standard of care at costs below the amount approved for the hospital under the global concept.
- It places more emphasis on hospital staff to assess quality of care and develop improvements within the funds available, thus encouraging evaluation of overall programs rather than in the context of each individual hospital.

Generally speaking, the global concept has only been partially accepted by provincial plans. In most cases, the hospitals do not have as much flexibility as would first seem apparent. For instance, in most provinces, salary rates are negotiated on a province-wide basis. With salary costs constituting such a large part of the total expenditures, the only flexibility is in the "mix" of staff employed, which is limited due to the standards required.

There is also concern at the provincial level where a hospital realizes a surplus on the established rates, and in many cases, the province recovers these surpluses. This seems to defeat the purpose of the global concept, in that to encourage efficiency, such efficiency must be rewarded.

Most provinces believe that they must reestablish the "globe" every three years or so, by a line-by-line review, and this reimposes the detailed assessment process that they supposedly were trying to move away from.

In general, it is fair to say that the provincial plans have been reluctant to give the hospitals the responsibility of the allocation of funds on the basis that appears best to the hospital, on other than a short-term basis, and that the global concept has only been partially implemented.

Professional trade-unionism

Within each province there exists a College of Physicians and Surgeons and a Medical Association. The medical associations are provincial chapters of the

Canadian Medical Association. Some provinces have modified the name and role somewhat but the basic raison d'être is the same and well defined by provincial medical statute; the Colleges are responsible for licensing, discipline and standards of service rendered by physicians and membership is mandatory.

Provincial medical associations concern themselves with the socioeconomic aspects of medical practice, physician education and matters of scientific importance. In general, membership is voluntary although most physicians do participate as members.

Before Canada's major national insurance programs were implemented, provincial governments had only a marginal involvement in the economic affairs of the medical profession. As public plans came into being, formal or informal arrangements developed for the negotiation of fees, the conditions of practice, and so on.

It is interesting to see what has happened in the Province of Quebec, although the next chapter elaborates on this. In Quebec, the activity of negotiation with the government is vested by charter between the Federation of General Practitioners and the Federation of Medical Specialists. The Federation of General Practitioners of Quebec received its charter in 1963. Today the federation consists of 16 regional associations throughout the province plus two associations of salaried physicians. The federation's chief activities are channelled into three main fields: a) negotiation on behalf of all Quebec's general practitioners, b) communications at all necessary levels, c) professional assistance to serve the needs of general practitioners in every way possible.

The federation has been recognized under the provincial medical care legislation as the sole agent for negotiating and entering into agreements on behalf of Quebec's general practitioners.

These agreements "determine in particular the manner in which the members of the medical profession may participate in such plan, the conditions for the practice of their profession and the standards respecting their remuneration for the purposes of such plan." The federation signed its first agreement with the government in 1966, when the Medical Assistance Plan was launched. The three main points covered were:

- A single fee schedule for general practitioners and specialists.
- A uniform fee structure for all regions of the province.
- Application of the agreement to all physicians whether or not members of the federation since the minister recognized the right of the medical association to negotiate on behalf of all Quebec physicians.

This agreement also recognized the following fundamental principles:

- Renunciation of any individual agreements between the minister and the physician.

- Adoption of a withdrawal or nonparticipating new procedure during which an individual physician could choose not to be bound by the terms of the collective agreement.
- The adoption of a system of retaining association fees. (Payment of dues is mandatory but membership is not.)

A further agreement in 1970 also provided for:

- Procedures to reopen negotiation on specific points.
- Establishment of a committee for appraisal of professional fee statements.
- Grievance and arbitration procedures.
- Mediation of any disagreement.

The Federation of Medical Specialists relates to the provincial government in a similar fashion. It represents all recognized specialists in the province who are members in good standing with the provincial College of Physicians and Surgeons.

In other provinces, it is not a professional union but the Medical Association which conducts negotiations with the government. In British Columbia, for example, the British Columbia Medical Association was the first to accept the concept of dealing with government through formal collective bargaining in 1965. At that time agreements were made governing the frequency of revisions of payment schedules, methods of increase and extent and nature of the revision which was related to the percentage change in the composite economic index compared to the previous two calendar years.

The composite index is the simple average of a) the industrial composite of average weekly wages and salaries in British Columbia and b) the consumer price index for the City of Vancouver. Revisions were to be made every two years thereafter and this basic agreement was used up to and including 1973.

Recently, the British Columbia Medical Association and the provincial government (B.C. Medical Plan) have concluded a new agreement incorporating the following highlights:

- The commission has agreed on the level of payments based on fees established as of April 1, 1973, plus any further revisions which are mutually agreeable.
- Agreement on the use of a standard account card and the right to opt out.
- The association has the sole right and responsibility of altering individual items of the schedule within the total medical claims cost where that cost is agreed upon by both parties.
- The association has the right and responsibility to examine and investigate abnormal payments to a physician and to refer to the

commission the action that the association deems proper and to expect prompt consideration by the commission.

- Agreement by the commission to provide the association with necessary statistical data to further their negotiations for revisions.
- The commission has agreed to make an annual payment of $1,800,000 as long as the current agreement is in effect for support of continuing educational programs for eligible physicians participating and receiving payment from the provincial plan.
- The commission and the profession also agree to the concept of disability insurance plans for eligible physicians whose services are paid for by the Medical Services Commission under the plan.

A very interesting innovation here is the acceptance by the government of the responsibility for continuing education of physicians and the concept of a disability insurance plan.

In Ontario, in an attempt to remove the "adversary" concept in negotiating for revisions of physicians' fees, the provincial government approved the appointment of a Joint Committee of Physicians Compensation. The concept of this committee evolved from the growing conviction among the Ontario Medical Association members that their own goals and the public interest would best be served within this sort of cooperative framework. Although this committee had been in existence for only several months, it was able to bring forth a recommendation for a revision of fees on May 1, 1974, which was approved by both the association and the government.

The changing hospital scene: sharing of facilities

The escalation of hospital costs in the late 1960's which followed the introduction of universal hospital insurance in Canada precipitated a variety of initiatives. These were designed to eliminate obvious duplication and multiplication of costly, highly-specialized clinical and laboratory services, hotel services such as laundry, food production and distribution, purchasing of equipment and supplies, and some administrative activities. While current and precise information is lacking, it is probably fair to say that while efforts have been varied, their application throughout the entire system has not been extensive. However, several significant attempts are being made to expand the practice of central laundries, bulk purchasing, controlled distribution of specialized clinics and services, and specialized laboratory and treatment services. Aside from the varied patterns of regionalization that are emerging, several provinces are encouraging various organizational and operational arrangements to deploy and use resources more effectively.

Hospitals have made reasonable progress in cooperative endeavors to share expensive services of specialized professional staff such as radiologists, pathologists, pharmacists, dietitians, physiatrists, etc. As for specialized clinical services, the provincial hospital authorities are cooperating with the federal government in the production of guidelines for minimum standards on a variety of special care units, which, if applied by the provinces will result in efficient distribution of specialized services (units) such as: intensive care, coronary care, cardiac surgery, hemodialysis, nuclear medicine, drug addiction treatment units, physical medicine and rehabilitation units, hostels, diabetic day care, nutrition, day care surgery, perinatal and inhalation therapy units. It should be emphasized that these guidelines will be variously applied by the provinces as they relate to their particular circumstances. But certainly the provinces recognize the principle that specialized services must be jointly shared when insufficient service load cannot economically justify separate facilities.

In the area of group purchasing, Canadian hospitals have generally recognized its value. A 1972 hospital symposium on group purchasing (bringing together administrators, purchasing agents, manufacturers and distributors) concluded that group purchasing is already a reality in the hospital industry and that the practice was spreading throughout Canada. It is seen as at least one method of abating the escalation of hospital costs as well as encouraging standardization, product quality improvements and evaluation.

One of the largest group purchasing arrangements operates in Metropolitan Toronto; it was incorporated in 1970 and serves 35 hospitals with a total of 14,000 beds. The corporation operates two laundries and a common laboratory. Other group purchasing and shared service arrangements exist in various parts of the country such as shared computer services among seven Montreal hospitals, a central biomedical engineering consultative and maintenance service for all New Brunswick hospitals, and province-wide laboratory services for high volume repetitive testing in Saskatchewan.

The provincial hospital authorities forcefully promote such arrangements as do the hospital associations. Of course, progress never is achieved easily and certain obstacles present themselves. For example, individual hospitals are reluctant to expand capital facilities from their own funds to serve a larger area and service load. Moreover, there is always the traditional competition between the medical staffs of different hospitals to attract and retain specialists. On the other hand, hospital insurance, particularly global budgets, serve as a vehicle through which provinces can influence hospitals and hence advance considerably the development of shared services and group purchasing arrangements.

Unionization and collective bargaining

With the introduction of government-sponsored hospital insurance, the demand for hospital services has increased substantially during the 1960's and 1970's. The hospital industry has been one of the economy's major growth areas and has a resource size that is of considerable economic importance. The magnitude of the hospital sector as an economic enterprise is reflected in the following recent approximate statistics. Canada has about 1,400 hospitals of all types (including general and allied special hospitals, mental hospitals, tuberculosis sanatoria and federal hospitals). They contain 200,000 beds and employ about 350,000 full-time and 60,000 part-time employees with total estimated costs for 1972 being 3.5 billion dollars.

Hospitals are also a labor-intensive industry with about 70 to 75 percent of hospital expenditures in the form of payroll costs. Complicating the matter of increasing employment in hospitals has been the spiralling increase in wage rates for hospital employees, i.e. during the period 1961-71, the average annual percentage increase for hospital wages was 14.7 percent. Further, during this period, 51 percent of the total increased cost of hospital services was attributable to increases in the labor cost per paid hour of work.

With the advent of government-assured financial support for hospitals came efforts of unions and professional associations to organize hospital employees (who were generally underpaid) and pressures for wage and benefit parity with the private sector. The union movement in the hospital sector has been increasingly vigorous whereby, presently, virtually all hospital employees in Canada (with limited exceptions) are represented for collective bargaining purposes by a union or association. Initially, the general service and clerical workers were organized. Subsequently in the late 1960's and early 1970's, nurses joined the collective bargaining movement with their provincial associations (where province-wide bargaining exists) serving as the bargaining agent for their membership. Most recently, allied health personnel, both professional and technical, are banding together for labor relations purposes.

Unionization has certainly increased employee wage and fringe benefits but the precise quantitative effect is not known. The 1960's were regarded as a "catch up" period for hospital wages, and unions were certainly an instrumental force in this process.

In collective bargaining, the trend in Canada has generally moved from individual hospital to local bargaining to regional and eventually province-wide bargaining.

Currently, province-wide bargaining exists in a number of provinces, e.g. British Columbia, Saskatchewan, Quebec, New Brunswick and Newfoundland. In these provinces the bargaining agents for hospitals are the provincial hospital associations with government usually represented at the bargaining table by "observers" or in some cases, as active participants. The influence of government at the bargaining table is important. Master agreements normally result from such negotiations and, initially at least, these resulted in considerable upward adjustment in wages and benefits. In one province (Quebec) a "common front" has developed whereby hospital employees, teachers and civil servants are components of an umbrella union organization although each group negotiates separately and simultaneously with their respective employers.

Labor negotiations in the other provinces, e.g. Ontario, Nova Scotia, Manitoba and Alberta, are generally conducted on a regional (group) or individual unit, local basis or a combination of these.

More and more hospitals are experiencing strikes and an even greater number are being threatened with strikes–in spite of the fact that, in most provinces, legislation exists denying hospital employees the right to strike. Recently, however, the right to strike has been restored in a few provinces, e.g. Manitoba, New Brunswick, Newfoundland and British Columbia (proposed). There is every indication, with or without supporting legislation, that hospital unions are more likely in the future to use the strike weapon to exert bargaining pressure on government.

Acute care hospital beds

A number of provinces are now trying to lower the bed-to-population ratio down to around 4 to 4½ beds per thousand from the 6½ to 7 that most provinces had. A great deal of emphasis is being placed on ambulatory care and ambulatory centers. The Castonguay report and the Hastings report have emphasized this and the next chapter deals with this issue.

One of the primary themes of a number of reports by federal and provincial commissions, task forces and working groups is the need to replace what is perceived as expensive acute hospital care wherever possible by the use of alternate facilities and services. These include development of different levels of institutional care, such as extended care hospitals, nursing homes, hostels and homes for the aged and ambulatory care facilities and services, such as home care programs, community health centers, outpatient units in acute general hospitals, etc.

Provinces can enforce a freeze through several mechanisms. First, provincial governments may withhold contributions to new projects or renovations since all provinces contribute heavily to these costs. These contributions range from a base of 40 percent for community hospitals to 60 percent for teaching hospitals in Saskatchewan, to a high of 100 percent of all costs (through one means or another) in New Brunswick, Quebec and Alberta, and 100 percent for teaching hospitals in Ontario and British Columbia.

A second mechanism which may be used involves productivity comparisons, either through utilization review and average length of stay studies, or productivity incentive schemes.

The planning guidelines for acute general hospital beds vary. In Ontario and New Brunswick, the goals are set at 4.0 beds per thousand population in urban areas and 4.5 beds per thousand in rural areas. The goal for Quebec is 3.2 beds per thousand population. British Columbia, Alberta, Manitoba and Nova Scotia have set targets at 4.5 beds per thousand population, while Saskatchewan has set a higher goal of 5.0 beds per thousand population. In Newfoundland, the bed standards depend upon the service performed: 2.0 where no surgery is performed, 2.5 where minor surgery is performed, 3.2 for regional hospitals and 4.0 beds per thousand population for provincial referral hospitals. These ratios vary considerably from province to province as they reflect practical recognition of several factors including the current inventory of facilities, the range of insured institutional alternatives (special rehabilitation, chronic, nursing home and personal care beds), the extent of ambulatory programs and services, as well as demographic factors such as age and sex distribution of the population. Also, the lack of a standard definition or classification of beds accounts for some of the variability in formulae.

Recent indications suggest that the "freeze" has begun to be lifted, but largely to allow construction of replacements. In some cases, this has appeared after a change in provincial government. In individual cases, decisions to close what were previously viewed as small, inefficient hospitals have been reversed. In Ontario, apparently with a "maturing" of hospital planning councils together with an increase in population, the number of hospital beds is approaching a level viewed as acceptable by the provincial government.

In all cases, however, the machinery for the "freeze" is still present. Across the country there is a provincial downward pressure on the planning for acute care beds. Beds are currently being taken out of service through attrition or amalgamation of services, particularly maternity and obstetrical beds. This is being accomplished by closing small hospitals, by removing beds from service in larger hospitals, or redesignating formerly acute care beds for alternative care needs. The roles of acute general hospitals are being subjected to closer scrutiny than at any time in the past. Thus, by continual review and analysis of the actual health care needs of Canadians, provinces are gradually and proportionately reducing the number of acute care beds in service relative to the population.

Use of statistics and data base

One of the most important spinoff benefits accruing from Hospital Insurance and Medicare has been the tremendous bulk of statistics and data which can be used for planning and evaluation. The federal government has played a major role in standardization across the country of this data base. It has provided expertise for the provinces to set up a comprehensive data gathering and analysis system and the majority of provinces now have sophisticated computer application of these statistics.

These data are required in a standardized format to be used by Statistics Canada and the Health Insurance Directorate of the Department of National Health and Welfare on a mandatory basis. Several volumes of hospital statistics on a regular basis for use by the hospital industry or other interested parties are now published every year. The same holds true for Medicare. At the hospital level, the data are used for local administrative and planning purposes. At the provincial level, the data are used among other things to make comparisons of the activities of similar hospitals, to assess kinds of care, to estimate future costs, for program planning, for research, evaluation, interpretation and ongoing administrative control. For example, as a control on utilization most provinces require long-stay reports to be submitted on inpatients occupying a bed for longer than a specified period of time, say anywhere between fifteen to thirty days. Sophisticated computer programs have been devised in some provinces to compare utilization of services for comparably-sized hospitals.

The Health Systems Group in the Health Programs Branch of the Department of National Health and Welfare is engaged in an active program of studies on the patterns of the flow of patients particularly in respect to hospitalization. The purpose is to make facility planning and reorganization of services a more meaningful exercise. This is largely possible because of the wealth of data on patients which are being assembled continuously on computer tapes. All aspects of provincial health care, including hospital utilization, medical care utilization and supporting social programs, are examined.

As a byproduct of a fee-for-service mechanism a record is automatically obtained for virtually every medical act rendered to a resident of Canada indicating what service was rendered, to whom, by whom, when, where and why; the resulting data can be put to use in a variety of ways including research in universities.

These studies provide very valuable information on the incidence of specific surgical procedures in relation to the age and sex composition of the beneficiaries as well as data on the location and provider of service. As a result, special committees are set up to determine whether the procedures are in fact necessary and if so, if they are carried out with the requisite quality considerations. For example, the rate of hysterectomies or tonsillectomies varies very much between communities, in relation to the proximity to academic centers, etc.

The cost of laboratory services for hospitalized patients and for ambulatory patients within governmental institutions, within hospitals or in private labs can be obtained, analyzed and evaluated.

Monitoring of professional care as an active function of the medical care plans has a long history in Canada. But the advent of Medicare and the introduction of computers as an administrative tool in the processing of claims has actually broadened the potential not only for the processing and paying of claims but also for the compilation of a reliable data base, with the accompanying opportunities for the retrieval and manipulation of services for the nation.

A governmental professional Committee on Standard Nomenclature has been working since 1971 on a uniform nomenclature of medical acts. The adoption of the uniform preamble and the standard nomenclature will facilitate estimating the cost of insured services and permit meaningful comparisons between the experiences of the various provincial plans. It would also allow analysis of professional workloads and contribute toward rational planning of the required numbers of the various kinds of specialists.

Other governmental agencies also use the collected data. For example, the Occupational Health Division of the Saskatchewan Department of Labor is conducting a study at this time on the incidence of poisoning through misuse of agricultural chemicals. This has involved keying in on specific diagnostic codes identifying claims and identifying the physician treating the particular case.

Through a followup interview the magnitude of the problem was determined and a campaign to acquaint farmers of the dangers was implemented. The Federal Department of Transport recently has approached some provincial health insurance commissions for the use of their computer tapes to have access to the histories of persons involved in car accidents.

Physicians' profiles

In the profile of a physician's practice there are three key items which are particularly significant and to which statistical measures can be readily applied: cost per patient, the generated cost per patient and the generated services per patient. While these are the main items in most physicians' profiles as many as 70 additional items may be added at the discretion of the plan and its facility of retrieval of data. Selections of individual profiles for examination by a Peer Review Committee are determined by setting an arbitrary tolerance in relation to the appropriate average for the key items commonly graded in two standard deviations.

Terms of reference for the Peer Review Committees generally provide wide investigative powers but no disciplinary powers. The committees make their recommendations to the governmental paying agencies which have the statutory powers to reassess accounts and impose fiscal penalties as they deem necessary. In many instances the College of Physicians and Surgeons may impose sanctions. A further technique which has been employed in certain specific instances is to reconstruct a physician's day book.

The Peer Review Committees are using gross indicators such as: services per patient, cost per patient, laboratory and x-ray test per patient and consultations requested per patient. This is then used for more detailed analysis. As an example, recently, in one province 10 percent of the doctors or a hundred of them were reviewed. A letter was sent to 30, and 15 were interviewed. Of these 6 were penalized, 4 were referred to the provincial College, 2 were referred for detailed audit and no action was taken for the others.

Direct monetary benefit to the plan in reassessing and prorating paid claims is generally minimal, especially when related to the cost involved. Most observers agree that the main benefits stem directly from the psychological influence attendant upon the fact that peer review is being carried out on all practices. This influence may act as a deterrent to overservicing and to control quality of care. There are no precise norms which can be used to evaluate the quality of the care delivered. Professional experience and judgment must be applied to relate the statistics to practice and then to evaluate the pattern in terms of possible abuse.

While the emphasis in the past has been toward cost control, there is growing evidence in peer review activity that more interest is being directed toward the techniques of evaluating the quality of care. Overservicing by a physician may indicate greed, but it may also indicate uncertainty on his part or again overutilization by patients due to poor quality of care necessitating additional services. When the review committee encounters apparent poor quality of care, the case is referred to the licensing and regulatory body of the profession.

If and when prescribed drugs are being provided as a benefit, a drug profile can be developed to provide both a drug consumption profile for the patient and a prescribing profile for the physician. Physicians' profiles may also be used to determine the appropriateness of medical education.

Under conditions of universal coverage and a fee-for-service system, it also becomes possible to compare the average pattern of practice of the various specialties in relation to such variables as specialty to population ratio and types of physicians in relation to population.

By taking advantage of Medicare data there is some hope that rational planning for future manpower requirements can be achieved. Without the knowledge of the quantity and type of services being provided by physicians, the only solution that could be proposed for identified or apparent shortages is an increase in the supply based on intuition. However, with the increasing data becoming available from the provincial Medicare plans, it is now possible to analyze what physicians are doing by type and by mix of physicians, and it will become increasingly possible to arrive at a reasonable estimate of our needs. Since the number of physicians Canada can produce or afford is not infinite, care must be taken to avoid an oversupply.

A recent editorial on this subject in a very conservative medical newspaper read as follows:

> "The doctors of this country may still be apprehensive of their autonomy in the future but reasonable men will admit that stricter professional review such as is now evolving here is good for the profession and was long overdue. Although Canadian doctors are being prodded into more soul-searching on quality of care by government, nothing but good can come to the patient because of it. As long as the changes come from within the profession.
>
> So if we Canadians are a bit puzzled by the storm of controversy PSRO has generated in the U.S., we hope American doctors will understand why. We understand their fears; we have them too. But there is no turning back the clock. The public is demanding more accountability. PSRO and our own professional review committees are giving the profession a last chance to discipline itself."

Physicians' income studies

One of the major question marks when introducing a universal health program, either Hospital Insurance or more specifically, Medicare, is what effect this will have on the income of physicians. Certainly, this has been in Canada an important element in the debate prior to the introduction of Medicare and the opposition of the medical profession to this legislation. It is, therefore, justified to spend some time reviewing the data on the income of physicians and the influence of universal health insurance.

Changes in physicians' incomes may be a function of changes in the volume and the effect of prices of the services performed by physicians. Changes in the volume of the services rendered by physicians as a whole or by individual physicians may depend on many factors: changes in the number and distribution (by specialty and by location) of physicians, changes in the age, sex and urban-rural distribution of the population, changes in technology, illness and treatment patterns, and changes in the extent of insurance coverage. Changes in the effective prices of physicians' services depend largely upon changes in payment schedules under conditions of universal coverage.

With the advent of universal coverage and the virtual elimination of bad debts, considerable disparities in income have developed between the various types of practice and in particular between medical specialists and surgical specialists.

One important study being carried out at the federal level is the physician's income study, which commenced with 1965 data. It is an annual study of the professional earnings of physicians in full-time practice and is undertaken with the cooperation of the Department of National Revenue. The results of this study are made available by specialty, by size of community and by province. The average gross and net professional earnings and overhead costs are provided on a confidential basis to the particular provincial medical association or equivalent and to the corresponding medical care authorities to assist them in negotiating fee schedule changes or revisions. In provinces with an oversupply of certain specialties, it is commonly noted that their average earnings are rather less than for other specialties. This kind of information is essential if income disparities between various specialties are to be corrected and physicians encouraged to engage in the type of practice where the need is greatest.

Another ongoing study relates to the estimated average working life of different kinds of physicians. This was initiated in 1971 in response to a request from the Canadian Medical Association. This kind of information is necessary to assist the association in determining fee differentials based on the working lives of different types of physicians in order to give each group, on the average, an adequate standard of professional income, bearing in mind such factors as the variation in the working lives of different types of physicians.

Tables 9-12 are quite informative concerning the effect of Medicare on physicians' incomes, especially when read in conjunction with Table 13 (dates of entry of each province in the insurance programs). For most physicians, Medicare has meant a sizable increase in earnings. In one province a jump greater than 40 percent of net earnings occurred in one year.

TABLE 9

AVERAGE NET PROFESSIONAL EARNINGS[a] OF ACTIVE FEE PRACTICE PHYSICIANS, CANADA, BY PROVINCE, 1957 TO 1971

Province	1957 ($)	1958 ($)	1959 ($)	1960 ($)	1961 ($)	1962 ($)	1963 ($)	1964 ($)	1965 ($)	1966 ($)	1967 ($)	1968 ($)	1969 ($)	1970 ($)	1971 ($)
Newfoundland	16,084	16,807	16,776	19,902	18,640	18,042	19,455	21,523	23,028	23,304	25,578	30,488	37,817	41,562	38,846
Prince Edward Island	9,787	10,237	11,427	12,589	13,119	15,448	15,777	16,478	17,835	18,910	20,716	22,636	22,760	26,892	38,822
Nova Scotia	10,026	12,862	14,820	16,074	16,070	15,925	14,839	17,851	19,146	20,395	21,480	24,642	29,880	35,776	35,351
New Brunswick	10,023	12,409	12,372	15,535	16,288	16,418	17,701	19,255	20,251	20,807	24,662	27,544	29,678	33,083	39,944
Quebec	10,669	11,136	11,795	12,870	14,454	15,173	16,696	18,534	20,532	21,231	23,133	25,112	27,233	27,402	41,131
Ontario	13,914	14,993	15,605	16,754	17,682	18,306	20,492	22,247	24,188	25,456	29,354	32,098	33,903	38,993	41,363
Manitoba	13,515	14,151	15,442	16,000	15,829	16,742	18,178	18,270	19,681	21,565	23,229	26,108	31,678	38,657	38,803
Saskatchewan	13,900	14,527	15,096	15,955	15,843	14,619	21,625	23,879	23,530	24,274	24,697	25,175	27,657	31,228	32,314
Alberta	13,422	14,815	15,941	17,754	17,925	18,612	19,111	21,117	22,681	24,356	27,591	33,221	33,165	39,678	40,357
British Columbia	14,926	15,488	16,953	17,600	17,067	17,284	17,464	19,560	20,121	22,209	25,169	26,239	28,829	31,006	31,138
Canada	12,852	13,778	14,590	15,735	16,472	16,970	18,688	20,484	22,064	23,262	26,093	28,615	30,861	34,360	39,203

(a) Includes net professional fees, and earnings received in the form of wages and salaries incidental to professional practice. Excludes earnings of some salaried physicians in active practice, e.g. physicians employed on a salaried basis in private group practice, and physicians employed under the Cottage Hospital Medical Service and by subsidized voluntary prepayment plans in Newfoundland.

SOURCE: "Earnings of Physicians in Canada," various years.

TABLE 10

PERCENTAGE CHANGE FROM PREVIOUS YEAR IN AVERAGE NET PROFESSIONAL EARNINGS OF ACTIVE FEE PRACTICE PHYSICIANS, CANADA, BY PROVINCE, 1958 TO 1971

Province	1958 (%)	1959 (%)	1960 (%)	1961 (%)	1962 (%)	1963 (%)	1964 (%)	1965 (%)	1966 (%)	1967 (%)	1968 (%)	1969 (%)	1970 (%)	1971 (%)
Newfoundland	4.5	-0.2	18.6	-6.3	-3.2	7.8	10.6	7.0	1.2	9.8	19.2	24.0	9.9	-6.5
Prince Edward Island	4.6	11.6	10.2	4.2	17.8	2.1	4.4	8.2	6.0	9.6	9.3	0.6	18.2	44.4
Nova Scotia	28.3	15.2	8.5	-0.02	-0.9	-0.5	12.7	7.3	6.5	5.3	14.7	21.3	19.7	-1.2
New Brunswick	23.8	-0.3	25.6	4.8	0.8	7.8	8.8	5.2	2.7	18.5	11.7	7.8	11.5	20.7
Quebec	4.4	5.9	9.1	12.3	5.0	10.0	11.0	10.8	3.4	9.0	8.6	8.5	0.6	50.1
Ontario	7.8	4.1	7.4	5.5	3.5	11.9	8.6	8.7	5.2	15.3	9.3	5.6	15.0	6.1
Manitoba	4.7	9.1	3.6	-1.1	5.8	8.6	3.0	5.1	9.6	7.7	12.4	21.3	22.0	0.4
Saskatchewan	4.5	3.9	5.7	-0.7	-7.7	47.9	10.4	-1.5	3.2	1.7	1.9	9.9	13.1	3.3
Alberta	10.4	7.6	11.4	1.0	3.8	2.7	10.5	7.4	7.4	13.3	20.4	0.2	19.6	1.7
British Columbia	3.8	9.5	3.8	-3.0	1.3	1.0	12.0	2.9	10.4	13.3	4.3	9.9	7.6	0.4
Canada	7.2	5.9	7.8	4.7	3.0	10.1	9.6	7.7	5.4	12.2	9.7	7.8	11.3	14.1

SOURCE: Table 3

TABLE 11

AVERAGE GROSS PROFESSIONAL EARNINGS[a] OF ACTIVE FEE PRACTICE PHYSICIANS, CANADA, BY PROVINCE, 1957 TO 1971

Province	1957 ($)	1958 ($)	1959 ($)	1960 ($)	1961 ($)	1962 ($)	1963 ($)	1964 ($)	1965 ($)	1966 ($)	1967 ($)	1968 ($)	1969 ($)	1970 ($)	1971 ($)
Newfoundland	22,795	24,351	24,669	28,583	27,184	24,809	27,903	30,630	31,620	33,688	36,503	43,256	51,977	57,520	55,081
Prince Edward Island	15,517	17,809	18,854	20,177	20,001	19,676	23,413	23,157	25,596	26,284	28,720	32,584	37,501	37,769	51,271
Nova Scotia	19,640	19,667	21,341	22,802	23,242	23,302	23,455	25,739	27,486	29,960	30,391	35,820	41,116	48,790	48,865
New Brunswick	18,413	19,538	18,918	22,523	24,220	23,978	26,376	27,802	29,622	30,271	35,891	38,933	42,362	46,394	54,204
Quebec	16,887	18,264	18,721	19,656	22,118	23,418	25,748	26,813	29,010	30,901	33,455	36,187	39,058	38,882	53,992
Ontario	22,003	23,415	24,153	25,534	27,206	27,779	30,641	33,201	35,752	38,254	42,721	47,427	51,170	57,856	61,657
Manitoba	23,673	25,036	27,567	25,767	29,072	29,003	28,769	29,103	32,037	33,589	36,657	40,083	49,255	58,338	56,517
Saskatchewan	22,689	23,511	23,699	27,102	27,103	23,238	35,657	36,484	37,474	40,150	40,150	41,546	45,010	49,178	50,908
Alberta	23,368	24,828	25,254	28,032	29,221	31,187	30,912	32,690	35,397	37,871	43,819	51,894	52,383	59,457	62,188
British Columbia	23,736	24,909	26,628	28,066	27,867	27,493	27,670	30,510	31,675	36,063	38,609	41,848	44,716	48,882	49,872
Canada	20,804	22,103	22,910	24,288	25,862	26,322	28,690	30,586	32,799	35,223	38,675	42,783	46,328	50,819	56,824

(a) Includes net professional fees, and earnings received in the form of wages and salaries incidental to professional practice. Excludes earnings of some salaried physicians in active practice, e.g. physicians employed on a salaried basis in private group practice, and physicians employed under the Cottage Hospital Medical Service and by subsidized voluntary prepayment plans in Newfoundland.

SOURCE: "Earnings of Physicians in Canada," various years.

TABLE 12

PERCENTAGE CHANGE FROM PREVIOUS YEAR IN AVERAGE GROSS PROFESSIONAL EARNINGS OF ACTIVE FEE PRACTICE PHYSICIANS, CANADA, BY PROVINCE, 1958 TO 1971

Province	1958 (%)	1969 (%)	1960 (%)	1961 (%)	1962 (%)	1963 (%)	1964 (%)	1965 (%)	1966 (%)	1967 (%)	1968 (%)	1969 (%)	1970 (%)	1971 (%)
Newfoundland	6.8	1.3	15.9	-4.9	-8.7	12.5	9.8	3.2	6.5	8.4	18.5	20.2	10.7	-4.2
Prince Edward Island	11.5	5.9	7.0	-0.9	-1.6	19.0	-1.1	10.5	2.7	9.3	13.5	15.1	0.7	35.7
Nova Scotia	0.1	8.5	6.8	1.9	0.3	0.7	9.7	6.8	9.0	1.4	17.9	14.8	18.7	0.2
New Brunswick	6.1	-3.2	19.1	7.5	-1.0	10.0	5.4	6.5	2.2	18.6	8.5	8.8	9.5	16.8
Quebec	8.2	2.5	5.0	12.5	5.9	9.9	4.1	8.2	6.5	8.3	8.2	7.9	-0.5	38.9
Ontario	6.4	3.2	5.7	6.5	2.1	10.3	8.4	7.7	7.0	11.7	11.0	7.9	13.1	6.6
Manitoba	5.8	10.1	-6.5	12.9	-0.2	-0.8	1.2	10.1	4.8	9.1	9.3	22.9	18.4	-3.1
Saskatchewan	3.6	0.8	14.4	0.0	-14.3	53.4	2.3	2.7	7.1	—	3.5	8.3	9.3	3.5
Alberta	6.2	1.7	11.0	4.2	6.7	-0.9	5.8	8.3	7.0	15.7	18.4	0.9	13.5	4.6
British Columbia	4.9	6.9	5.4	-0.7	-1.3	0.6	10.3	3.8	13.9	7.1	8.4	6.9	9.3	2.0
Canada	6.2	3.7	6.0	6.5	1.8	9.0	6.6	7.2	7.4	9.8	10.6	8.3	9.7	11.8

TABLE 13

DATES OF ENTRY FOR EACH PROVINCE FOR HOSPITAL INSURANCE AND MEDICARE

Province	Date of Entry Hospital Insurance	Date of Entry Medical Care
Newfoundland	July 1, 1958	April 1, 1969
Prince Edward Island	October 1, 1959	December 1, 1970
Nova Scotia	January 1, 1959	April 1, 1969
New Brunswick	July 1, 1959	January 1, 1971
Quebec	January 1, 1961	November 1, 1970
Ontario	January 1, 1959	October 1, 1969
Manitoba	July 1, 1958	April 1, 1969
Saskatchewan	July 1, 1958	July 1, 1968
Alberta	July 1, 1958	July 1, 1969
British Columbia	July 1, 1958	July 1, 1968
Yukon	July 1, 1960	April 1, 1972
Northwest Territories	April 1, 1960	April 1, 1971

Physicians' supply and manpower planning

The implementation of the Hospital Insurance program in 1958 does not appear to have had any significant effect on the actual numbers of physicians in Canada. It appears, however, to have promoted medical specialization and contributed to the functional imbalance apparent today. During the first few years of the program, the number of graduates of the Canadian medical schools remained relatively constant at the level of the early 1950's, while the number of foreign physicians immigrating into Canada remained around 400 per annum, and the number of Canadian physicians emigrating to the United States at around 300 per annum. The appearance of the Hall Commission Report in 1964, the implementation of the Health Resources Fund and the announcement of the government's intention to implement a universal medical care insurance program, were followed by an increase in the output of Canadian medical schools, a very marked increase in the numbers of physicians immigrating into Canada and for several years a decline in the number of physicians emigrating from Canada to the United States.

It is possible that some of the temporary increases in emigration to the United States which occurred in the early 1960's may have been indirectly influenced by the Hospital Insurance Program. The Hospital Insurance Program certainly contributed to the trend for recent graduates to specialize, and in the pre-Medicare days many of the poorer provinces were unable to support the increasing number of specialists coming onto the market. Many of these emigrated to the United States during that period, others moved to wealthier provinces.

It would seem that these changes produced a marked increase in the physician-population ratio in Canada and related more to the Health Resources Fund and Medicare than to Hospital Insurance. In the case of Newfoundland, for example, in the first three years of the program, the supply of private medical practitioners in relation to population increased by about 20 percent; in fact, if one takes all physicians into account (because Newfoundland has a salaried service and a medical school as well) it is more like 30 percent. There was no way that an increase of this magnitude could happen in the absence of Medicare because the local resources were insufficient to support such an increase. There had to be a program which would iron out the economic difference to a practicing physician between a poor community and a wealthy one. All provinces have had a significant improvement in the physician-population ratio.

Before Medicare, Quebec had a steady decrease in the supply of general practitioners relative to population because of the nature of the private insurance coverage in that province which in effect encouraged specialization. That province has an 11 percent increase in the number of active GP's in the first year of the Medicare program and, of course, this made primary care more available to the public. Some provinces, Ontario in particular, have implemented programs to locate physicians in specified underserviced areas and with the advent of Medicare they were able to guarantee them a minimum professional income. In point of fact, provinces have very seldom had to actually pay any subsidy to these physicians as they were generally able to have enough work to satisfy their needs.

The Task Force Reports in 1969 (established to study the problem of the cost of health services), noted that in studying total physician-population ratios, medical schools and governments in Canada to that time had not seriously planned for the needs for different types of specialists in the country. Quite clearly, the number of people trained in a special field should bear a close relationship to the needs for qualified people in that specialty. In a free society the flow of people to a specialty can be best brought about by improvement in the working conditions and incomes in the specialties for which candidates are required. Fee schedules and other methods of payment can have direct relevance to the fulfillment of these needs. The pattern of remuneration of physicians must encourage optimum proportions of general practitioners and all kinds of specialists. The whole question of physician supply and supply by specialties is very complex and consideration must be given to many factors. These include the true need for services of a particular type, the effect of care upon health status, the type of physician, location and type of practice, recruitment, training capacity of the educational system, training costs, retention rates in particular specialties, working life, content of practice, immigration and emigration, practice trends and use of surrogates, average physician productivity for any particular specialty, and so on. These necessary studies are now possible because of the data coming from Hospital Insurance and Medicare.

On a national basis, because the physician-population ratio is now so good and because studies by the Medical Care Directorate on medical care utilization indicate that a saturation point for certain specialties is very close or has been reached in a number of provinces, it is now urgent that postgraduate training programs be reassessed and the desirability of a selective physician immigration policy be considered.

It was only the advent of the medical care program which has enabled us to scrutinize so closely the actual content of various types of medical practice on a broad basis. It has become apparent that physician utilization is not only a function of the number of physicians but also of the mix and geographical distribution. The optimum overall specialty-population ratio recommended some years ago on an intuitive basis now appears to be too high. Studies show that when numbers are in excess of requirement, they enter into fields of practice beyond that of their specialty to make up for the reduced surgical workload resulting from the oversupply. This is seen in neurosurgery, for example, where despite a 400 percent variation in the ratio of neurosurgeons to population among Canadian provinces, the variation in the incidence of neurosurgery per 1,000 residents in most provinces does not exceed about 30 percent and this under a fee-for-service system where remuneration results only from professional activity. Thus, the market for the services of certain types of specialists is not unlimited and we are now beginning a joint undertaking with the various professional bodies to reexamine the old recommended specialists to population ratio. We hope that it will lead to a more rational determination of the number of residencies in each specialty which should be supported under the Hospital Insurance Program.

In the past the number of residencies in the different specialties of medical practice has been influenced and determined by local and regional needs for different types of physicians. In addition, residencies have been influenced by medical schools, hospitals and by the students themselves, according to the popularity and attraction of a specialty at a particular point in time in a different region of the country. The number and types of residencies which should be supported under the Hospital Insurance Program must be determined in a more rational way.

COSTS

The nature of the problem

I will not deal with the subject of costs extensively since this part is covered in detail in Chapter 3 of this book. However, there are a few points to be made to explain the recent change in the philosophy of the federal government with regard to cost-sharing.

Cost escalation has become a major problem, especially in the hospital field; this led, in 1969, to the appointment of a task force to look specifically at this problem. Many of the recommendations contained in the report have been implemented and we seem to have reached a plateau in the rate of increase in the hospital field (at least up to this year).

There is no doubt that the 10-year delay in the implementation of the second program contributed to an incentive for both the physician and the patient to use the hospital whenever possible. Canada has 7 general and allied special hospital beds per thousand population compared approximately to 5 per thousand in the United States. And Canadians, of course, with their program have considerably greater financial access to those beds than does the average citizen in the United States. The net result was exactly what we would have predicted. We use our hospitals more, our admission rate per thousand is higher (although the gap seems to be closing lately) and the days of hospital care per thousand population are also greater, the average length of stay being approximately two days greater.

In the three years 1966, 1967 and 1968, the average rate of increase was approximately 17 percent. For 1968, which was effectively a pre-Medicare year, it was over 20 percent. With the introduction of Medicare in most provinces during 1969, the rate of increase in hospital costs began to decline and recently was running less than 12 percent per annum, gross. (The 1974 figures, because of inflation, may not be that encouraging!) Of course, with this demand for the use of hospital beds, hospitals continued to be built. We realize now that we have too many general hospital beds. That fact is going to cost us a great deal of money, even if we had them sitting empty (which is not the case). Many of the acute general hospitals are not ideally laid out for conversion into some other type of hospital. It might have been better if we had left some of the older ones up so that we could now close them and in that way reduce the bed-to-population ratio a little more quickly. Once a modern hospital is built, it is politically very difficult to close. Often it is the sole industry in a small community, the major local source of employment and the only means of attracting a physician. It is not hard to diagnose the cause of high health costs or escalating health costs. What is very difficult is how to do something about it that the public will support.

There were many other factors in cost-escalation: technological improvements, improved services, unionization and inflation. Massive unionization of the hospital workers and, in one province, common front negotiations raised the salaries and benefits of all hospital workers at one collective bargaining session. Another factor was also the delay seen in many provinces in introducing diagnostic services on an insured basis outside the hospital setting or available to ambulatory patients.

The problem in cost-escalation has been mostly that of hospitals and the yearly increase in Medicare has been running approximately as predicted (Table 14).

TABLE 14

MEDICAL CARE ACT
COST OF INSURED SERVICES BY PROVINCE
1968-69 TO 1971-72

	Estimated Costs as used for Calculation of Advance Payments					Final Costs for Calculating of Final Contributions				
	1968-69	1969-70	1970-71	1971-72	TOTAL	1968-69	1969-70	1970-71	1971-72	TOTAL
Newfoundland	–	12,285,800	15,125,895	16,695,000	44,106,695	–	12,262,217	14,969,628	15,763,046	42,994,891
% increase								*100.0%*	*105.3%*	
Prince Edward Island	–	–	603,075	3,978,335	4,581,410	–	–	606,410	4,294,957	4,901,367
% increase									*100.0%*	
Nova Scotia	–	23,579,100	30,507,258	33,356,774	87,443,132	–	21,581,606	30,339,834	32,935,739	84,857,179
% increase								*100.0%*	*108.6%*	
New Brunswick	–	–	1,859,618	25,016,433	26,876,051	–	–	2,105,138	21,139,685	23,244,823
% increase									*100.0%*	
Quebec	–	–	81,406,966	336,729,000	418,135,966	–	–	66,877,475	303,441,409	370,318,884
% increase									*100.0%*	
Ontario	–	132,455,834	428,687,082	472,148,340	1,033,291,256	–	124,067,686	441,452,947	479,716,124†	1,045,236,757
% increase								*100.0%*	*108.7%*	
Manitoba	–	41,909,747	50,800,000	56,556,730	149,266,477	–	39,423,819	53,040,698	54,957,880	147,422,397
% increase								*100.0%*	*103.6%*	
Saskatchewan	20,929,879	32,755,008	33,950,034	38,573,360	126,208,281	17,877,073	30,788,926	34,571,462	40,025,240*	123,262,701
% increase							*100.0%*	*112.3%*	*130.0%*	
Alberta	–	44,241,854	80,226,179	89,983,943	214,451,976	–	41,756,736	82,582,484	86,572,984	210,912,204
% increase								*100.0%*	*104.8%*	
British Columbia	52,329,000	105,995,660	117,647,000	135,123,570	411,095,230	50,058,739	106,942,396	121,863,469	132,459,901†	411,324,505
% increase							*100.0%*	*114.0%*	*123.9%*	
Northwest Territories	–	–	–	1,384,000	1,384,000	–	–	–	1,028,687	1,028,687
% increase										
TOTAL	73,258,879	393,223,003	840,813,107	1,209,545,585	2,516,840,474	67,935,812	376,823,386	848,409,545	1,172,335,652	2,465,504,395

* Utilization fees removed in August 1971.

† The covered population was less than 95% during the first year of participation, but reached about 100% in 1972-73. Consequently the cost per insured person increased at substantially lower ratio than aggregate costs.

It is interesting that since Medicare, the increase in the physician-population ratio has been running at more than double the rate of increase in the years before Medicare and despite that, the rate of increase in the cost of physicians' services has been running somewhere between one fourth and one third less per annum. It is also a fact that in a number of provinces, if one takes the per capita cost of physicians' services the year before Medicare came in, and escalates it at the average rate of increase for physicians' costs in that province in the several years leading up to Medicare, the hypothetical cost today would be higher than these provinces are actually paying under the universal program.

Prior to Medicare it was predicted by many that it would be quite impossible to estimate costs with such an open-ended program. The Medicare Act was passed in December 1966. In early 1967, 1968 and 1969, the federal government prepared estimates covering the next five-year period of the hypothetical cost of Medicare with all provinces participating for the full year. The first year that this happened was 1971-72 and the average variance between the estimates of 1967, 1968 and 1969 for 1971-72 with the audited final report for that year was 0.4 percent (a fairly accurate estimate!) Table 14 shows that for the first four years of the program, in three out of those four years the actual total costs turned out to be lower than estimated. In one province, British Columbia, the four-year cost was estimated at $411,000,000 and the actual cost was $411,000,000! However, in the hospital field the estimation of cost was not that accurate.

Even though the hospital costs are the largest category of public expenditure on health, the most important determinant of total health cost is the number of physicians practicing in thc system. The costs attributable to physicians are not only their remuneration but also a sum, greater in amount, reflecting expenditures elsewhere in the system which result from their professional decisions. The physician decides admission to hospital, duration of stay, the use of diagnostic and therapeutic procedures, prescription of drugs, referral to specialists and the pattern of further examinations. These services together probably represent 80 percent of health costs. In the absence of financial barriers to physicians' services, both the volume of services rendered and the cost per service tend to increase with the number of physicians in practice, contrary to the usual supply and demand relationships. As health economists have observed, the quantity of medical services delivered can be increased almost indefinitely by demands from the consumer and by expansion of the types of care offered by physicians. In a health insurance system with no direct financial burden on the patient, the only deterrents to seeking care are the time and trouble involved, and there is a large untapped reserve of "beneficial" services which can be offered. A surplus of physicians, therefore, will increase the cost of health services without necessarily improving health. In several of the larger Canadian provinces with a rapidly increasing ratio of physicians to population, the prospect of a significant surplus of physicians is imminent. If there is no limit to the number of physicians who may register in a province, then the added costs of health services from a surplus of physicians will almost certainly negate attempts to achieve economies in other sectors.

Another problem area in cost increase relates to diagnostic services, particularly lab tests. These have been increasing in volume in most provinces at rates in the order of 20 percent or even higher per annum and I am referring here to outpatient diagnostic services. Because of this rapid rate of volume increase, it has proven to be a rather lucrative business to operate private laboratories and there has been quite an expansion of them in the last few years. All provinces are now attempting to control these by limiting the numbers which operate and licensing them rather strictly. Diagnostic services continue to be perhaps the single most rapidly escalating area in the field of health costs.

New formula in financing

At this time in Canada the present concerns regarding Hospital Insurance and Medicare are: a) the rising costs relative to gross national product, b) the rigidities and complexities of present arrangements, c) the limitations on and type of health care eligible for federal financial support, and d) the minimal returns to provinces for cost-saving innovations.

It has been recognized by the federal government that provincial efforts at cost containment cannot be maximized unless sufficient flexibility and incentives are provided under the federal-provincial cost-sharing arrangements. In the aftermath of the Task Force Reports, the federal minister of National Health and Welfare advised his provincial counterparts at a Conference of Health Ministers, held in December 1970, that the federal government was prepared to explore with the provinces the possibility of revising the current sharing approach to hospital and medical care insurance. This step was taken in the hope that the revised arrangements would not only help to contain the escalation of health care costs, but also result in the provinces having greater flexibility in determining their own priorities in health care, and in pursuing the most effective approach in line with these priorities. All ministers of health agreed that a comprehensive review of the existing cost-sharing arrangements was both timely and appropriate.

The existing arrangements while encouraging high quality services have focused professional attention on the costly services for which federal financial contributions are available. The federal government has been preaching along with the provinces, that a patient should not be hospitalized in acute general beds unless absolutely necessary. Yet, we do not cost-share any other facilities such as nursing homes (unless the patient is on welfare). Also, we have been urging use of allied health professionals such as nurse practitioners and the health care team concept and yet, we only cost-share the services of the most costly of health professionals, namely, the physicians.

All of this has tended to discourage efforts to increase efficiency and economy through the development of alternate approaches. In fact, in some provinces, especially the poorer ones, a new health care expenditure is guaranteed to bring more than $0.50 on the dollar from outside the province to the economy of that province (Table 2). In some provinces, namely the Atlantic Provinces, the governments in fact almost have a $0.20 dollar guarantee in that increasing their own expenditures by $0.20 will bring $0.80 from the federal government. Conversely, a cost-reduction of $1 is equivalent only to a provincial saving of $0.50 in some provinces and $0.20 in others. There is, therefore, very little incentive for the provinces to contain cost.

Also there are complex arrangements, including detailed auditing, which are necessary to control the administration of the present programs. A simpler approach has, therefore, real attraction to both levels of government although there is still quite a debate on the exact dollar value of the new cost-sharing formula.

If the brakes are not applied judiciously to the cost spiral, the health care system will simply price itself out of the market. The Economic Council of Canada has predicted that at the present level of cost escalation, by year 2000, 100 percent of our gross national product will be spent in the fields of health and education!

The objectives of the new arrangements were therefore:

a) cost control,
b) flexibility,
c) effectiveness,
d) fostering reorganization,
e) simplification of relations,
f) guaranteed standards.

Toward a total health system, it was proposed that future federal financial contributions for the provinces with respect to health insurance take the form of a per capita payment. This would replace contributions presently payable under the Hospital Insurance and Medicare Act with no province receiving less in the initial year than it would have received under the pre-existing arrangements. Flexibility would be achieved through each province being free to use the federal contributions in accordance with its own priorities provided that national standards for coverage are maintained. Federal payments, therefore, could be applied to the total range of provincial health services in the way deemed most effective by the individual province and without incurring financial penalties as a result of cost-saving innovations.

Another major objective of the new arrangements would be to foster reorganization. Traditional organization and methods of providing care will have to change if they are incapable of providing quality service within the rate of increase of the economy. A special fund would have to be instituted for this purpose.

The federal proposal would also include an escalation formula that would avoid complicated federal-provincial agreements such as those under the Hospital Insurance and Diagnostic Services Act. Financial relations between both levels of government would be simplified through the avoidance of much of the present auditing requirements.

There would be a requirement to maintain the existing basic standards of comprehensiveness, universality, portability and public accountability for hospital and medical services incorporated into the current programs.

Any new major program in which the federal government might in future accept a role would be the subject of separate negotiations and financing. The new financial arrangements should not result in a lessening of federal-provincial cooperation in health matters, particularly with respect to the development of improvements in the health care delivery system. The federal government would continue, and if necessary, expand, its role in promoting federal-provincial cooperation and in the coordination of health programs, in the exchange of information, in the provision of consultative services and in support of studies, surveys and research.

In May 1971, a firm proposal was presented to the provinces. There have been many meetings since then but essentially the basic payment features of the proposals are as follows:

a) the federal payment would be made on a per capita basis per insured resident of each province.
b) this payment would be revised annually in accordance with changes in the insured population of each province and of the economy generally.
c) the per capita payment would not be dependent upon the way funds are disbursed by the province. It could be used anywhere within the total health system provided that nationally acceptable standards were maintained.
d) the per capita payment would escalate by the rate of growth of the gross national product (excluding the population component of that index) rather than by a specific relationship to the cost changes provincially or nationally in the two major component programs for health insurance.
e) the per capita payment would be protected against year-to-year fluctuation of the GNP by being based upon the moving average of five consecutive yearly indices.
f) the per capita payment would be standardized among the provinces over a period of five years.
g) there would be a thrust fund equivalent to $30 per capita paid entirely by the federal government to finance the reorganization of the health care delivery system according to the particular needs of each province.

The provinces could use this money for any part of the health care system, but new major programs such as dental or pharmaceutical care would have to be negotiated as such between the provinces and the federal government. The thrust fund would be an investment which, through promoting improvement in the system for providing health care, would permit the rate of cost escalation to be contained within the overall level of change in the economy and with no loss of quality for the people of a province.

At this time it is fair to say that the next move is in the hands of the provinces. The federal government has said it has gone as far as it can in terms of enriching the formula; most provinces seemed to agree on the principle at the beginning. Some provinces, however, have now reversed their original stand and hope that the old formula be kept because they say this is the best way to keep the federal government involved in health. The major difference of opinion is probably still the amount of money that is to be attached to the new formula as well as the method of payment–direct payment versus tax points.

PROBLEMS IN HEALTH CARE DELIVERY

Universal health insurance is an important step in eliminating financial barriers to necessary health care, but it does not guarantee an adequate system of health services. Indeed, it tends to highlight other defects in the system such as the organization and distribution of health services which previously seemed to be of lesser significance. Two major deficiencies have been recognized in the organization of health services. The first is the lack of an organized framework for the delivery of primary or first line health care to ambulatory patients of the community and the second is in the organization of health services to be found at the regional level. The supply and distribution of medical manpower is also a major problem at this time.

Community health centers

This level of organization is needed to provide a more readily accessible and available entry point into the system of health services other than through hospital emergency rooms. In addition, community health centers would serve as a mechanism for maintaining continuity of care without dislocation of the patient from the working or home environment. They also offer the potential for coordination of the contribution of different types of health personnel and transfer of functions from physicians to other health and social service workers.

The concept

The following definition is proposed by the Community Health Center Project Committee established by the Minister of National Health and Welfare in 1971 on behalf of the Conference of Health Ministers of Canada. The function of this committee was to examine the role and organization of community health centers, and represents the concept of community health centers in

Canada today. I have previously referred to this committee under its more informal name of the Hastings Committee.

> "The community health centre is a facility or intimately linked group of facilities, enabling individuals and families to obtain initial and continuing health care of high quality. Such care must be provided in an acceptable manner through a team of health professionals and other personnel working in an accessible and well managed setting. The community health centre must form part of a responsive and accountable health services system. In turn, the health services must be closely and effectively coordinated with the social and related services to help individuals, families, and communities deal with the many sided problems of living."

The reasons

Community health centers are considered to be an acceptable alternative to some of the present forms of health care delivery. They may help to curb the accelerating cost of health services in many ways. With their emphasis on health promotion and prevention as a primary contact, community health centers are expected to reduce the demand for hospital facilities and utilization of inpatient services. They may also facilitate earlier discharge from hospital through coordinated discharge planning and home care services and provision for monitoring the total health needs of the discharged patient.

Coordination of many services in one facility should result in increased productivity and effectiveness. The benefits of using less highly trained personnel (i.e. dental hygienists working under the supervision of dentists, and nurse practitioners working with physicians) are twofold. The overall cost of salaries may be less, as well as more time available to give individual patient care and counseling.

The public has expressed concern about lack of access to health services, especially after normal working hours. This deficiency has created mounting pressure on outpatient and emergency hospital departments. In a community health center, continuity and availability of medical care should be assured. Flexible and innovative uses of manpower and multidisciplinary teamwork can result in more comprehensive care to the patient. Community health centers can be instrumental in coordinating health and social services, making better use of the resources available in the community.

The implications

There will have to be appropriate legislation, as the concept of the community health center requires "cooperative" or "collective" responsibility for the joint professional actions of all its personnel. Minimum staffing requirements and broad personnel policies should be set by negotiation at the provincial level.

Salaries for personnel must meet the personal expectation of the team member of adequate, fair and competitive remuneration for professional status and professional independence. Although fee-for-service is a more accepted form of remuneration for physicians, a third of the physicians in Canada receive remuneration for their services in some other way. If the physicians are paid on a fee-for-service basis and the rest of the team is on salary, it creates almost insurmountable problems and conflicts.

There should be some incentives to attract personnel to the center. These may be in the form of regularly revised and negotiated minimum levels of basic income, shared cost pensions, life and disability insurance, etc. Additional incentives should be available to attract personnel to isolated or unattractive areas. These could be in the form of incentive payments, adequate housing, etc. Funding of community health centers should be part of the broader financing arrangements for health services in the province. Continuing education of the health care team should be provided by inservice education. The health center should also be a training center for students in the health sciences.

The issues

The basic problem faced by many community health centers is how to finance them within the present payment system. Capital financing is needed to construct and equip a building, and to provide funds for planning and development. Some provinces have specific legislation concerning funding of community health centers (i.e. Quebec). Many others are working on new legislation to try and cope with this problem.

Many community health centers find it difficult to attract physicians to work there. The general practitioner is not attracted by a lower income, and often fears loss of autonomy. There is often conflict with hospital boards when trying to attract specialists to work at the center. The cost of hiring specialists is too great for some centers.

One of the major issues concerning community health centers is control of the clinic by a community board. Physicians are often in conflict with the board, the main problems being disagreement between the physicians and the board on management rights.

Regionalization of health services

Wasteful competition between hospitals, duplication of specialized facilities and failure to coordinate effectively the full spectrum of institutional and ambulatory services have strengthened the conviction that a comprehensive approach to the planning and management of health services on an area-wide or regional basis is necessary. Regionalization has been endorsed in principle by all the provinces in Canada and has been enacted by legislation in the Province of Quebec, but the process of implementation has been slow. In some cases the geographic area or population concerned has been too large and diverse to be identified as a cohesive unit for planning or management purposes. The influence of the regional council or group in rationalizing service and introducing changes has been severely limited by the reluctance of government to delegate financial or other authority. The strong identification of lay boards and medical staff with their own hospitals, and the desire to have them totally self-sufficient in terms of the services provided, has impeded cooperative planning, differentiation of role of individual hospitals and rationalization of highly specialized services on an area-wide basis. For the physician, particularly the specialist, regionalization involves reorientation of thinking toward the needs of the community as a whole rather than identification with the interests of a specific hospital. For the hospital which has functioned as an autonomous institution, regionalization involves relinquishing a substantial measure of independence and subordination of institutional aspirations to priorities determined on an area-wide basis. Although these difficulties have impeded the implementation of formal structures for regionalization, the concepts have gained increasing acceptance by individuals and by institutions and substantial progress has been made in area-wide planning on an informal basis.

Supply and distribution of medical manpower

The supply of physicians in Canada is increasing dramatically. This is a result of the increase in domestic production, stimulated by the Health Resources Fund program and the increase in immigration brought about by improvements in the professional environment and the good and relatively improving social environment. On December 31, 1972, the physician-population ratio was 1 to 633. For the first time in Canada, it would appear that Canadian universities are producing sufficient physicians to maintain and even improve our physician-population ratio, taking into account attrition from all causes including losses by emigration to the United States even if one assumes a zero immigration situation for physicians. The overall attrition rate is actually going down, a phenomenon which may be due to a return flow of physicians who had emigrated to the United States.

Physicians continue to immigrate into Canada at the rate of about 1,000 a year and the pool of Canadian students applying for admission to medical colleges is great. A total of 1,178 acceptable applicants were turned away in 1972. Given a lead time of four to five years, if need be, the output of Canadian medical colleges could be substantially increased beyond what is already tentatively planned. If nothing is done to influence the flow of immigrant physicians or to change current firm plans in Canadian medical colleges, then the number of physicians in Canada will continue to increase at a much greater rate than the population and we will probably have a physician-population ratio of 1 to 488 by 1981 if there is no great change from the recent attrition rate (Figure 2). All the evidence now points to the fact that for most types of medical

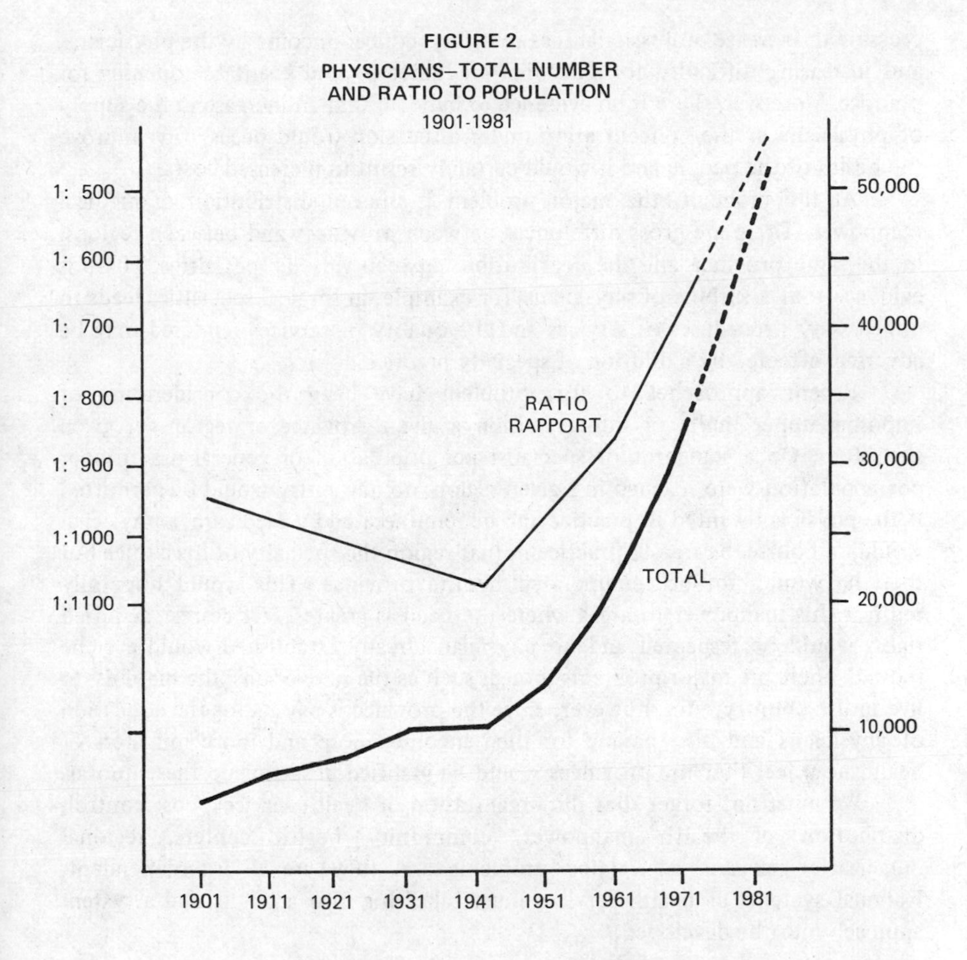

practice, and in most provinces, the physician supply is increasing more rapidly than present utilization demand and consequently, the very real possibility exists of an oversupply of underemployed physicians—at least in certain specialties in the short run and of most specialties in the long run, and in geographical areas in particular.

It is anticipated with some conviction that the Canadian consensus will call, in gross terms, for one active physician for each 600 people in Canada. This concentration of physicians will, in all probability, be enough to provide an excellent health care service if perfective measures are taken to improve their distribution on a geographical and functional basis, and to improve their efficiency through more use of allied health manpower.

There is evidence that unless there are major technological breakthroughs, further increases in the physician supply in most specialties and most provinces would mainly result in a lower volume of work per physician. This would bring pressure to increase professional fees to offset reduced income by the physicians, and increasing difficulty for Canadian graduates to find a suitable opening for practice. Moreover, there is no evidence to indicate that an increase in the supply of physicians at the concentration under discussion would necessarily improve the health of the people and it would certainly result in increased costs.

At the moment, the major problem is uneven distribution of medical manpower. There are gross differences between provinces and between regions, in the same province and the distribution between various specialties. There is evidence that a surplus of physicians, for example, in surgical specialties leads to unnecessary procedures or services and the quality of services rendered may be adversely affected by a dilution of specialty practice.

Recent approaches to this problem have been the consideration of imposing upper limits or quotas within a given province or region for given specialties. Once standards of specialist per population or general practitioner per population were reached in a given region, no new entry would be permitted if the physician wanted to practice and be remunerated by Medicare; a physician would, of course, be free to practice in that region the specialty of his choice but then he would not be remunerated by the province. This would hopefully redirect this manpower to areas where the need is greatest. Of course, acquired rights would be respected and no physician already established would ever be moved. There are major problems though such as the native sons, the inability to live in the country, etc.; however, since the province is paying for the education of physicians and also paying for their income, more and more ministers of health now feel that the provinces would be justified in setting up these quotas.

We must not forget that the organization of health services, cost control, distribution of health manpower, community health centers, regional organization all are interrelated problems and they are all interdependent. Rational systems of health services must take this into account and a system approach must be developed.

THE ADVANTAGE OF HINDSIGHT

The Canadian experience with universal health insurance, both Hospital Insurance and Medicare, is a positive one. It is fairly clear, however, that if one had to do it over again, we would probably do the same as before, given the social and political climate of the time. It is, of course, easy now to speculate on how differently things could have been done but I doubt that much could have been changed at the time of implementation of these programs. However, if one leaves aside the social, financial and political constraints of the time, there are theoretically a few things which could have been done differently.

a) Simultaneous introduction of coverage for inpatient hospital care, outpatient diagnostic and treatment services and physicians' services as a mandatory benefit would have prevented many problems. The reasons for this have been mentioned previously.

b) One might also permit the use of authorized charges to encourage patients and physicians to use the type of facility best suited to patient needs. Permitting differing levels of authorized charges between levels of institutional care would encourage the use of appropriate levels of care. However, there might be major political constraints to these charges.

c) One should try to avoid detailed listing of facilities in federal-provincial agreements by covering all levels of care whether they be inpatient or outpatient.

d) Mandatory portability for all benefits for emergency care anywhere in the world and for elective care within Canada might have been instituted at the very beginning as a condition of cost-sharing.

e) The cost-sharing formula should take social, economic and demographic characteristics of a provincial population as well as incorporating a reasonable bed population level according to age, sex, etc., although allowing flexibility within this overall budget.

f) There might be provision for conversion, after a reasonable period, to an indirect rate of cost increase such as the new financing formula described earlier as opposed to continuation of direct open-ended cost-sharing indefinitely.

g) The acceptance and the problem of implementation are easier if done at smaller levels of political jurisdictions such as a province or a region rather than for a larger population such as a federal one.

h) More participation in decision-making by those affected by the decision such as the providers of health insurance and the consumers would have prevented many problems.

I have not attempted to give an exhaustive list of the things which should have been done differently. Reading of this chapter will certainly indicate problems that have been encountered and how they might be resolved differently in the United States. It should be realized that governmental involvement in the financing of universal health programs will not result in health matters becoming no longer an active political issue. Quite to the contrary, while the universal programs have resolved some of the major problems, the advent of universal hospital and medical care insurance has made the public and the politicians more aware of deficiencies in the health care system. The consumers have become more militant and vociferous in their demands and the providers are finding out that in all these matters, it is usually the general population which has the last word.

A NEW PERSPECTIVE ON THE HEALTH OF CANADIANS

In the field of health we are in Canada now approaching the "post-health care" stage. The overall resources and financing of personal health care are generally sufficient even though greater efficiency can still be achieved through their improved organization and use. If our experience in Canada can be generalized to other countries, it would appear that we need to turn our attention to the health problems we impose on ourselves both as a society and as individuals.

A major departmental study has shown that while death and sickness in Canada are attributable mostly to environmental and lifestyle hazards, which could have been prevented, some 95 percent of health expenditures are directed at curing existing illness with only some 5 percent being spent on prevention. Health care costs have been increasing at a rate that has caused concern to both levels of government and to other interested organizations without a satisfactory off-setting improvement in the health of Canadians. Most major health problems of today result not from lack of services and facilities but from a combination of social, biological, environmental and lifestyle factors.

An analysis of mortality and hospital morbidity statistics for recent years has revealed the following: taking mortality statistics first, for Canadians age 5 to 35 in 1971, the principal cause of death was motor vehicle accidents. The second most important cause was all other types of accidents and the third was suicide. These three taken together account for 6,200 of the 9,700 deaths for this age group in 1971. These deaths were mainly due to human, environmental and social factors and were preventable. Our health system, defined as the quantity and quality of services and facilities, is almost powerless in preventing death by accident and its power in preventing suicide is negligible.

The statistics for 1971 show that at age 35, coronary artery disease first appeared as a significant cause of death (over 5 percent). By age 40, it became the principal cause and held this position in increasing ascendancy through all subsequent age groups. For the age group 35 to 70, diseases of the cardiovascular system accounted for 25,700 deaths out of a total of 58,000. While the causes of circulatory diseases are various, there is no doubt that obesity, smoking, stress, lack of exercise and high-fat diets, in combination, make a dominant contribution. These also cannot be linked to the health delivery system per se; the root causes are to be found elsewhere.

Turning to morbidity, the hospital statistics show that diseases of the cardiovascular system were by far the principal cause of hospitalization in acute general hospitals, accounting for 6,800,000 acute hospital days out of a total 37,600,000 in 1969. Fractures, head injuries, burns and all other causes arising from accidents and violence accounted for 3,100,000 hospital days. For these causes of hospitalization, individual behavior and carelessness are the principal underlying factors. Mental illness accounted for 2,000,000 hospital days in acute general hospitals. Diseases of the cardiovascular system, injuries due to accidents, respiratory diseases and mental illness, in that order, are the four principal causes of hospitalization accounting for some 45 percent of all hospital days. The significance of mental illness is further underlined by the fact that 23,400,000 patient days were utilized in psychiatric inpatient facilities in 1970.

The solutions to the major causes of death and suffering are largely preventable and the solutions thereto are found to be largely outside the capabilities of the health care system. Yet, when one examines direct expenditures on health, one finds that they are mostly physician-centered, including medical care, hospital care, laboratory tests and prescription drugs. Adding dental care and the services of such other professionals as optometrists and chiropractors, close to seven billion dollars a year are spent in Canada on a personal health care system which is mainly oriented to curing what in many cases could have been prevented.

A basic problem encountered in the analysis of the health field was the absence of an agreed conceptual framework for subdividing the field into its principal elements amenable to analysis and evaluation. It was keenly felt that there was a need to organize the thousands of pieces into an orderly pattern that was both intellectually acceptable and sufficiently simple to permit a quick location in the pattern of almost any idea, problem or activity related to health: a sort of map of the health territory.

Such a Health Field Concept has been developed and it envisages that the health field can be broken up into four broad elements: *Human Biology, Environment, Lifestyle* and *Health Care Organization.* These four elements were identified mainly through an examination of the causes and underlying factors of sickness and death in Canada, and from an assessment of the parts the elements play in affecting the level of health in Canada.

The *Human Biology* element includes all those aspects of health which are developed within the human body as a consequence of the basic biology of man and the organic make-up of the individual. This element includes the genetic inheritance of the individual, the processes of maturation and aging, and the many complex internal systems in the body, such as skeletal, nervous, muscular, cardiovascular, endocrine, digestive and so on. The human body being such a complicated organism, the health implications of human biology are numerous, varied and serious and the things that can go wrong with it are legion. This element contributes to all kinds of ill health and mortality, including many chronic diseases (such as arthritis, diabetes, atherosclerosis, cancer) and others (genetic disorders, congenital malformation, mental retardation). Health problems originating from human biology are causing untold miseries and costing billions of dollars in treatment services.

The *Environment* category includes all those matters related to health which are external to the human body and over which the individual has little or no control. These include the safety of food, drugs, cosmetics, devices, water supply, etc.; the control of health hazards resulting from air, water and noise pollution; the containment of communicable diseases, effective garbage and sewage disposal; and the health effects of rapid societal changes.

The *Lifestyle* category, in the Health Field Concept, consists of the aggregation of decisions taken by individuals which affect their health and over which they more or less have control. Personal decisions and habits that are bad, from a health point of view, create self-imposed risks. When those risks result in illness or death, the victim's lifestyle can be said to have contributed to, or caused his own illness or death.

The fourth and last element in the concept is the one to which 95 percent of health resources are allocated: *Health Care Organization*; it consists of the quantity, quality, arrangement, nature and relationships of people and resources in the provision of health care. It includes medical practice, nursing, hospitals, nursing homes, drugs, public and community health care services, ambulances, dental treatment and other health services such as optometry, chiropractics and podiatry.

The *Health Field Concept* has many characteristics which make it a powerful tool for analyzing health problems. The concept is comprehensive. Any health problem can be traced to one or a combination of the four elements and the role and influence of all contributors to health: patient, physician, scientist and government can be identified. Another feature of the concept is its inherent analytical possibilities.

For example, the underlying causes of death from traffic accidents can be found to be due mainly to risks taken by individuals, with lesser importance given to the design of cars and roads, and to the availability of emergency treatment; therefore, lifestyle, environment and health care organization can be said to contribute to traffic deaths in the proportions of, say, something like 75 percent, 20 percent and 5 percent respectively. Similarly, the concept permits a subdivision of factors; again, for traffic deaths in the lifestyle category, the risks taken by individuals can be subdivided under impaired driving, carelessness, failure to use seat belts and speeding. The concept thus provides a map showing the most direct links between health problems and their underlying causes and the relative significance of various contributing factors. However, the concept is not an end in itself; as mentioned previously, it is merely an analytical tool and clearly its most important contribution has been the realization that the health care delivery system is no longer the fount from which all health improvements will flow. The concept will enable policy makers and planners to identify the contributing factors to suffering and premature death in Canada and will facilitate the selection and design of preventive measures.

The need for a redirection of resources, over time, is self-evident: taking coronary artery disease as an example, one finds that it is the major killer and the major cause of hospital days. Contributing factors are well known and include genetic inheritance, the relative absence of the hormone estrogen in men, smoking, obesity, high-fat diets, high serum cholesterol, lack of exercise and stress as well as such morbid conditions as atherosclerosis, diabetes and high blood pressure. Yet when one looks for programs aimed at reducing the prevalence of coronary artery disease through an abatement of known contributing factors, one finds that they are weak or nonexistent. Deaths and injuries due to automobile accidents could probably be reduced by 50 percent if everyone wore seat belts, and if stricter measures were taken to reduce the number of impaired drivers. In spite of this knowledge, the rate of seat-belt wearing stays at about 10 percent and alcohol continues to be a factor in half the traffic accidents. Cigarette smoking contributes heavily to respiratory diseases and lung cancer. Education campaigns have succeeded in reducing the number of smokers in the 20 years of age and over bracket from 58 percent to 50 percent, but the recruitment of new smokers among teenagers has increased alarmingly, especially among teenage girls.

Some 40 percent of all alcoholic beverages in Canada are purchased by but 7 percent of the drinking population, the alcohol abusers. One quarter of all first male admissions to psychiatric hospitals are due to alcoholism, and the heavy contribution of alcohol abuse to motor vehicle accidents, poisonings, accidental fire deaths, cirrhosis of the liver and falls has been ascertained. Yet, the control and treatment of alcohol abuse in Canada is fragmented and weak.

The lack of physical fitness of the Canadian population is well known. A study in 1972 showed that 76 percent of Canada's population over age thirteen spent less than one hour a week participating in a sport, and that 79 percent had less than one hour per week in other physical activity such as walking. This same survey shows that 84 percent of the population over age thirteen watches four or more hours a week of television. Some 36 percent watch in excess of fifteen hours a week. This pattern of living, dominated by indolence, explains why so few Canadians are fit.

It is estimated that in Canada, about half the burden of illness is psychological in origin and this proportion is growing. An indication of the seriousness of the problem can be seen from the following facts: one third of all hospital beds and hospital days are for mental care patients; three out of 1,000 Canadians are hospitalized in psychiatric institutions at any given time; between 5 percent and 10 percent of school children suffer from mental and learning disorders; there is a significant increase in alcoholism and drug addiction, homicide and suicide, crime, anxiety neuroses and depressive psychoses. And yet, mental health as opposed to physical health has been a neglected area for years.

When one looks at the foregoing major health problems of Canada and their underlying causes, it is obvious that we are failing to act on the information we already have.

The Working Paper called "A New Perspective on the Health of Canadians" is an attempt to deal with these problems on a comprehensive basis and this is now our challenge in Canada.

DISCUSSION

JOHN I. EVANS: Dr. LeClair has presented a balanced and comprehensive review of the history and current status of health insurance in Canada from the federal viewpoint. From this historical perspective it is worth emphasizing the long period of staged evolution of health insurance in Canada and the extensive decentralization of authority and accountability for the administration of health insurance and health service programs.

Staged evolution

The period of evolution of national health insurance in Canada spans more than 20 years. The succession of staged programs included hospital construction (1948), hospital insurance (1958), health manpower development (1965) and medical care insurance (1968). This long period of evolution proved an opportunity for the development of structures and administrative machinery at the federal and provincial level, and allowed time for those affected by the new processes to gain an understanding of them. Furthermore, implementation was carried out by each province in relation to its social, economic and political circumstances rather than as a single national plan. Since some provinces introduced health insurance before the national plan, there was an opportunity for the federal government and the other provincial governments to learn from their experiences.

Decentralization and pluralism

In Canada the provinces have primary responsibility in the field of health by constitutional right and so the 10 provinces provided an established regional framework for the development of health services. The provinces showed considerable individuality in evolving their health insurance programs in terms of timing, extent of benefits, remuneration of physicians, financing of hospitals, use of private insurance carriers and the nature of government administrative machinery. The decentralization of health programs to the provincial level provided a more manageable size of administrative jurisdiction, allowed adaptation to local needs and brought the administration of the programs closer to those served. The disadvantages of pluralism were largely overcome by federal guidelines and financial assistance to offset the disparity in resources among the provinces.

A further level of decentralization is now under way within the larger provinces, with the aim of coordinating all health resources and programs on an area-wide or district basis. The purpose of the district level of organization is to coordinate all planning, to reconcile competing demands for resources and to provide an opportunity for the providers and recipients of health services in that district to participate in establishing the policies and priorities. This second level of decentralization has been difficult to establish because the districts lack a political base, taxing power, accepted boundaries and administrative machinery which is respected by the institutions within the district and by other levels of government.

Current problems

National health insurance as it has been developed in Canada removes all financial barriers to access to health care but it does not assure a satisfactory system of health services. There are still major problems of geographic accessibility, particularly in sparsely populated areas, availability of services and imbalance in the type of facilities.

With national health insurance the public looked to the insuring agent, government, to meet their expectations and rectify these deficiencies. The hospital construction program began in anticipation of national hospital insurance and the 10-year interval between the introduction of hospital insurance and medical care insurance undoubtedly contributed to the overbuilding and overutilization of active treatment hospital beds. Access to hospital and medical services has been improved by the insurance programs for disadvantaged groups in the population and for residents in rural areas, but equitable distribution of facilities and manpower involves other important factors.

When hospital insurance was introduced no mechanisms were established to ensure a balanced pattern of health service facilities, to reduce duplication of facilities and to rationalize the distribution of highly specialized services. Similarly, outside the institutional setting medical care insurance reinforced the existing system of medical practice and now there is much less incentive for the citizen or the physician to evolve more effective and economical approaches to the delivery of primary care. Health insurance has a powerful steering effect and should, therefore, be introduced in relation to an overall health plan. In Canada, the health plan and organizational structure has been evolved in the years following the introduction of health insurance and it is partly for this reason that the system of administrative controls established in conjunction with health insurance has not been very effective.

The second major problem in Canada and the United States is the distribution of physicians in relation to location and type of practice. It seems likely that health insurance has improved the distribution of physicians to the poorer, rural areas, particularly in New Brunswick and Newfoundland, by increasing the economic returns of practice. Apart from this it is difficult to attribute to health insurance any specific effects, either positive or negative, on the distribution of physicians. The existence of publicly sponsored health insurance almost certainly increased the sense of responsibility of government to respond to medical manpower problems, with specific measures designed to increase the number of family physicians and to ration the training of specialists. In addition, under the health insurance plan some provinces have introduced return of service educational grants, establishment of practice grants and guaranteed income as incentives for physicians and dentists to locate in underserviced areas.

There is little doubt that the escalation of health costs is the most serious problem now facing government and inflation has intensified this concern. Control of costs will undoubtedly mean denying most demands for new services and cutting back on existing hospital beds and other health services. But control mechanisms at the provincial level are blunt instruments and a more successful adaptation to limited resources is likely to result if the decisions can be made at district level by those who will be most directly affected. Although hospitals account for nearly two thirds of expenditures on health, the most important single determinant of these expenditures is the behavior of doctors. It has been estimated that costs attributable to doctors represent nearly 80 percent of total health expenditures and it follows that a surplus of doctors, particularly procedurally oriented specialists, will increase health costs without necessarily improving health. This matter is of immediate concern in some provinces where a surplus of physicians is imminent or already exists. In Canada, national health insurance was introduced at a time when the primary consideration was to improve access to good quality services by eliminating financial barriers. Cost control was a consideration but it was secondary. Now escalating expenditures are of great concern, and the visibility of these expenditures has been highlighted by national health insurance because the financial burden has been transferred from the individual to the state.

CHAPTER 2 • CLAUDE CASTONGUAY

The Quebec Experience: Effects on Accessibility

To establish how national health insurance was implemented in Quebec, and to understand the problems of accessibility, their importance and the setting in which solutions have been attempted, it is necessary to give a brief outlook of Quebec before this measure was adopted.

Quebec has an area of 600,000 square miles. Its population is just over 6,000,000, eighty percent of which speaks French. The population is generally concentrated in the St. Lawrence Valley, on a belt going from west to east on the southern portion of the land. Montreal, whose metropolitan population exceeds the 3,000,000 mark, is located on the western edge of this belt. Clustered along the St. Lawrence is the city of Quebec which has more than 400,000 inhabitants, and on the eastern edge, 700 miles from Montreal, lies Blanc Sablon whose population is no more than 2,000 inhabitants.

To the north of the St. Lawrence Valley, there are a number of towns relatively distant from one another which, for the most part, are directly linked to the exploitation of natural resources. Finally, further to the north, there are villages inhabited by approximately 3,500 Eskimos and 2,000 American Indians; some of these villages are located more than 1,000 miles from the City of Quebec.

The largest portion of the province of Quebec is dotted by thousands of lakes and rivers and the climate, even in the southern portion, is relatively rigorous during winter. To understand the significance of these dimensions, one might compare the area of Quebec to the combined areas of the states of New York, Vermont, New Hampshire, Maine, Massachusetts, Rhode Island, New Jersey, Pennsylvania, California . . . and Texas (590,000 square miles).

The evolution toward health insurance

During the 1950's, the constant increase in the cost of health services gave rise to more and more acute problems with reference to the financing of hospitals. At the individual's level, this increase very often meant almost insoluble financial problems. In addition, it limited access to hospital care for a significant portion of the population. Faced with this situation, in 1961 the government established the Hospital Insurance Plan. Under this plan, any resident can receive free hospital care as required, from all hospitals under contract with the provincial government. While the objectives intended by Hospital Insurance have generally been attained, the resulting costs were much higher than anticipated. Moreover, the increased demand for services required a rapid increase in the number of beds for the treatment of acute illness.

With respect to training of personnel, problems became gradually more numerous and more diversified. On the one hand, the general reform in medical education which had been under way since the beginning of the 1960's raised very fundamental questions. While, on the other hand, the rapid growth of knowledge and the multiplication of the categories of professional personnel placed the system of professional corporations under severe strains. Finally, the government declared itself powerless to provide the answers to the numerous questions arising from these two types of problems. In 1965, the government requested a moratorium and froze all requests to change the legislation related to professional corporations.

After the establishment of Hospital Insurance in Quebec, attention was gradually focused on the growing increases in the cost of health services such as medical care, drugs, etc. The eventual implementation of a health insurance plan appeared a certainty. To facilitate financial access to medical care for the most underprivileged categories and, at the same time, establish an experimental program, the government in the Spring of 1966 set up a full medical care plan for beneficiaries of social assistance.

A few months later, during the Summer of 1966, negotiations of the collective agreement for nonmedical personnel gave rise to a general strike in the hospitals of Quebec. This strike lasted nearly three weeks and gave further evidence of the existence of numerous problems in the health sector and the lack of clear-cut approaches to solve them.

It was in this context that the federal government, in 1966, unveiled its bill on medical care insurance. Through this bill, beginning on July 1, 1967,[1] the federal government undertook to bear approximately 50 percent of the costs of any medical care plan established by a provincial government. Certain general criteria were provided to establish admissibility to cost-sharing: universal access, complete medical care coverage, transferability of coverage from one province to another, and public control of the utilization of financial resources.

Confronted at once by the rapid growth and multiplication of problems, and the need to adopt a position or policy in relation to the federal bill on medical care, in November 1966 the government of Quebec established a commission of inquiry whose mandate included not only the health sector but also that of social welfare.

In July 1967, at the government's request, this commission submitted the first part of its report. It recommended establishment of a universal health insurance plan.[2] According to the commission, the plan was to be financed by contributions, which varied according to wages and paid by workers and their employers, and by federal government contributions. The commission submitted its general report on health services to the government in the Summer of 1970 following a long study, consultation and visits to bodies and establishments in Quebec as well as outside the province.[3]

I will now describe the major steps in the reform of health services undertaken following the commission report. After reviewing health insurance with respect to the general health policy, I will then analyze its main provisions. Finally, in the last section, I will present an evaluation of the results to be followed by a proposal likely to improve the system.

THE REPORT OF THE COMMISSION OF INQUIRY ON HEALTH AND SOCIAL WELFARE

In its report on health services, the commission demonstrates that in spite of the improvement of the state of health of Quebec's inhabitants over the years, there continue to be significant differences in mortality and morbidity statistics between regions and various zones within urban areas. On the positive side, the commission notes the improvement in the general level of mortality, the increased life expectancy, the decline in infant mortality and in the mortality due to certain forms of cancer. Nevertheless, the difference in comparison to certain countries of a comparable economic level demonstrates that important progress remains to be made especially with reference to regional disparities. In fact, and particularly with reference to infant mortality and coronary disease, there continue to be notable variations between the many regions of Quebec. In the case of coronary disease, the commission points to an increase in premature deaths among men in all regions except in Metropolitan Montreal.

In discussing policies, programs and the organization of services, the commission identifies many deficiencies and notes a preponderant emphasis being placed on the treatment of illnesses and not on the individual in the context of his family and work. It underscores the disproportionate resources committed to the treatment of illness in comparison to those committed to its prevention and the promotion of health. Finally, the commission expresses apprehension at the very rapid increase in the costs of health services compared to the various indexes on the growth of the resources of society, as well as the growing difference between the resources and needs of primary services, services for the chronically ill and for the aged, etc.

The commission concludes its assessment of the situation in the following terms:

> "Analysis of the present situation of health organization emphasizes the lack of an integrated care distribution system. In the absence of

a veritable policy based on precise objectives which orient the development of a total health organization, it is natural that several parallel systems emerged, one isolated from the other and each filling part of the people's needs. It is natural, normal too, that each of the components of the plan does not preoccupy itself with reconciling and integrating its objectives with those of the overall system: the latter constitutes, taking everything into account, simply an addition of individual interests and objectives of the institutions which make it up. The absence of a coherent health policy and of a master plan which serve as guides during decisions with regard to development and investment is, according to all evidence, the fundamental shortcoming of the present Quebec health system."[4]

Problems of accessibility

With reference to the problems of accessibility, the commission adopted a very broad approach aimed at the causes of morbidity and mortality and their relation with poverty, unsanitary dwellings, deterioration of urban areas, certain life and nutritional habits, pollution under its various forms, etc. Consequently, its recommendations constitute a program of action which, in the opinion of the commission, must be pursued vigorously. Unless this is done, efforts in the more limited area of access to health services will merely become extremely expensive palliatives.

With the aid of available data, the commission also traces as completely as possible a portrait of the population's state of health. It puts into evidence the evolution of coronary disease, various forms of cancer, accidents, infant mortality, psychic and mental disorders, the consumption of alcohol, tobacco, drugs, etc. By doing so, the commission wants to lay the foundations necessary for the development of programs geared toward the main causes of mortality and morbidity, taking into account the training of personnel, the organization of services and research. It also wishes to put into evidence the need for systematic epidemiological studies without which efforts with respect to accessibility to services cannot be but inappropriate and inefficient.

Having demonstrated through detailed data that the professional and technical manpower as well as hospital resources are numerically and qualitatively comparable to those of most industrialized countries, including the United States, the commission tackles the more closely related aspects of accessibility to health services. According to the commission's findings, these problems or obstacles are of three different types: physical, psychosocial and financial.

Physical obstacles. Distance constitutes a major problem for a considerable portion of the population. In fact, the dispersion of the population over a large territory into pockets of inhabitants gives rise to difficulties of access to care due both to distances and time involved. To these constraints must be added the high cost of transportation, the deficiencies or lack of a specialized ambulance system and climatic conditions which are particularly severe in the less populated areas. As for the services themselves, the commission notes that among the types of care which are most deficient in comparison to the needs of the whole population of Quebec, one must include preventive care, primary care, rehabilitation, mental health, and care for chronic and convalescent patients.

Finally, with reference to this subject the commission notes that it is easier to identify than to quantify the types of care which are lacking.[5]

Psychosocial obstacles. Fear of the unknown, deficiencies in medical education, lack of information on the nature and availability of care, the difficulty of identifying the most appropriate way to have access to services and the difficulty of communicating with the doctor and other health professionals are, in the commission's opinion, if not obstacles at least resistances capable of hindering access to care or differentiating the demand for services. Such obstacles are compounded by problems of the same nature with respect to treatment. The fragmentation of psychic and physical components of health and their rigorous division introduces a barrier between these two closely related aspects of illness. Due to its increasingly scientific and technical character, medical specialization involves a similar form of fragmentation with respect to the physical component of health. The doctor's interest is being increasingly shifted toward the affected part of the body and this to the detriment of the individual. For example, the commission notes the difficulty of alcoholics to obtain care due to the lack of interest in the person or his family.

With respect to the social obstacles, the commission notes that hospitals and other institutions take for granted, without any analysis of the situation, that all citizens have identical needs and equal opportunities of access to health care. Nevertheless, it is obvious that the state of health of underprivileged groups is not as good as that of the population in general. For that reason, it concludes that in the name of distributive justice it is necessary to facilitate access to health services for the underprivileged and that the organization of health services be adapted to their specific needs.

Financial obstacles. The commission notes that since the introduction of the Hospital Insurance Plan, the problems of access to services due to financial reasons have been reduced.

However, it points out that in 1964 only 43 percent of the population, that is, 2,400,000 persons in Quebec, were insured against medical expenses and that among those who were insured only 1,000,000 benefited from relatively complete protection. The commission also notes that those who were insured were mainly concentrated among persons in the middle and upper income brackets. To assess the progress made by the insurers, one must remember that Quebec was eighth in rank among Canadian provinces with reference to the number of persons insured and the extent of their coverage.

The commission's report stresses that for a significant portion of the population the costs of drugs, dental care, eyeglasses and protheses constitute almost insurmountable obstacles. Beside the immediate costs of disease one must also take into account indirect expenditures (inability to earn an income due to an interruption of employment, transportation expenses, child care costs, etc.), which also weigh heavily on a family's budget.

Bearing these factors in mind, the commission concludes that an important portion of the population does not have access to the services it needs and finds itself somewhat permanently trapped in a vicious circle.

To identify all the dimensions of the problems of accessibility, it is useful to recall certain elements contained in the commission's analysis of the modes of distribution of services. This analysis, as we have seen, reveals numerous deficiencies. They indicate a lack of a systematic organization in the distribution of services and the need for major changes. In other words, the commission sees the establishment of health insurance as only one measure among many intended to improve access to health services.

It is interesting that the commission does not consider the situation described above as being unique to Quebec. To support this assertion, it cites the following passage from the Report by the National Advisory Commission on Health Manpower to the President of the United States:

> "As members of the Commission and as American citizens, the indications of such a crisis are evident to us: long delays in non-urgent examinations and treatments; long waiting periods in the inevitable 'waiting rooms,' to obtain hasty and sometimes impersonal attention during a very brief visit; difficulty in obtaining care during the night and weekends, except in hospital emergency services; overcrowding of certain hospitals while beds are vacant in other institutions; reduction of hospital services through lack of nursing personnel; redundancy in certain specialized services in a single locality; uneven division of care, as indicated by health statistics with respect to inhabitants of rural regions and poor urban sectors, to migrating workers and other minority groups, which sometimes recall the statistics of a developing country; desuetude of certain hospitals in our largest cities; rapid rise in care costs on the basis of levels which are already prohibitive for some and which create heavy financial burdens for many others."[6]

THE REFORM OF THE HEALTH SECTOR

The analysis of the situation in terms of access to health services requires some general information on the health policy adopted by the government of Quebec following the commission report. This policy constitutes the general setting against which the more specific measures with respect to the problems of accessibility can be analyzed.

This health policy was defined in the following manner:

- The need to establish a coherent and integrated health care delivery system based on comprehensive health care founded on the individual person.

- The development and orientation of services toward geographic, financial and social accessibility to continuous care.
- The decentralization of management in the health and social services sector, namely through the establishment of regional councils representative of the various regions of Quebec and the introduction of the regionalization of services and of the concept of the levels of care (primary, specialized and highly specialized care).
- The participation of all those involved, including the beneficiaries, in identifying needs as well as in managing health services.
- The withdrawal by the department from its role of administrator of public health services in order to concentrate on planning, on the location and utilization of resources and on the elaboration and enforcement of norms and standards.
- The introduction of the concept of programs, and the development of mechanisms for the permanent evaluation of the utilization of resources and of the efficiency of such programs.
- The reorientation of research in accordance with clearly-defined objectives.
- Finally, the limitation of the growth of public expenditures at a level not exceeding that of the government's fiscal revenues.

It can be seen that the government opted not to merely add health insurance to existing programs, but rather to undertake an in-depth reform of health services with the objective of improving the state of health of the population. The objective of financial accessibility through health insurance became only one dimension in the overall effort. In fact, most of the elements of the health policy bore either directly or indirectly on the broadly defined question of access to services. The government also took the option, although the stated objectives do not make it explicit, not to modify the status of the physicians into that of civil servants nor to transform the structure of the public institutions into government services.

The new health policy involved a series of measures that I will now review briefly.

The Health Insurance Act

On November 1, 1970, a health insurance plan covering all Quebec residents was implemented. Initially, this plan covered all medical care[7] and optometric services; at the same time the government announced its intention of gradually extending coverage to other services. Since then, the coverage has been extended to prescribed drugs for the beneficiaries of social assistance as well as for the low-income aged, to dental care for children under eight years of age[8] and to prostheses other than dental, optical and auditory for the whole population.

The administration of the health insurance plan in Quebec is entrusted to an autonomous public body whose board of directors allows for broad participation. As it was the case with hospital insurance, private insurers withdrew for all practical purposes from this field of activities. The legislation prohibits them from insuring services already covered by the public plan.

The financing of the plan is provided by the contributions from the federal government and by contributions payable by workers and employers. The amount of the latter's contributions is related to the worker's taxable income, which has the effect of excluding a large number of workers from the payment of contributions. A maximum is also applied on the amount of the worker's contribution and the nonpayment of a contribution does not result in the cancellation of the right to health services but rather in the obligation to pay the income tax penalties.

The fees paid to doctors and other professionals under the plan have been established through negotiations with the syndical associations representing the various categories of health professionals.[9] Since the plan was established, costs have been largely in line with the initial projections and the health insurance board has been able to build a surplus fund for contingency purposes.

The Department of Social Affairs

On January 1, 1971, the Department of Health was merged with the Department of Family and Social Welfare and became the Department of Social Affairs. This Department was entrusted with the responsibility for the following sectors: health services, social services and income security. Through the merger, it became possible to develop policies and programs in terms of the individuals rather than the episodes of illness, and to stimulate, or whenever necessary, to assume the coordination of health and social services, particularly at the primary level.

When the new department was created, the government announced it would relinquish its role of direct distributor of personal public hygiene services (prevention, immunization, etc.). This was done so that governmental efforts could be devoted strictly to the functions of planning, programming, resource allocation, development of standards and supervision of their application, and program evaluation. In summary, the new Department of Social Affairs undertook resolutely the application of the health policy and its regular updating.

The development of resources

At the same time, the Department of Social Affairs went through the first stage in the reorientation of the development of physical and human resources. This stage consisted of the establishment of a ceiling on the number of beds for the treatment of acute cases. It was done by taking the then existing level as ceiling and by cancelling nearly all current construction or expansion projects for this type of service. Subsequently, the department has authorized only those programs which have been developed in consultation with all involved parties. These bear on the development of outpatient clinics, emergency hospital services, resources for chronic and convalescent patients and the new local community service centers. The department also undertook to develop and implement programs intended to adapt resources to regional needs for specialized and ultraspecialized services, to the requirements of other levels of care, and to specific needs such as a perinatal policy.

As far as the development of human resources is concerned, the department has undertaken an in-depth review of the question of training various categories of health professionals and workers. This review, which is broadly based on the findings of the Commission of Inquiry, is carried out in close collaboration with the Department of Education, the educational institutions at the university and college levels and the professional corporations and associations. It seeks to establish the different categories of personnel to be trained, the content of training as well as the level at which it is to be given. Finally, the department has undertaken to establish a mechanism for the periodic evaluation of future needs using as a starting point the manpower projection developed by the Commission of Inquiry.

Also with respect to human resources, the legislation under which professional corporations issue licenses to practice and supervise the various professions has been completely revised. Among the many changes and innovations introduced, some are especially important from the point of view of access to services.

The criteria for admission or refusal to practice a profession were clarified and simplified so as to avoid their being used to artificially limit the number of health professionals. Representatives of the beneficiaires or of the general public are now members of the boards of administrators of the various professional corporations to make sure the public is always protected by their decisions. To reduce conflict between professional corporations and educational institutions with reference to the development of education and training programs, the new legislation requires both types of organizations to join together in such effort including the elaboration and application of evaluation mechanisms.

Henceforth, the legislation imposes on professional corporations more clearly defined obligations with respect to discipline. It requires them to put into operation permanent mechanisms for the evaluation of the professional activity of their members.

The new legislation also contains provisions which allow the legal definition of the sphere of practice of each profession to be adapted in a more dynamic way than in the past, depending on the evolution of knowledge and the greater demands of a health system based on the satisfaction of the various needs of the population. For example, the professional corporations representing physicians and nurses must jointly restablish and periodically revise a list of medical procedures which nurses are legally entitled to perform under given conditions.

The global budget

In 1971 and 1972 a new type of relationship was established at the financial level between the Department of Social Affairs and the establishments responsible for the distribution of health services. It must be remembered that since the implementation of hospital insurance, nearly all of the operating costs of these establishments, with the exclusion of the cost of medical services, were being assumed by the government for hospitalized patients as well as for ambulatory patients.[10] Due to a rigid approach to the need to control expenditures of public funds and in view of the rapid increases in the costs of hospital services, ever more detailed budgetary and control procedures were gradually introduced. While the objective was obviously to contain or limit increases in costs, these procedures and controls eventually came to have the opposite effect. On the one hand, they were applied without distinction to all establishments irrespective of their efficiency and, on the other hand, they removed from the establishments the autonomy needed for the improvement of their management and operation.

In collaboration with the hospital administrations, a new method of financing intended to give to each establishment the responsibility for its own current operations was first tried and then applied to all establishments. Through the method of the global budget, the level of the operating budget for each establishment is determined in advance in relation to the anticipated volume and type of services to be rendered. Each establishment then has the freedom or latitude, within certain broad guidelines, to use this budget in the most appropriate manner to attain objectives defined with respect to the needs of the population. If, at the end of a financial year, an establishment develops an operating surplus, this surplus is not necessarily claimed by the government.

This modification in the method of financing was also accompanied by changes in the statistical and financial reports which establishments are required to submit. Besides the simplification of reporting, a comparative evaluation mechanism of the various functions or activities in all the establishments has been introduced. It has, therefore, become possible for the establishments as well as for the Department of Social Affairs to concentrate the efforts for improvement strictly where such efforts are most needed.

The Health Services and Social Services Act

Adopted at the end of 1971, the Health Services and Social Services Act constitutes at the legislative level the foundation of the reform of the health and social services. A description of the aims of this legislation gives a better understanding of its importance:

1) improve the state of the health of the population, the state of the social environment in which they live and the social conditions of individuals, families and groups;
2) make accessible to every person, continuously and throughout his lifetime, the complete range of health services and social services, including prevention and rehabilitation, to meet the needs of individuals, families and groups from a physical, mental and social standpoint;
3) encourage the population and the groups which compose it to participate in the founding, administration and development of establishments so as to ensure their vital growth and renewal;
4) better adapt the health services and social services to the needs of the population taking into account regional characteristics and apportion among such services the human and financial resources in the most equitable and rational manner possible;
5) promote recourse to modern methods of organization and management to render the services offered to the population more efficient;
6) promote research and education.

For the purposes of the present analysis, I will only review the provisions of the Act related to the question of access to services.

The right to health services and social services

The Act explicitly proclaims the right of every individual "to receive adequate, continuous and personal health services and social services from a scientific, human and social standpoint, taking into account the organization and resources of the establishments providing such services." It prohibits any discrimination based "on race, color, sex, religion, language, national extraction, social origin, customs or political convictions." Finally, it gives to every individual the freedom "to choose the professional or establishment from whom or which he wishes to receive health services or social service, (and) the freedom of a professional to accept or refuse to treat such person."

The philosophy of the health policy with respect to accessibility is clearly expressed by the provisions contained in the legislation, both as far as individuals, families and professionals are concerned. Since this legislation is the basis for the organization and operation of health services in Quebec, it is obvious that the situation with respect to access to services will continue to evolve in the future, even if it will do so in a less spectacular manner than when hospital and health insurance were established.

The Regional Health and Social Services Councils

In accordance with the Health Services and Social Services Act, a regional council has been set up in each of the 12 regions of Quebec. It should be emphasized these councils emanate from each region since their members are nominated or elected by the institutions of each region, namely by the mayors of municipalities, the local community service centers, the hospitals and reception centers, the social services centers and the educational establishments.

The main functions of the regional councils are the following:

i) to encourage the participation of the population in defining its own needs in health services and social services and in the administration and operation of the establishments providing these services;
ii) to ensure sustained communication between the public, the minister and the establishments;
iii) to receive and hear complaints of persons for whom an establishment situated in the region for which the regional council is established has not provided the health services and social services that the legislation entitles them to receive, and to make the recommendations it considers appropriate in this regard to the establishment concerned and the minister;
iv) to advise and assist the establishments in the preparation of their programs, to develop and operate health services and social services and to assume the duties that the minister entrusts it with to carry out such programs;
v) to promote the setting up of common services for such establishments, the exchange of services between them, the elimination of duplication of services, and a better apportionment of services in the region;
vi) to send the minister, at least once a year, its recommendations to ensure adequate apportionment in its territory of the resources devoted to health services and social services and the best possible use of them.

The regional councils must also regulate and supervise the election of a number of members of the board of directors of the establishments in their respective region. They are also required to hold at least once a year a public meeting to report on their activities, and they must submit an annual report to the National Assembly.

Since their recent creation, the regional councils have been given the task of developing a complete emergency services system for each region.[11] The councils are expected to be called upon to participate in the operation of these services.

The hospitals

The legislation entrusts the management of the hospitals to boards of administrators in spite of the fact that almost all of their operating expenses are assumed by the government. These boards are meant to represent all the interested groups. They are composed of individuals representing the corporations which previously had the responsibility of the establishments, the beneficiaries, the socioeconomic groups, the physicians and other professionals affiliated with the hospital, nonprofessional personnel, local community service centers linked by contract to the hospital, the university or college with which the hospital is affiliated, and interns and residents.

In accordance with the Act, more than 30 hospitals have been asked to develop a department of community health. The fundamental objective consists in:

1) making these hospitals responsible for the protection and promotion of the health of a given population in addition to the normal responsibilities with respect to treatment and hospitalization;
2) widening the range of activities of the designated hospitals by assigning them new and original responsibilities in the area of prevention and promotion of public health;
3) bringing preventive services nearer to curative services in order to progressively integrate this preoccupation in the distribution of general services;
4) orienting hospitals to move closer to the community and less toward the treatment of individual cases.

Among the functions entrusted to the departments of community health in line with the general objective, is their responsibility to develop preventive care programs (perinatal, nutrition, etc.), to ensure the propoer operation of hospital outpatient clinics and emergency services, to organize home care services adapted to the need of the population and the patients upon their dismissal from hospital, and to carry out studies on trends of physical and mental illness within the population, and to develop appropriate methods of intervention.

Finally, it should be mentioned that the conditions for the admission of physicians to practice medicine in the hospitals of Quebec have been clearly defined by the Act. The decision is taken by the board of administrators which, in case of refusal, must communicate its reasons in writing. A hospital cannot refuse a candidate on the basis that it does not have a sufficient number of beds. Provisions are also made for a review and appeal procedure.

The Local Community Service Centers

The enactment of the Health Services and Social Services Act has given rise to the establishment of a network of local community service centers called upon to provide integrated primary care services. These community centers constitute a level of services midway between the doctors' private offices and the hospitals, and are designated eventually to become the main form of entry into the services network.

The local community service centers are intended to provide basic services to individuals, families and local communities. These services are intended to be easily accessible and continuous, and to these ends the centers must maintain constant communication with the other establishments within the network.

The decisions as to their location are based on the studies on the state of health of the population and on available resources. Priority is given to underprivileged areas in terms of available services.

With respect to their organizational structure, the management of the community centers is vested on boards of administrators composed of nine members, five of whom are elected by the users of the services of the center, two represent socioeconomic groups and are nominated by the government, one represents the professionals practicing in the center and one represents the nonprofessional personnel. The staffs of the centers function as multidisciplinary teams.

The allocation of resources

To ensure a proper balance in the allocation of resources, the new Act contains the provision, introduced in 1962 in the Hospital Act, under which the government's prior authorization is required to establish, transform, expand, or cease to operate in whole or in part an establishment.

This general review of the major stages which have characterized the implementation of the new health policy in Quebec emphasizes that accessibility to services has not been approached by means of one measure only but rather by a series of complementary policies and programs embodying all aspects of accessibility to health services.

HEALTH INSURANCE

As mentioned previously the Health Insurance Plan, established in November 1970, covers for all practical purposes all Quebec residents. With the exception of provisions relating to the level of contributions, all the other provisions of the plan apply uniformly to all Quebec residents without regard to their income or other characteristics.

Although it was estimated that approximately 60 percent of the population was insured in 1970, the government replaced private plans with a single plan to simplify administration, obtain appropriate statistical data and, above all, avoid any distinction between beneficiaries capable of perpetuating different standards of access to or of quality of medical care. With reference to this last aspect, the government was taking an analogous approach to that taken when hospital insurance was introduced. This has effected the elimination of "public wards" and "dispensaries" previously reserved for low income people. In taking this approach, the government knew it would be criticized in the future by persons who previously had no problems of access to services. In the government's opinion, this approach was the sole one compatible with the objective of a single level of access and of quality of health care.

In the establishment of health insurance, the option to negotiate with the medical profession and the other health professionals was chosen. For the purposes of these negotiations, the government decided to distinguish between *long-term* principles and conditions bearing on the practice of professions (such as supervision of professional activities, therapeutic freedom, professional confidentiality, freedom to provide services, conditions with respect to opting out) and the *short-term* issues related to fee schedules and working conditions. The long-term conditions and principles were included in the Health Insurance Act while the short-term conditions were left to be negotiated within the established framework.

For discussion purposes, the government sought to delineate the short-term issues affecting the professionals and the beneficiaries of the plan from fundamental aspects of health insurance. But part of the medical profession saw in the provisions of the Act the possibility that the government would eventually determine the manner in which medicine would be practiced; this possibility appeared even more critical because the plan provides no remuneration to the professional who does not wish to participate. These features of the plan plus the level of the fee schedule proposed by the government gave rise to a strike in Quebec by medical specialists in the Fall of 1970. The Act was amended to eliminate any ambiguity with reference to the therapeutic freedom of physicians, and a temporary schedule of fees was imposed through legislation after which the National Assembly ordered the physicians back to work. Shortly after, negotiated agreements, which included an increase in some of the proposed fees, were signed with the syndical federations representing general practitioners and specialists.

While it would have been desirable to avoid the confrontation, nevertheless, certain positive aspects have been identified in retrospect. The confrontation has allowed Quebec to establish the necessary primacy of the legislator and the government in defining the main elements of the health policy. It has also made clear that provisions dealing with the practice of medicine need to be fully clarified so that they would lead to maintenance and improvement of the quality of accessible services. The medical profession's reaction following the return-to-work legislation has been described as follows:

> "Among some specialists the initial response was one of petulance; it is even said that patients (who were guilty of voting the culprit politicians into office) were deliberately inconvenienced and delayed, but their general reaction was one of calm acceptance, and therefore the folly was abandoned. A second response was what one

would expect of a leading profession: more attention was paid to the Castonguay Report and there was an increasing acceptance of both its findings of inadequacies in the health delivery system and of its goals for future development. The Federation (of medical specialists) itself established a consulting agency to initiate and assist in the development of poly-clinics. Hospital medical staffs undertook ways and means of rationalizing and removing duplication of services in hospitals."[12]

With reference to the remuneration of physicians and other professionals, the plan and the negotiated agreements include various provisions intended to facilitate access to services. In spite of the deficiencies of the fee-for-service system of remuneration, it was retained for all those professionals remunerated in this manner when the plan was established. In doing so, an abrupt change which might have seriously reduced the volume of services was averted. The government, however, retained as an objective the negotiation of other methods of remuneration that might be better adapted to certain establishments, to the local community service centers, etc.

A number of provisions of the fee-for-service system of remuneration were determined in relation to the objectives of access and quality of care. Thus, with the exception of a few nonparticipating physicians who receive no remuneration from the plan, all the physicians are remunerated directly by the Health Insurance Board and cannot claim any additional fees beyond those covered by the negotiated agreements. Moreover, a single rate of fee is provided for a given procedure whether it is carried out by a general practitioner or by a specialist, and this rate applies uniformly throughout the province of Quebec. Finally, no deterrent fees are payable by the beneficiaries of the plan.

The fee schedule may also be modified through negotiation to influence the volume of services and improve the overall quality of care or to reduce the volume of unnecessary services. The data gathered and analyzed by the Health Insurance Board constitute a very useful tool for this purpose, both for the government as well as for the professionals.

The provisions of the Act and of the agreements are binding on all Quebec physicians, with the exception of those choosing to practice outside the plan. In such a case, neither the patient nor the physician receives payment under the plan. The maintenance of different standards of access and of quality as well as the development of a health services "black market" can be avoided when almost all professionals whose services are covered participate in the plan.

EVALUATION AND IMPROVEMENT

At this stage, an assessment of the results of health insurance can only be incomplete. In fact, some of the objectives are mainly of a qualitative nature. It is only through much more detailed and complete analyses and evaluations that it will be possible to judge more rigorously and objectively all of the negative and positive results. It should also be remembered that the data on services rendered provide only an incomplete picture since, in the final analysis, the results in terms of health improvement and reduction in mortality and morbidity are the most significant. It is with these restrictions in mind that the limited data presented below on the overall comprehensive results with respect to access to services must be interpreted.

Hospitalization

When speaking of access to hospital care, it must be remembered that the hospital insurance plan in Quebec has been in operation for the last 13 years and constitutes now a well-established program. The numerous analyses of the results obtained through the hospital insurance plan indicate that generally the initial objectives, particularly in terms of access to care, have been attained. For those reasons, I present only some statistics which illustrate the situation in that respect.

Table 1 shows that in terms of access, rural regions are not underprivileged

TABLE 1
HOSPITAL STATISTICS—1971

	Region	Rate of hospitalization per 10,000 inhabitants	Average length of stay (days)	Hospitalization in the region ($)
1	Bas St-Laurent — Gaspésie	2,020	10.5	86.4
2	Saguenay — Lac St-Jean	1,792	12.4	95.9
3	Quebec	1,534	13.0	95.0
4	Trois-Rivières	1,567	12.4	89.0
5	Cantons de l'Est	1,913	11.8	95.0
6A	Montréal*	1,382	13.7	97.1
6B	Laurentides	1,217	13.5	97.1
6C	Rive-Sud	1,266	13.2	97.1
7	Outaouais†	1,633	11.2	68.8
8	Nord-Ouest	2,125	10.4	84.4
	Quebec as a whole	1,515	12.8	92.3

SOURCE: Statistics compiled by the Department of Social Affairs on the hospitalization of the physically ill in short duration and long-term care hospitals.

*Regions 6A, 6B and 6C cover the whole metropolitan Montreal.

†This region is in the immediate vicinity of Ottawa in which about 25% of hospitalization took place.

when compared to urban areas. Regions 3 and 6A, 6B and 6C, which are the most urbanized, have, in fact, hospitalization rates clearly below the average. It can be noted, however, that the average length of stay is longer. This indicates that in the context of a better balance in the resources, there is less frequent recourse to hospitalization, but when it does occur, it is for longer durations; hospitalizations in the immediate region are also more frequent.

On the basis of Table 1, it is also possible to conclude that in general, low-income people are not discriminated against when compared to those with higher incomes. Regions whose per capita incomes are the highest, have, in fact, the lowest rates of hospitalization. A more detailed analysis of some underprivileged zones within the large urban centers would indicate, however, lower rates of hospitalization and, consequently, the existence of some problems of accessibility.

Medical care

The implementation of medical care insurance, having been more controversial than that of hospital insurance, provides a more detailed picture of the changes which have resulted in terms of access to services. I have reproduced data drawn from the 1972 Annual Report of the Health Insurance Board relating to a relatively stabilized operation of the plan.[13] Unfortunately no similar data which would enable comparisons with the situation prior to the establishment of the plan are available.

Out of the 34,375,513 insured services provided by physicians in 1972, 53.5 percent were provided by general practitioners and 46.5 percent by medical specialists; the volume of services increased by 7 percent in comparison to that of 1971.

Table 2 shows that from a regional perspective, there were marked differences in the volume of services rendered. These differences were particularly evident in the regions having a high density of physicians and those with a lower concentration.

It must be mentioned, however, that the statistics in Table 2 reflect the number of medical services provided by physicians of each region and not the number of services received by the residents of each region. In the regions where the number of physicians is lower, residents tend to receive part of their services outside their region. This has the effect of increasing the number of services per capita rendered in urban areas. The Report of the Health Insurance Board also shows that in general, the lower the number of physicians per 100,000 inhabitants in a region, the greater the number of services provided by these physicians. For example, physicians in the Nore Ouest region provided an average 7,197 services in 1972 while those in Cote-Nord provided 7,200. At the other extreme, the region of Quebec had an average number of services per physician of 4,194, Montreal 4,008 and les Cantons de l'Est 3,994.

The data indicate, therefore, clearly that the health insurance plan, in its

TABLE 2
REGIONAL PERSPECTIVE OF MEDICAL SERVICES—QUEBEC

	Region	Number of medical services by region (per capita)
1	Bas St-Laurent – Gaspésie	3.7
2	Saguenay – Lac St-Jean	5.3
3	Québec	5.6
4	Trois-Rivières	4.7
5	Cantons de l'Est	5.8
6	Montréal	6.2
7	Outaouais	3.9
8	Nord-Ouest	3.4
9 & 10	Cote Nord and Nouveau Québec	3.4
	Quebec as a whole	5.6

(1) Quebec Health Insurance Board, Annual Statistics 1972.

second full year of operation, has not enabled the population of the various regions to receive in their own region a relatively equal volume of medical services. In other words, the assumption that physicians would eliminate by themselves the regional disparities, since with health insurance their income can be as high in the rural areas as in the urban areas, has not proven correct to date.

On the other hand, the results obtained thus far are much more positive with reference to the distribution of services according to age and income, general access to services, satisfaction of the beneficiaries as well as with reference to the health of the population. These conclusions have been clearly drawn from a study carried out by a group of researchers from the University of Pittsburgh and McGill University.[14] The predominating features of this study as presented by the authors themselves as well as the conclusions were the following:

> "Household interviews were conducted before and after the introduction in Quebec of a government sponsored compulsory insurance program covering physician services. Physician visits per person per year remained constant at about five but were markedly shifted from persons in higher to lower income groups. The percentage of selected medical symptoms seen by a doctor increased from 62 percent to 73 percent with all of the increases in lower income groups. Average waiting time for a doctor's appointment increased from 5.3 to 10.2 days, with the largest increases in higher

income groups. Waiting time in the doctor's office also increased, again with the largest increase in higher income groups. Eight percent of the population felt the quality of medical care improved while 30 percent thought it got worse. For those who saw a doctor in the previous year, however, about 90 percent were satisfied with the services received, the same proportion as before Medicare.

"Clearly, economic barriers existed and were removed by Medicare, so that a considerable increase in utilization of physician services by person in lower income groups took place. Given a relatively fixed supply of services, there was a shift in services from higher income to lower income groups. Since waiting time for appointments and in doctors' offices increased most for persons in higher income groups, they may have been unable or unwilling to compete with lower income groups. This resulted in some dissatisfaction–probably with the system but not with individual services.

"Of particular significance is the increased frequency with which patients were seen for a series of common and important medical symptoms. This suggests that the removal of economic barriers to medical care may actually improve the general level of health of the population."

Tables 3, 4 and 5 allow for a more detailed appreciation of the results. Finally, here is how Taylor concludes his analysis of the implementation of

TABLE 3

PHYSICIAN VISITS PER PERSON PER YEAR BEFORE AND AFTER MEDICARE BY TYPE OF VISIT SHOWING PERCENT CHANGE MONTREAL METROPOLITAN AREA

Type of Visit	First Survey (1969-70)	Second Survey (1971-72)	Percent Change
All Visits	5.04	5.04	None
Telephone	.81	.70	-13.6
Face-to-Face Contacts	4.23	4.34	- 2.6
Office	2.34	2.73	+16.7
Hospital Outpatient and Emergency Room	1.17	1.17	None
Home	.44	.18	-59.1
Other Visits*	.28	.26	- 7.1

*Includes visits at school and at work.

SOURCE: The distribution of medical services before and after "free" medical care—The Quebec Experience

TABLE 4

PHYSICIAN VISITS PER PERSON PER YEAR BEFORE AND AFTER MEDICARE BY ANNUAL FAMILY INCOME SHOWING PERCENT CHANGE, MONTREAL METROPOLITAN AREA

	First Survey 1969-70		Second Survey 1971-72		
Annual Family Income	Interviews	Person Per Year	Interviews	Person Per Year	Percent Change
< 3,000	1,590	6.6	1,231	7.8	+ 18.2
3 - 4,999	2,400	5.5	1,741	6.0	+ 9.1
5 - 8,999	6,921	4.7	6,098	4.7	None
9 - 14,999	3,889	5.1	4,716	4.9	- 3.9
15,000 +	1,372	5.3	2,274	4.8	- 9.4
Unknown Income	2,360	4.4	2,273	4.2	- 4.5
Total	18,532	5.0	18,333	5.0	None

SOURCE: The distribution of medical services before and after "free" medical care—The Quebec Experience.

TABLE 5

PHYSICIAN VISITS PER PERSON PER YEAR BEFORE AND AFTER MEDICARE BY AGE AND ANNUAL FAMILY INCOME SHOWING PERCENT CHANGE, MONTREAL METROPOLITAN AREA

	Annual Family Income						
	Under $9,000			$9,000 and Above			
Age	First Survey	Second Survey	Percent Change	First Survey	Second Survey	Percent Change	Total Percent Change*
Under 17	4.5	4.2	- 6.7	5.4	4.6	-14.8	- 6.8
17 - 64	5.2	5.6	+ 7.7	4.9	4.9	None	+ 2.0
65 and Over	7.5	8.5	+13.3	7.8	7.1	- 9.0	+ 5.2

*Including unknown income.

SOURCE: The distribution of medical services before and after "free" medical care. The Quebec Experience.

health insurance in Quebec:

> "Quebec residents have had removed whatever economic barrier intervened between their medical need and their access to care. That barrier was both incalculable and in dispute. The medical profession would argue that their sliding scale of fees system barred no one; spokesmen for the public would argue that the very act of asking for free or cut-rate services inhibited thousands until need was desperate. In any event increased utilization, assuming every medical "act" a necessary one, clearly indicates that latent and unmet need has been translated into effective demand."[15]

In addition to these conclusions, it is worth mentioning that the population of Quebec certainly does not question the principle or the application of universal health insurance. On the contrary, interest has gradually shifted to the improvement of other significant aspects of health services. The resulting shift in pressure may also be considered as a positive result of health insurance since without such a plan, concern would still be focused on the question of financial access to health care. We can, therefore, conclude that on the whole, the health insurance plan has reached its objectives.

Improving the system

Health insurance in Quebec was implemented in a context of numerous constraints. To illustrate, one might mention the framework established by the federal Medical Care Insurance Act, the limitations of the budgetary allocation, the need to limit the average remuneration of physicians at a level lower than in the neighboring province of Ontario, threats of an exodus of physicians, the concern in the population with a possible lowering of the quality of medical care and its depersonalization, the fear that health insurance gives rise to too rapid an increase in the cost of medical services, etc.

Most of these constraints, due to their nature had to be the subject of political judgments. For that reason, rather than identify in retrospect what might have been done differently, I believe it more useful to analyze one aspect of the health insurance plan which, in my opinion, should be modified.

By proceeding in this manner, I wish to illustrate, with the benefit of past experience, the need not to consider health insurance merely as a mechanism for the payment of costs and fees but rather as a measure, among others, that can improve health services and as a consequence the level of health of the population.

The change which, in my opinion, has to be made is intended to provide a solution to a series of problems which have not been sufficiently resolved in spite of the progress realized through health insurance. Briefly, these problems are:

a) the slow improvement in the geographical balance of the distribution of physicians;
b) the deficiencies in the volume and quality of care to the chronically ill and to the aged, at home as well as in institutions;
c) the maintenance if not the accentuation of the disproportion in the allocation of resources to curative services as compared to prevention, promotion of health, education, research and evaluation;
d) the abnormally high frequency of some types of medical procedures (tonsillectomy, appendectomy, certain forms of injections, etc.);
e) the lack of interest on the part of too many physicians in the efficient operation of outpatient clinics and emergency services;
f) the obligation to remunerate all physicians, even those who decide to practice in already saturated areas;
g) the resistance to regionalization of health services, to attain better utilization of resources, and to improve the quality of care. This problem is due to the system of remuneration under which the majority of physicians tend to consider hospitals and other establishments as resources at their disposal in the pursuit of their own personal objectives.

Since 1971 attention has, therefore, gradually shifted toward most of these problems. Although they are the consequence of many factors, the present system of remuneration of medical services is in each case, in my opinion, one of them. Indeed, among the various characteristics of the system of remuneration of medical services under health insurance, there are two aspects which have a definite influence on the activities of physicians and indirectly on the distribution of services.

First, there is the fee-for-service system which is generally used for curative services. Since there exist analyses of the problems and abuses related to this system of remuneration, I will only state that it constitutes a very inadequate system.

The second characteristic of the system of remuneration of health services is a direct legacy of the liberal practice of medicine. While the physician should normally be remunerated by the establishment in which he practices, he is remunerated under health insurance by a third party; in Quebec the physician is remunerated by the Health Insurance Board. This is due to the fact that when health insurance was implemented, the patient (or his private insurer which amounts to the same thing) was replaced for the purposes of fee payment by the government through the Health Insurance Board. The physician's status as a free entrepreneur, together with the positive and negative attributes related to this status, were not, therefore, fundamentally changed. Thus, the health insurance plan allows the physician to establish himself in the location that appears to him the most appropriate in terms of his preferences rather than in accordance with the needs of the population. The plan also allows the physician who wishes to do so to determine the utilization of his time in the least exacting and most profitable manner. Finally, the plan also allows the physician to consider hospitals and their personnel as resources at his disposal in the pursuit of his objectives.

While this status of free entrepreneur, to which is added financial security, perhaps constitutes a positive element in the maintenance of a certain level of scientific quality of medical care, it should not be forgotten that even with national health insurance the physician continues to practice his profession strictly in accordance with his objectives. While valid from the physician's point of view, these objectives can only correspond inadequately with the objectives of the establishment in which he practices his profession. Moreover, the sum of the individual objectives of physicians cannot correspond to a greater degree with the objectives of a health policy defined in terms of population needs and of the resulting programs which require a concerted participation of many institutions and several categories of personnel.

It is for these reasons that the channel through which flows the remuneration of the physicians constitutes, with the fee-for-service system, one of the causes of the problems in the distribution of services and access that have not been resolved by health insurance. I believe that improvement of the situation requires modifications to these two aspects of the system of remuneration.

Modification to the fee-for-service system

To begin with, I do not think that the fee-for-service system should be replaced abruptly by a straight salary system. Such change would obviously cause a serious confrontation with the medical profession, with negative consequences. Besides salary is not always an appropriate or better form of remuneration. Solutions must rather be sought through a modification of the methods of fee-for-service payment and the structure of fee schedules. It is also necessary that we seek such changes through an evolutionary process. There are, for instance, many physicians engaged in prevention and teaching or working in teaching hospitals and community health centers. For such physicians the fee-for-service method might be inappropriate and could be replaced by other modes of payment—for example, salary plus an additional amount determined according to institutional objectives, fixed fees for a given period of work, and so on.

Modification to the channeling of the remuneration

With respect to the channeling of payment, I think it is necessary that budgets for medical services be allocated to the hospitals and institutions in the same manner as for other functions. A hospital or a community health center would be able, with such a budget, to contract in a more balanced way with the physicians, and be able to set the modalities of their practice in such a way as to ensure the pursuit of the institutional objectives. The contracts, however, would have to respect the collective agreements with the associations representing the medical profession.

Budgets for medical services would also be allocated to regional councils for the remuneration of physicians practicing wholly or partly in private offices. While regional councils would also have to respect the collective agreements with the medical profession, it would be possible for them to negotiate with the physicians to arrive at a better geographical distribution, a better balance between the various medical specialties, to set certain service objectives, etc.

The Health Insurance Board would continue to pay the remuneration of physicians on behalf of the establishments and the regional councils. However, the Board would make no payments to physicians unless approved by the institutions and the regional councils which must verify that the services have been provided in accordance with the physicians' contractual obligations.

Since the full health insurance budget would be channeled through the regional councils and the health care institutions, the latter would be in a position to contract validly with the physicians in return for the indispensable resources and services which they put at their disposal. Such a modification would, therefore, provide the missing element in the solution of the problems of allocation of resources and of distribution of services.

Although such a modification in the system of remuneration of physicians raises problems in terms of application, it does nevertheless possess the great advantage of allowing to introduce necessary improvements without raising an "ideological" debate or bluntly replacing the fee-for-service system.

Relying on Quebec's experience, which on the whole appears positive, I have sought to illustrate the importance of avoiding to consider health insurance as an isolated measure intended only to solve the problem of financial access to medical services and health care in general. To the extent that there is a desire to solve the various problems of accessibility, it is necessary to conceive consequently health insurance and to insert it in the complex of policies and programs having as a common goal the improvement of the health of the population. If this avenue is not taken, such a decision limits for the future the options available to solve the problems not tackled initially.

FOOTNOTES

1. The initial date on which the medical care insurance bill was to become effective was later changed to July 1, 1968.

2. Report of the Commission of Inquiry on Health and Social Welfare, Vol. I, *Health Insurance,* Quebec Official Publisher, Quebec, 1967.

3. Report of the Commission of Inquiry on Health and Social Welfare, Vol. IV, *Health Insurance,* Quebec Official Publisher, Quebec, 1970.

4. *Op. Cit.,* tome 1.

5. On this subject, in 1970 Quebec was in the same situation as the United States. This is clear if one considers the statement made by the National Advisory Commission on Health Manpower in its Report to the President of the United States: "We should recall that our conclusions and recommendations are necessarily limited because we could not obtain truly adequate data on the medical care system based on available resources. Even though information possibilities have increased appreciably as a result of the growing use of computers and automatic data processing methods, the health industry, in government departments as elsewhere, has not been sufficiently affected by those innovations. Consequently, complete and uniform statistical data, vital to rational analysis and planning, are lacking and this despite an overabundance of statistics dealing with health.

   Report of the National Advisory Commission on Health Manpower, Vol. I, U.S. Government Printing Office, Washington, D.C., 1967.

6. *Op. Cit.*, Vol. I, p. 15.

7. Only medical services not related to health such as examinations for employment purposes, insurance, etc. are excluded from the plan's coverage.

8. This age limit for dental care will be gradually increased from year to year.

9. It is important to distinguish clearly syndical associations from professional corporations.

10. In accordance with the federal Hospitalization Insurance and Diagnostic Services Act, the federal government in Canada assumes approximately one half of the operating costs of hospitals other than psychiatric hospitals.

11. The emergency services system under development includes the means of communication, the establishment of standards for equiment and the training of personnel, and the distribution and operation of emergency services in hospitals.

12. Taylor, M. G., Quebec medicare: policy formulation in conflict and crisis. Public Administration of Canada, 1972, p. 247.

13. Quebec Health Insurance Board, *Annual Statistics,* 1972.

14. Enterline, P. E., Salta, V., McDonald, A. D., and McDonald, J. C., The distribution of medical services before and after "free" medical care. The Quebec Experience, Department of Biostatistics, University of Pittsburgh and Department of Epidemiology and Health, McGill University.

15. Taylor, M. G., *Op. Cit.*, p. 249.

DISCUSSION

JOHN G. VENEMAN: Had there been a similar symposium 10 years ago, I would predict that the thrust of the discussion would have been costs—just as costs have been the predominant topic at this forum. But the discussion would have been from an entirely different perspective. It would have centered around cost as a barrier to equal access to health care, instead of the cost to government.

In both Canada and the United States we have seen the evolution of health policies—all with the objective of providing equal access to the health system. The parallels in the evolution of health policy are worth noting. Mr. Castonguay points out that high costs were a deterrent to hospital care for a significant portion of the population—and that this was a factor in the establishment of the national insurance plan in 1961.

During the same era Congress passed the Kerr-Mills Bill—to cover certain health care costs for the low-income aged and the PAMC program for other public assistance recipients. In 1965 the United States Congress passed Medicare and Medicaid. The following year Canada passed its Medical Care Act.

Similar concerns in both countries—specifically equal access—motivated changes in policy. And there were similar points of resistance to those changes stemming from medical societies and other professional groups.

The prevalent voices of the 1960's were those who argued for equality and access to health care services at any cost.

When Medicaid passed in California, the theme was "Mainstream Medical Care" and the elimination of the county hospital or a "dual level of care system."

Those were the concerns of the time and, therefore, the politics of the time.

At this conference, however, we heard an entirely different theme—costs from the other perspective. It was suggested by some of the participants that we put the population at both financial and a clinical risk.

One participant suggested that we may have to ration medical care. Another pointed out that Canada has not been able to control the *demand* for health care. Still another argued that there are cost controls in the U.S. Medicare law which are not being administered. The point being that the high cost of health care to the public sector is the concern today and, therefore, the politics of today. It was also correctly pointed out that we do not have a national health policy in the United States.

While serving as undersecretary of the Department of Health, Education and Welfare I argued the same point. Before Congress and in public appearances I suggested that we cannot continue to approach health policy on a piecemeal basis. We can't just look at facilities, manpower, financing, distribution, etc. as separate entities. We must have a national health policy.

I would still argue that we *should* have—but I doubt that we will ever have a single agreed-upon document to follow. As we review what has transpired during the past 10 years, we have made great strides toward sorting out responsibilities between the public and private sectors and among the governmental entities. But health policy, like any other—be it environment, land use or whatever—will continue to be, as it has been in the past, an evolutionary process. As health policy evolves it will be the concerns of today—real or unreal—that will dictate the politics of health. I use the phrase "real or unreal" because the concerns of the populace may not necessarily correspond with the concerns of the politicians.

A case in point is national health insurance. I met with groups throughout California for the past year and the subject of national health insurance was never a topic of discussion unless I initiated it—with the exception of two groups:

1) health providers and insurers who were concerned about the effect on their way of doing business, and
2) some state and local officials who saw a national health insurance program as a way of relieving them of the burden of Medicaid.

There is no clamoring for national health insurance among the populace—as there is for control of inflation, of concerns over employment. The most vocal support is in the federal sector, and appropriately so. It is its responsibility to generate interest in, and support for necessary social change. I would hasten to add that there is no indication of major opposition. In fact, most people are receptive to some form of national health insurance. It is a "popular" issue—but not a paramount one.

There is one interesting movement taking place in California. *Some* of the same elements of the population who were arguing for a single level of care during the '60s, are now arguing for the reestablishment of county hospitals and locally-supported outpatient clinics as a means of assuring access to care for the low-income population. I don't believe there is any significant amount of support for this effort—but I am concerned that *if* local government officials yield to this kind of pressure, it would be a regressive step. It is difficult enough to achieve balance in access because of political barriers, without creating new ones.

The Canadian experience has confirmed that the enactment of national health insurance and "global budgeting" will require the elimination of some of the traditional methods of delivery and of providing access. As has been mentioned previously, taking something away creates a considerable amount of political heat.

While at HEW, I testified before Congress for the elimination of the Hill-Burton hospital construction grant program, and the closing of some antiquated Public Health Service hospitals. Some of the members depicted me as a moss-backed Republican who wanted sick people thrown out in the street and our merchant seamen to be left without medical attention. I would still argue that the rational establishment of a health delivery system may require the breaking of even more antique china. This could include a hard look at our system of veterans hospitals.

One thing that interested me in the Canadian system is the absence of any Health Maintenance Organization (HMO) or prepaid method of health delivery, with the exception of the community health centers. I am not suggesting that HMO's are the panacea to health delivery—but the option does offer some promise. Nor is National Health Insurance the panacea.

In his paper, Mr. Castonguay lists problems which have not been sufficiently resolved. First among these, he cites the "slow improvement in the geographical balance of the distribution of physicians." This has traditionally been a problem in the United States and may continue to be a gnawing problem for a long time to come. It is difficult to develop a system of financial rewards that will cause someone to remove his roots from a community.

Manpower utilization is also a sticky problem—because it affects traditional professional turf. A review of state licensure laws to determine if they are for the protection of the patient or the preservation of the provider may be appropriate.

There are a couple of other areas where I believe we are falling short in our efforts to assure access to the system.

Health education in its broadest definition is one of these. We can have all the components for a good health system in place, but if people are unaware of the presence or entry points it is of little use. This is a particular problem to low-income groups, but not exclusively. Canada's involvement of consumers is a move to alleviate this as a problem.

Secondly, I believe we lack the expertise to implement new (or existing) programs. Too often Congress will pass a bill, put it in an effective date and assume things will happen.

One participant at the symposium asked if there was adequate capacity on the part of federal civil servants in the United States to carry out federal health policy. I would have to question our capacity on a federal level. What's even more discouraging is that there isn't the capacity on the state and local level either, and that's where the action is. We have lots of qualified planners but few qualified implementers.

It is fair to say that both countries have gone a long way in the past decade in improving our health systems and access to it. But there is still much to be done. I appreciate and respect the need for solid information on what's happening in the world of health and for an indisputable data base. I would only hope that we refrain from getting so bogged down in health economics and statistics that we ignore the political realities. Health policy, good or bad, will be made or evolve, by those in positions of power and with political considerations.

II ECONOMIC PERSPECTIVE

CHAPTER 3 • ROBERT G. EVANS

Beyond the Medical Marketplace: Expenditure, Utilization and Pricing Of Insured Health in Canada

To understand the structure of health care legislation in Canada, one must begin with federal-provincial relations. The division of powers between the federal government in Ottawa and the 10 provincial governments is Canada's longest and most carefully defended border. This division of powers, based on Sections 91 and 92 of the British North America Act, clearly designates health as a matter for provincial jurisdiction.[1] In a strict sense, there cannot be "national" health insurance in Canada; rather there are 10 separate "provincial" health insurance plans. Federal jurisdiction, as was pointed out in an earlier chapter, is limited to Indians, Eskimos, sick mariners, and the Armed Forces, and to a variety of specific services such as quarantine, immigration, food and drug control, and many other small items.

And yet quite obviously, there exists a national health program covering hospital and medical care (with minimal specific exclusions) for almost all Canadian residents. It came about through a constitutional subterfuge which enabled the federal government to contribute a significant share of the total operating costs to any provincial plan meeting certain specified federal standards. The constitutional niceties thus are preserved, and indeed no province was forced to follow the federal lead and set up a conforming plan. Since the formulae for cost sharing cover roughly 50 percent of each provincial plan's total operating costs, it is clear that the financial pressures on the provinces to set up qualifying plans were irresistible.[2] The Hospital Insurance and Diagnostic Services Act of 1957 specified July 1, 1958 as the earliest date at which federal cost-sharing for hospital care became available; Newfoundland, Saskatchewan, Alberta, and British Columbia already had operating hospital plans which qualified for cost-sharing and Manitoba initiated a plan on that date. The pressure on the remaining provinces brought in Prince Edward Island, Nova

Scotia, New Brunswick, and Ontario in 1959, and finally Quebec in 1961. A similar scenario followed the passage of the Medical Care Act; British Columbia and Saskatchewan had qualifying plans on July 1, 1968 while Manitoba, Nova Scotia, Newfoundland, Alberta, and Ontario initiated plans at various dates during 1969. Quebec and Prince Edward Island set up plans toward the end of 1970, and New Brunswick joined at the beginning of 1971. Thus 1971 is the first complete year of Canadian experience with both hospital and medical insurance; it is also the latest year for which expenditure data of all forms are currently available.[3]

The federal standard–shared funding and provincial administration structure–required by the Canadian constitutional system is very clearly a mixed blessing. On the positive side, national average-based cost-sharing makes possible a more uniform level of service availability to the degree that the federal contribution rises proportionately in the poorer provinces. Relating the federal contribution to national averages of expenditure brings it up over 60 percent of hospital spending and over 80 percent of medical spending in the poorest provinces,[4] permitting a national standard of health services which would have been quite out of reach of the provinces alone.[5] But the total effects of the minimum criteria for eligibility are much less clear.

In brief, these criteria are portability of coverage across provinces, universal access on equal terms and conditions to all, comprehensive coverage, and administration by a nonprofit public agency.[6] Portability clearly works to the general interest by preventing cost-conscious provincial agencies from finding ways of dropping migrants out of the system, while the requirement of public, nonprofit administration specified the initial form of organization believed most likely to achieve the other objectives with minimal overhead cost.[7] Universal access is becoming less relevant as provinces are recognizing that "premiums" represent a rather regressive poll tax and are shifting over time to total general revenue financing. But "equal terms and conditions" and "comprehensive coverage" do in fact impose significant limitations on the modifications that can be made on the supply side, to the extent they can be interpreted as prohibiting incentives directed at consumers to choose one form of delivery over another. A user of a closed panel plan, e.g., could not receive a premium rebate if his plan were shown to use fewer hospital days, nor could one earn such a rebate by signing up with a well-baby clinic and agreeing not to use a pediatrician unless referred by the clinic.

Furthermore, cost-sharing both distorts the structure of care delivery and dilutes incentives to economize. Provincial agencies are acutely aware of what services are or are not cost shareable; no provincial bureaucrat worthy of the name would allocate funds for a nonshreable program if the same result could be attained through a shareable route. Even if the former were cheaper the latter only draws 50¢ dollars. This problem creates steady pressure to expand the coverage of the provincial plans–ambulatory care in hospitals must be insured since otherwise the insurance plan leads to excess hospitalization; extended care facilities should be covered to reduce acute care hospital use. Home care programs should also be subsidized with federal cost-sharing. Thus the open-ended nature of the federal commitment to currently covered services, combined with the steady pressure to "rationalize" utilization by expanding coverage, has led to growing interest in ways of dismantling the cost-sharing system and transferring full fiscal responsibility to the provincial governments. In return, the federal government would release to the provinces a larger share of personal income tax revenues, and/or revenues from other federal taxes (alcohol and tobacco). As yet, however, no package acceptable to both sides has been worked out.[8]

The provinces finance their share of the cost of hospital and medical care by a mix of taxes. Many provinces introduced retail sales taxes at the time the hospital plans were set up, and in some cases these were initially labelled hospital taxes. This revenue is not earmarked, however, and merely flows into general revenue. All provinces receive a share of the federal personal and corporate income tax collected from their residents. Quebec also levies its own personal income tax as well as an 0.8 percent payroll tax introduced along with Medicare. The federal income tax was augmented by a "Social Development" surtax of 2 percent ($100 max) at the introduction of Medicare.

Revenue sources specifically associated with the hospital and medical insurance plans include "premiums" in some provinces and in a few, "utilization charges," but the universal access condition of federal participation restricts the role of such charges.[9] Thus the "premium" must not interfere with the requirement that 99 percent of the population should be insured. This can be achieved by compulsion (making the premium a poll tax), by setting premiums well below expected cost per family (which would exclude nonpayers who have already paid most of the cost through other taxes), or by relatively high premiums combined with subsidies to low-income families (making the poll tax less regressive but more costly to administer). The regressive nature, expense of administration, and general pointlessness of the premium system is slowly leading provincial governments toward full general revenue financing of integrated medical and hospital "insurance." There are still a few voices raised arguing that premiums are desirable as a utilization control; if people are aware of the costs of the plans they may use less. However, no evidence for this has been adduced, any more than for the contrary position that visible premiums lead people to "get their money's worth." In any case, current premiums in no way reflect plan costs and could not be made to do so. They appear to be a transitional feature only.

A scattering of utilization charges persists, without clear rationale; thus British Columbia charges $1 per day of hospital inpatient stay, and $2 per visit to a hospital outpatient department. Saskatchewan experimented with a $2.50 physician office visit fee and $2.50 per day hospital charge in 1968 but dropped both in 1971; on balance it appears the results of the medical charge was to reduce utilization by lowering use on the part of lower income groups and raising that of upper income groups.[10] In general, the purpose of the public plans is to reduce the inequality of access to services by income class.[11] And the "universal access on equal terms and conditions" principle is not consistent with utilization fees having a significant effect on use. Thus, they are restricted to specific circumstances; it is proposed, for example, that elderly patients in British Columbia's extended care facilities should be charged a daily rate sufficient to mop up their monthly federal old age pensions rather than cumulating these payments for their heirs. But most utilization charges are said to cost as much to collect as they return in revenue—although, of course, the costing has never been done so no one really knows.

There is, however, a patchwork of arrangements, differing in each province, governing physician bills to the patient. When the plans were introduced, many provinces reimbursed physicians at a discount from the fee schedule (90 percent or 85 percent) to allow for the reduced uncollectable ratio. Treatment of the remaining 10 percent or 15 percent varied, and in some provinces the physician was allowed to try to collect this from the patient. Furthermore, some provinces permit physicians to bill the patient above the fee schedule. In Ontario physicians began after 1969 to bill the province for 90 percent and then bill the patient for whatever they might get. This was prohibited in 1971; now if a physician submits a bill to the plan, he is not permitted to bill the patient as well. If he chooses, he may bill the patient directly and let the patient bill the plan. In Quebec, physicians may bill the plan or the patient at plan rates; in the latter case the patient is reimbursed. Only "nonparticipating" physicians may bill patients above plan rates, and their patients will not be reimbursed at all. In British Columbia the physician may bill the patient directly, up to or above the fee schedule, if he has notified the patient in advance and obtained written consent. Otherwise the patient is not obligated to pay, and the British Columbia Medical Association must disallow the bill if challenged. But the patient doesn't know this. It is not known how significant the practice of extra-billing directly to the patient is in those provinces where it is permitted; but informed opinion is that it is a trivial phenomenon. This would seem to agree with the public perception of Canadian medical care as "free."

If the economic relationships between third-party and consumer are relatively uninteresting in the Canadian insurance system, those between payment agency and provider are the heart of the whole system. Initially, it appears to have been the intent of the designers of both hospital and medical insurance plans to intervene as little as possible in the process of health service supply, and merely to pay legitimate charges arising from an independent transaction between patient and provider. This may be an oversimplified view of the hospital insurance plan, since the federal requirements went beyond mere audit to ensure legitimacy of charges and included inspection and supervision to upgrade the quality of hospital services. However, it appears to have been believed that so long as hospitals and paying agencies were organized as not-for-profit entities, their economic behavior could safely be disregarded. In establishing the medical care plan, economic behavior of providers seems to have been ignored without even the safeguard of not-for-profit providers!

The implicit model of the delivery system underlying this approach was the naive medico-technical view of disease conditions arising independently in the population, requiring necessary care as defined by medical technology, and generating costs again according to a fairly well-defined production technology and price structure. Expenditures for medical and hospital care were, of course, expected to rise. It was believed that in the pre-insurance period patients were failing to seek "needed" care due to financial barriers, or providers were giving "charity" services on a volunteer basis. But nowhere in the legislation or procedures establishing either insurance plan was there any recognition that all three components of the delivery process—care seeking, choice of technique, and input costs, might shift in response to insurance coverage.

Care-seeking in response to health status stimuli is likely to increase; this is the obvious response of demand to price but appears to be a relatively small component of the Canadian insurance experience. Shifts also occur in definitions of best-practice health technology because more is performed at greater expense for any given disease state. And most difficult of all to deal with, health providers at all levels, from physicians down through hospital janitors, seem to have revised their income aspirations upward in response to the observation that the payment process was open-ended. If medical care payments were to be made according to fee schedules promulgated by medical associations alone, what besides adjustment lags limits physicians' fees and incomes? If hospital budgets are increased as required to cover wages negotiated by an increasingly unionized labor force, what besides the public spirit of trustees and administrators limits wage levels? And so it has turned out that the single most prominent influence of health insurance in Canada has been to increase the earnings of health providers.[12]

If one examines the net earnings of physicians, comparing their first full year of experience under insurance with their last year of earnings prior to insurance (a two-year span, except for New Brunswick which began its plan January 1, 1971), the following picture emerges.

Province	Time Period	Change in Net Physician Earnings	Change in Weekly Wages & Salaries	Relative Income Gain
Saskatchewan	1961-63	36.5%	6.6%	28.0%
British Columbia	1967-69	14.5%	13.0%	1.3%
Newfoundland	1968-70	36.3%	18.7%	14.8%
Nova Scotia	1968-70	45.2%	18.2%	22.8%
Ontario	1968-70	21.5%	15.9%	4.8%
Manitoba	1968-70	48.1%	15.3%	28.4%
Alberta	1968-70	19.4%	18.6%	0.7%
Quebec	1969-71	51.0%	15.6%	30.6%
Prince Edward Island	1969-71	70.1%	11.2%	53.0%
New Brunswick	1969-71	34.6%	17.1%	14.9%

SOURCES: Data appendix

The final column adjusts for changes in the overall rate of inflation, which was accelerating in the late sixties, and brings out the dramatic gain in the relative income status of physicians which took place since the insurance plans went into effect. As will emerge below the same pattern of dramatic income gains has also been true for hospital workers but over a longer time perspective.[13]

In fact, the peculiar federal-provincial structure of the Canadian insurance scheme militates against expenditure controls. In adopting a policy of "pay the bills," the federal government merely recognized its lack of constitutional authority to engage in regulatory activity with respect to the provincial plans. It could, of course, impose requirements to check fraud or raise quality standards as conditions for federal funding, and it went further to permit disallowance of claims for "medically unnecessary" procedures. But other than placing some limits on elective surgery, this provision has been empty. There is no limit of payment for, e.g., removal of healthy appendices or ritual tonsillectomies.

The uniform hospital accounting standards, required by the federal participation agreement have, however, led to the generation of a formidable data base. It details the operations of each of the "budget review" hospitals in Canada whose services are reimbursed by the provincial agencies. This set of data is remarkable, not only for the vast amount of detailed information it provides on the activities of hospitals, levels and patterns of output, utilization and cost of inputs, and so on, but also for the surprisingly weak management tool and control which it has turned out to be. When the need arises to make estimates of the full costs of particular activities in Canadian hospitals, or the relative costs of hospitals engaged in similar activities, the data require vigorous massage to yield approximate answers. The reporting systems put in place at the time hospital insurance was initiated are descriptive and epidemiological rather than managerial control systems. They are suitable for a strategy of minimal intervention by the public agency in spite of their level of detail.

Standard hospital reports in Canada are of several types. Each hospital returns annually federal reports HS-1 and HS-2 providing information on facilities, services, and finances. In addition, each patient discharged generates a form documenting the episode for reimbursement purposes and returned to the provincial agency. The basic content of these returns is standardized nationwide. Each provincial payment agency may impose its own budgetary returns, overlapping or extending the HS-1 and HS-2. Finally, hospitals may participate in a quarterly federal survey of major hospital indicators (partial HS-1 and HS-2) or return data to nonprofit agencies such as PAS or HMRI. But the federal statistical returns and the patient discharge forms, covering the whole population of hospitals and patients respectively, form the backbone of the system.

The discharge forms report patient name, age, address, dates of admission and discharge, attending physician, discharge diagnosis (primary and secondary), and surgery and/or anesthesia, if any. They provide a comprehensive picture of the inhospital morbidity patterns of the Canadian population, as well as of the case-mix structure of each hospital. Unfortunately, none of the data can be directly linked either to ambulatory care or to the cost structures of specific hospitals. Much work can be done on the age and regional structure of morbidity, regional patterns of patient flow, etc., but it is only within the past five years that provinces have seriously tackled the problems of machine-processing these data. Within another five years most provinces will have established common patient and physician identifiers linking ambulatory and hospital records. But current ambulatory reporting is by fee schedule item and thus it is specific to procedure rather than diagnosis.

The hospital statistical returns are institution-specific, keyed to line-item input budgets. They have been modified over time, but in their present form they divide all hospital expenditure into Nursing Services (wards, operating and recovery rooms, emergency, central supply, labor and delivery rooms and nursery); Special Services (diagnostic and investigative units, special clinics, ambulatory services, and services such as pharmacy, physiotherapy, etc.); Educational Services (direct costs only of salaries or stipends to staff or students in medical, nursing, or other educational programs); and General Services (administration, laundry, linen, records, physical plant, and all other nonclinical services). Each area reports direct expense for salaries and paid hours (medical and nonmedical) and supplies and other expenses. Separate totals for drugs and medical and surgical supplies are reported hospital-wide but not allocated. Reports include not only cost and personnel input by area, but also a range of physical outputs—patient days (short and long term), admissions, discharges, deliveries, lab tests done (on a standard unit basis), radiological films taken, visits to each class of clinic, pounds of laundry processed, meal days produced, etc. (Not, however, stamps licked by administrative staff.)[14]

Compared to this vast array of data, much of which is tabulated and published and all of which is now on tape, the records of the medical plans are relatively sketchy. Medical data are generated by provider/patient contacts only, while hospital data report both contacts and annual descriptions of providers. The medical plans grew out of private, nonprofit, often physician-sponsored prepayment plans (see Shillington, *op. cit.*) in which participating physicians had agreed to accept payment according to uniform provincial fee schedules promulgated independently by the provincial medical association. These plans recorded only who did what to whom and paid accordingly.

These schedules vary from province to province, and definitions of procedures tend to shift both over time and across provinces. Thus, one can be fairly sure about how many surgical operations of a particular type were performed; but the line, for example, between first and subsequent office visits (same condition), or general and partial examinations, is very blurred and seems to shift over time. Data are not generally collected on why procedures were carried out, although some provinces also request diagnostic data. And no data at all are collected on provider units (employees, capital, etc.) except for the information required by medical associations and the payment agency in reimbursing claims. This information includes name, age, residence, date and place of medical graduation, specialty[15] as well as data on billing (whether the physician is in solo practice, grouped but billing separately, or grouped but billing jointly, whether or not eligible to bill as a specialist) and so on.

The weakness of both of these data collection systems is that they provide no link between costs and inputs, and any meaningful measure of output. Hospitals measure direct costs by department, but departmental services are not independently costed out or related back to patients and no allocation of overhead cost is made. Thus one can calculate direct laundry cost per pound of laundry processed for any hospital in the land, but in no hospital can one do more than estimate (rather crudely) the division of budget into inpatient, outpatient, and educational expense. Moreover, linkages between cost structure and patterns of patient output seem to have been examined only by academics. The public reimbursing agencies have not generally tried to relate cost to diagnostic mix in any systematic way in spite of the fact that they are consequently unable to make any but very crude cross-hospital or cross-time comparisons.[16] "Similarities" among hospitals for budget review purposes are assumed on the basis of indicators like size and location, rather than specific information on workload. Budgetary overruns or requests for further funding are difficult to evaluate since changes in output patterns (diagnostic mix, length of stay or occupancy) are not related to changes in cost patterns. Thus, when the initial relatively permissive attitude toward hospital expenditure began to harden in the mid-sixties, adequate informational tools to interpret and control cost escalation were simply not available.

A similar problem underlies medical care statistics. At first glance it might appear that fee schedules provide a firm price fixed to levels of output. Initially, it was argued that fee schedules should remain the prerogative of medical associations, with government carrying on the "hands off" policy of its private, physician-sponsored predecessors.[17] The enormous increases in physician incomes and effective (though not list) prices before and during the introduction of Medicare, eliminated that idea rather swiftly. In most provinces now, fee schedules are *de facto* negotiated with provincial governments although the process is often obscure to preserve the appearance of professional autonomy.[18]

The weakness in the process is that, of course, fee schedules price procedures, not care episodes. The mix and definition of procedures, used during an episode, can be and are varied at the discretion of the physician. Hence rates of payment to physicians tend to climb steadily over time even given constant fee schedules; prior to Medicare this phenomenon could be explained by changing collection ratios but it has persisted since. Moreover, levels of procedures seem to be dependent on the available supply of physicians, as much as on the demographic structure of the population.[19] The profession and the paying agencies have responded in some provinces by developing "provider profiles." These show the patterns of procedures performed by individual physicians relative to groups of similar physicians (by region and specialty). These monitoring systems identify practitioners with unusual billing patterns (rates more than two standard deviations away from norm) and help to draw all providers toward uniform patterns. But they leave unanswered crucial questions such as: How well are procedures performed? Should they be performed at all? What is happening to patterns over time? Profile monitoring provides information neither on quality of care nor on the benefit from steady increases over time in procedural volume. It merely isolates a very few cases of apparent malfeasance. Like hospital audit it is an instrument to detect fraud, not to manage performance.

The spectacular movements in hospital and medical expenditures in Canada can be related first, to a relatively naive initial policy of paying the legitimate bills and minimizing management intervention on the supply side.[20] Second, they are related to an inadequate information structure on which to base efforts at management. The statistical record can be analyzed to try to observe what did (and did not) happen as national insurance was introduced; this will provide a backdrop for discussion of the policy responses which have been attempted and which are now recommended.

THE QUANTITATIVE IMPACT OF NATIONAL HEALTH INSURANCE

Historial patterns of health care expenditure

The interpretation of patterns of use of and expenditure on health care in Canada, before, during and after the introduction of the two National Health Insurance plans, is a complex problem which must be pursued at the level of particular classes of institutions and often of individual provinces. But an initial overview of the industry is provided by the data in Tables 1 to 3, showing the distribution of personal health care spending from 1953 to 1971 in current dollars, current dollars per capita, and percentage of personal income. The

TABLE 1

EXPENDITURE ON PERSONAL HEALTH CARE IN CANADA, 1953-1971

($ Million)

Year	General and Allied Special Hospitals	Other Hospitals	Physicians	Dentists	Prescription Drugs	Total
1953	280.4	123.6	176.6	60.5	48.8	689.9
1954	314.0	132.8	188.6	66.4	52.1	753.9
1955	342.4	137.6	206.5	68.6	59.5	814.6
1956	380.8	149.0	240.1	81.5	71.8	923.2
1957	422.9	164.5	271.8	85.0	103.2*	1047.4*
1958	462.3	178.3	301.3	90.5	112.4	1144.9
1959	543.7	191.9	325.7	99.0	130.2	1290.5
1960	640.6	204.4	355.0	109.6	132.6	1442.2
1961	722.1	226.9	388.3	116.7	135.8	1589.9
1962	811.8	242.3	406.1	121.5	144.4	1726.2
1963	909.8	265.1	453.4	136.9	161.7	1922.0
1964	1015.1	285.1	495.7	147.8	178.6	2122.3
1965	1144.5	317.4	545.1	160.1	211.5	2378.6
1966	1319.0	349.0	605.2	176.4	232.0	2682.3
1967	1523.0	393.3	686.2	187.2	265.5	3055.1
1968	1790.0	428.4	788.1	213.7	297.3	3517.5
1969	2024.7	476.6	901.4	239.7	318.5	3960.9
1970	2302.6	523.5	1028.9	262.1	360.4	4477.5
1971	2594.6	557.4	1236.2	298.8	422.5	5109.5
Annual % Change						
1953-59	11.7	7.6	10.7	8.6	12.3	11.0
1959-65	13.2	8.7	9.0	8.3	8.4	10.7
1965-71	14.6	9.8	14.6	11.0	12.2	13.6
1953-71	13.2	8.7	11.4	9.3	10.6	12.0

* The definitions underlying the prescription drug expense series changed in this year. Annual average rates are from 1957 on.

TABLE 2

EXPENDITURE ON PERSONAL HEALTH CARE IN CANADA, PER CAPITA 1953-1971

($ Million)

Year	General and Allied Special Hospitals	Other Hospitals	Physicians	Dentists	Prescription Drugs	Total
1953	18.89	8.32	11.90	4.08	3.29	46.47
1954	20.54	8.69	12.34	4.34	3.41	49.32
1955	21.81	8.77	13.15	4.37	3.79	51.90
1956	23.68	9.27	14.93	5.07	4.46	57.41
1957	25.46	9.90	16.36	5.12	6.21*	63.06*
1958	27.07	10.44	17.64	5.30	6.58	67.03
1959	31.09	10.98	18.63	5.66	7.45	73.01
1960	35.77	11.41	19.82	6.12	7.40	80.53
1961	39.52	12.42	21.25	6.39	7.43	87.02
1962	43.61	13.02	21.82	6.53	7.76	92.74
1963	47.97	13.98	23.91	7.22	8.53	101.61
1964	52.53	14.75	25.65	7.65	9.24	109.82
1965	58.16	16.12	27.70	8.13	10.75	120.87
1966	65.79	17.44	30.19	8.80	11.57	133.80
1967	74.61	19.27	33.62	9.17	13.01	149.67
1968	86.35	20.67	38.02	10.31	14.34	169.69
1969	96.29	22.66	42.87	11.40	15.15	188.36
1970	107.96	24.54	48.24	12.29	16.90	209.94
1971	120.15	25.82	57.24	13.84	19.56	236.61
Annual % Change						
1953-59	8.7	4.7	7.8	5.6	9.5	8.2
1959-65	11.0	6.6	6.8	6.2	6.3	8.6
1965-71	12.9	8.2	12.9	9.3	10.5	11.8
1953-71	10.8	6.5	9.1	7.0	8.5	9.9

*See note to Table 1.

TABLE 3

EXPENDITURE ON PERSONAL HEALTH CARE IN CANADA, 1953-1971

(As a Percent of Personal Income)

Year	General and Allied Special Hospitals	Other Hospitals	Physicians	Dentists	Prescription Drugs	Total
1953	1.43	0.63	0.90	0.31	0.25	3.53
1954	1.59	0.67	0.96	0.34	0.26	3.82
1955	1.61	0.65	0.97	0.32	0.28	3.83
1956	1.62	0.63	1.02	0.35	0.31	3.92
1957	1.68	0.65	1.08	0.34	0.41*	4.16*
1958	1.73	0.67	1.13	0.34	0.42	4.30
1959	1.93	0.68	1.16	0.35	0.46	4.59
1960	2.17	0.69	1.20	0.37	0.45	4.88
1961	2.40	0.75	1.29	0.39	0.45	5.29
1962	2.48	0.74	1.24	0.37	0.44	5.28
1963	2.62	0.76	1.30	0.39	0.47	5.54
1964	2.73	0.76	1.33	0.40	0.48	5.70
1965	2.79	0.77	1.33	0.39	0.52	5.80
1966	2.87	0.76	1.32	0.38	0.50	5.83
1967	3.02	0.78	1.36	0.37	0.53	6.05
1968	3.22	0.77	1.42	0.38	0.53	6.33
1969	3.28	0.77	1.46	0.39	0.52	6.42
1970	3.46	0.79	1.55	0.39	0.54	6.74
1971	3.54	0.76	1.68	0.41	0.58	6.96
Annual % Change						
1953-59	5.1	1.3	4.3	2.0	5.9	5.0
1959-65	6.3	2.1	2.3	1.8	2.1	4.0
1965-71	4.0	-0.2	4.0	0.8	1.8	3.1
1953-71	5.2	1.0	3.5	1.6	2.5	3.7

*See Note to Table 1.

effects of introducing first hospital and then medical insurance show up in the expenditure series for general and allied special hospitals and for physicians, which dominate personal health care spending. Personal health care spending, in turn, makes up about three quarters of national health expenditures in Canada (the conceptual differences are discussed in the data sources at the end of this chapter).

The first thing which commands attention in the Canadian health care industry is the rapid growth in its level of expenditures. This increase is, of course, an international phenomenon; but in Canada the pattern of increase correlates well with extensions in insurance. The insured components, hospital and medical care, are the largest and fastest growing. Moreover, in each case the introduction of the national insurance plan is associated with significant increases in expenditure. In 1959 hospital insurance covered all provinces except Quebec. In 1959 and 1960 hospital expenditures were up nearly 18 percent in each year. No other year in the period matches these. Medical care insurance was phased in province by province from 1968 to 1971. In 1969 and 1970 annual expenditure increases were over 14 percent and in 1971 they jumped to 20 percent. If we look only at these "leading sectors," and compute the share of total hospital and medical expenditures going to hospitals over this period, the movements in this share correlate precisely with the introduction of the two national plans. The hospital share drifted from 61.4 percent in 1953 to 60.5 percent in 1958, then began a steady rise until 1968 when it peaked at 69.4 percent. By 1971 it was down to 67.7 percent.

The same coincidence of timing appears in Table 3; the total expenditure and expenditure per capita data are muddled by accelerating general inflation trends but the personal income share series corrects for this. Hospital spending increased its share of income fastest in the 1959-65 period, whereas medical spending moved up fastest in the 1965-71 period. From 1958 to 1961 the hospital share rose 38.7 percent or 11.5 percent per year; from 1953 to 1958 and from 1961 to 1971 it rose about 4 percent per year. The physician series is less dramatic, but it is easily seen that the upward trend was accelerating after 1966. Clearly public insurance has been closely associated with significant jumps in spending.[21]

But the *mechanism* is less obvious. Conventional economic explanations might focus on the pressure of increased demand on relatively inelastic supply, leading to a combination of utilization and price increase. There is reason to believe that demand-driven adjustments were not very important in the Canadian experience; this will emerge from more detailed discussion below. A suggestion, however, emerges that supply-side factors may be of considerable importance if we note that the relative availability of physicians and hospital beds also shifted over this period. General and Allied Special beds per fee-practice physician reached a peak of 7.18 in 1966, having drifted up slowly from 7.00 in 1958. From 1968 to 1971, however, they dropped over 10 percent from 7.12 to 6.38. The increase in physician share was associated with a rapid *increase* in the relative availability of physicians, a response far too rapid to be associated to insurance-induced demand. Noting also that the mid-1950s saw a rapid increase in the relative availability of hospital beds (Table 4), it rather looks as if plans were made to expand the supply of beds in the 1950s and of physicians in the 1960s (recalling that these are, to a large degree, policy variables in Canada) in anticipation of insurance. The mere observation of increased expenditure may be

TABLE 4

CANADIAN PUBLIC HOSPITALS, SELECTED OPERATING STATISTICS, 1953-1971

Year	Hospitals	No. of Beds	Beds Per 000 Pop.	Expense per Patient-Day	Patient-Days per 000 Pop.	Admissions per 000 Pop.
1953	857	76224	5.13	12.47	1473.1	130.2
1954	870	79281	5.19	13.30	1532.7	132.0
1955	897	84761	5.40	14.05	1530.6	134.9
1956	909	86433	5.37	14.91	1578.1	141.4
1957	924	90154	5.43	16.11	1578.5	142.1
1958	955	94665	5.54	17.84	1624.1	143.0
1959	982	100059	5.72	18.88	1649.7	144.8
1960	972	101352	5.67	21.32	1643.2	146.1
1961	946	100506*	5.51*	23.10	1639.5	145.9
1962	964	106718	5.74	24.82	1721.0	149.7
1963	976	111165	5.87	26.87	1753.4	151.1
1964	996	114545	5.94	29.18	1762.4	152.8
1965	1011	117021	5.96	31.92	1778.3	152.2
1966	1027	122315	6.11	36.06	1793.9	152.0
1967	1036	126182	6.18	40.38	1806.2	151.6
1968	1043	129856	6.26	45.01	1850.8	155.1
1969	1040	132340	6.28	50.69	1854.9	156.4
1970	1039	135877	6.36	56.24	1880.2	161.1
1971	1043	138280	6.41	61.58	1896.6	164.9
% Change						
1953-59	14.6	31.3	11.5	51.4	12.0	11.2
1959-65	3.0	17.0	4.2	69.1	7.8	5.1
1965-71	3.2	18.2	7.6	92.9	6.7	8.3
1953-71	21.7	81.4	25.0	393.8	28.7	26.7

*The beds total for this year appears to be too low due to a classification error; neither beds nor per capita appears reliable.

telling us more about supplier behavior than about increased demand, and we cannot resolve the issue without more detailed data.

The response of the hospital industry–administered inflation

Expenditure on general and allied special hospitals dominates Canadian health spending. This sector is also the first to have been covered by universal health insurance. The dramatic increase in expenditure, from $280.4 million in 1953 to $2,594.6 million in 1971 or nearly 10 times, is the product of a combination of many factors which may or may not be associated with insurance coverage. It is thus of some interest to sort out the quantitative effects of population growth, utilization, general price inflation, sectoral price inflation, and changes in service mix over this period. It is not possible, due to changes in the reporting procedures and reliability of data, to present a detailed picture of what happened, but several major trends are evident.

First of all, the 9.25 ratio of 1971 expenditures to 1953 is the outcome of a 45.3 percent increase in population and an increase from $18.89 to $120.15 in expenditure per capita (Table 2). Moreover, patient days per thousand population rose from 1,473.1 in 1953 to 1,896.6 in 1971 or 28.7 percent. The expenditure per patient day implicit in these data increased from $12.82 to $63.35 or by 9.3 percent per year. The reported data are $12.47 and $61.58 (Table 4, see data sources) also yielding 9.3 percent increase annually. The increase of 13.2 percent annually in hospital expenditure in Canada between 1953 and 1971 thus resolves into increases of 2.1 percent in population, 1.4 percent in patient-day utilization, and 9.3 percent in expenditure per patient day.

This increase has, of course, several sources. Ideally, one would like to trace out its shifts through the full accounting detail provided in present-day hospital statistics; but that would be a major paper in itself and in any case could not be driven back to 1953 where the detail does not exist. Certain clear trends, however, emerge. In 1953 the cost per patient day of $12.47 was divided into $7.20 gross wages and salaries, 51¢ medical and surgical supplies, 53¢ drugs, and $4.23 other supplies and expense. By 1971 these components were $41.82, $1.93, $1.78, and $16.06, or increased by 10.3 percent, 7.7 percent, 7.0 percent, and 7.7 percent annually. Wages and salaries rose from 57.7 percent of the hospital budget to 67.9 percent.[22]

The wage and salary component can be split into "price" and "quantity" components (if we assume that hours are a homogeneous commodity) since in 1953 the hours worked per patient day were 9.18 and in 1971 this had risen to 13.29 paid hours per patient day. A difficulty is that in 1953 the 1.62 hours per patient day of work were contributed by student nurses or interns who were then paid little or nothing. If these are treated as part of hours worked in both years, the increase in wages and salaries is made up of a 44.8 percent increase in hours worked and a 303.8 percent increase in wages and salaries per hour worked (from 78¢ to $3.14 at an average of 8.1 percent per year).

Comparing these shifts with general trends in the Canadian economy, we find that from 1953 to 1971 the Consumer Price Index rose 2.2 percent annually, the G.N.E. deflator rose 2.5 percent, and average weekly wages and salaries (industrial composite) were up 5.0 percent. Price indices are not available for the various components of hospital expenditure, now or in 1953, but if we assumed that prices of hospital goods rose more or less in line with the rest of the economy, we would estimate quantity increases of 5.4 percent annually for medical and surgical supplies, 4.7 percent for drugs, 5.4 percent for supplies and other expense, and about 2.1 percent annually for labor input. These figures should not be taken too seriously, however, as no real price indices exist. Still, they suggest a tendency for real resource use in hospitals to have increased fastest in supplies and drugs, less rapidly in labor input. The single largest component of the cost increase is clearly the change in levels of remuneration of hospital workers.

If we take the increase in average weekly wages of 139.2 percent and assume that due to changes in hours worked per week, a "true" hourly index might have increased 150 percent, then assuming that hospital workers had merely moved up in line with workers generally, the wage bill in 1971 would have been $25.92 per patient day, instead of $41.82. Out of expense per patient day of $61.58 in 1971, $15.90 or 25.8 percent is due to the increase in average hourly wages of hospital workers *relative* to all other workers. This observation, of course, says nothing at all about the division of this increase into differences in skill mix, "catch-up" effects left over from the period of charity hospitals, or pure inflation.

There are, of course, certain other effects that one can look for in the longer-term data. One might expect that changes in the pattern of the care episode, or in the mix of hospitals examined, might affect these results. Yet, in fact, such shifts in the relation between patient day and care episode have not had much effect. Average lengths of stay per separation and occupancy rates have both fluctuated somewhat, but stays were 10.9 days in 1953, 11.3 in 1971, and occupancy rates were 81.2 percent and 81.3 percent. Corresponding to these sluggish movements, admissions per bed fell from 26.3 to 25.7. Thus changes in patient-day costs are clearly not explicable by changes in short-run capacity utilization.

Changes in hospital class of activity are a bit more complex. General and allied special hospitals includes chronic and convalescent, specialty, and teaching hospitals, all of whom have relatively different activity patterns and cost experience. Chronic and convalescent hospitals are too small a portion of the total for shifts in their share to affect costs, for general (acute care) hospitals alone, costs per day rose from $12.79 to $65.58 or 9.5 percent annually. It is more difficult, however, to sort out the effects on patient-day costs of growth in educational and outpatient expense since the departmental distribution of reported expenditure in 1953 was still relatively loose. Separate expenditures were reported for nursing schools, outpatients, emergency, and social service, laboratory, and radiology, the latter two departments having a significant proportion of outpatient work. These groups accounted for 1.76 percent, 1.05 percent, 2.49 percent, and 3.34 percent of total hospital expenditure. The difficulty is that 17.44 percent of total expenditure is "unattributed" in 1953; if that component were equally spread over all departments the above percentages become 2.13 percent, 1.27 percent, 3.02 percent, and 4.05 percent.

By 1971 nursing education had increased to 3.41 percent of total budget, and total education was up to 6.48 percent. If one assumed that education costs other than nursing were zero in 1953, the increase in direct educational costs per patient day would be from 27¢ to $3.99 or nearly 15 times. But in fact this is too small a budget component to matter. Patient-day expense net of education and special research projects is reported as $58.44 in 1971 compared with $12.20 expense net of nursing schools in 1953. Even assuming medical education and research at zero in 1953, the increase in expense net of education is 9.1 percent annually. This line of argument, however, ignores the large indirect costs associated with education. Thus one could be underestimating the effects of expanding the educational sector.

In 1971, teaching hospitals of 500 beds or more had expenses per patient day of $83.70 if full teaching and $67.56 if partial teaching, while in 1953, all 500+bed hospitals had costs per patient day of $15.93. If we assume that 500-bed full teaching hospitals in 1971 are roughly equivalent to 500+bed hospitals in 1953, it appears that costs have risen somewhat faster for this group–9.7 percent annually compared with 9.3 percent. But the difference is not large, and is probably upward-biased since not all 500+bed hospitals are full teaching. Nor has there been any major shift in the numbers of hospitals with full or partial teaching programs, and the share of such hospitals in total patient activity has not expanded significantly. Hence we may tentatively conclude that while educational programs are undoubtedly much more expensive to operate than their direct costs would indicate, the *increase* in costs from 1953 to 1971 does not seem to be traceable to the expansion of educational programs.

Turning to outpatient clinics (which include short-stay or day care surgery where relevant), we find that in 1971, outpatient clinics, emergency, and social service account for $1.82 per patient day. This compares with 16¢ per patient day in 1953, confirming the widespread view that such activity has increased in importance substantially faster than the regular inpatient service. These data also show clearly, however, that quantitatively the effects of this increase are trivial. Even after due allowance is made for indirect costs and overheads associated with an outpatient department, it appears that this sort of activity, like education, does not affect the conclusions reached above.

The above discussion suggests that the reported increases in expenditures per patient day really do reflect shifts in the cost of providing inpatient services, rather than being a result of shifts in the heterogeneous mix of hospital activities which are reflected in "per diems." To relate these increases to changes in insurance coverage, we must examine the behavior of expenses by sub-periods and draw on some additional data on wages and hours worked. For this purpose we have divided the 18-year span into three equal sub-periods: a pre-insurance phase 1953-59, a "digestion" phase 1959-65, and a post-insurance phase 1965-71. The initial period is not really pre-insurance, since several provincial plans were in operation during that period; but the two largest provinces, Ontario and Quebec, began their plans in 1959 and 1961 respectively so that 1959 rather than 1958 may be treated as a transitional year. This is supported by the observation that cost per day rose at an average rate of 7.2 percent annually, 1953-59, but only 5.8 percent from 1958 to 1959. In 1960 it took off, 12.9 percent.

In these three sub-periods, costs per day rose at average rates of 7.2 percent, 9.2 percent, and 11.6 percent. Relative to the Consumer Price Index these reduce to 5.6 percent, 7.5 percent, and 7.6 percent. There is of course no particular rationale for using the CPI as a deflator–except that no hospital price index exists. This pattern suggests that the apparent cost surge after 1966 is, in fact, tied in with the general rate of inflation, but that a break in behavior did take place at the time national insurance was introduced. Hospital costs per day were rising substantially faster than general inflation rates prior to national health insurance, but their relative increase speeded up both during and after the period of introduction of the public plans. The fact that the share of personal income going to hospitals increased much faster in the 1959-61 period than subsequently, in spite of the observations that both utilization and (price-adjusted) cost per day increases are relatively similar from 1959-65 to 1965-71, may be traced to the recession in 1961 which held down personal income growth. Whether national insurance served to insulate the hospital sector against this downturn, or whether hospital expenditures would have climbed through the recession without public insurance, we do not know.

What is fairly clear from Table 4 is that national insurance did not have any observable effect on utilization. Patient days and admissions per thousand population grew almost twice as fast annually in the pre-insurance period 1953-59 and have generally been slowing down since the public plans were introduced. Increases continue, but are now less than 1 percent per year. If not correlated with insurance, utilization does move very closely with bed availability. It seems in fact to be responding to new bed construction, partially stimulated by a federal building subsidy program started in 1948. This program provided a fixed dollar grant per bed, so was progressively eroded by inflation and finally terminated in 1970, but it had some effect in the 1950s.

More information emerges if we look at the components of cost per day by sub-periods. The share of total expense accounted for by gross wages and salaries, and its relation to hours worked, is as follows:

	Per Patient Day							
Year	Gross Salaries and Wages	% Change	% of Total Budget	Hours Worked	% Change	Implicit Wage	% Change	Relative Wage Gain %
1953	$ 7.20		57.7	9.2		$ 0.78		
1959	$11.72	62.8	62.1	10.6	15.2	$ 1.11	42.3	11.4
1965	$20.77	77.2	65.1	13.0	22.6	$ 1.60	44.1	16.2
1971	$41.82	101.3	67.9	13.3	2.2	$ 3.14	96.3	29.9

Relative wage gain is the percent increase in hospital wages relative to the average weekly wage (industrial composite); it measures the improvement in the relative income status of hospital workers.

This table suggests that there were some differences in behavior over these sub-periods. The share of hospital budget going to wages and salaries has been growing but at a reducing rate; the relative earnings of hospital workers have grown at an accelerating rate; and inputs of hours worked have first increased rapidly and then slowed down. In fact, hours worked per patient day rose after 1965 and then fell to their present level.

This suggests a behavior pattern of a rapidly expanding hospital sector in the 1950s, perhaps driven by the new funds made available through private and provincial insurance plans. Hospital workers were making income gains; labor inputs were rising; federal funds were adding new beds; and physicians were generating patients to fill them. Since the nonlabor budget share rose from $5.27 to $7.16 over this period, or 35.9 percent, and prices generally only rose 9.5 percent, it would appear that nonlabor inputs rose even faster than labor inputs. But our lack of any sort of hospital nonlabor price index is a hindrance here.

In the phase of introduction of national insurance, all cost increases speeded up while utilization increases slowed down. Labor input increased 22.6 percent compared to 15.2 percent in the previous six years; relative hospital workers' wages rose 16.2 percent faster than the general wage rate, and nonwage expense rose from $7.16 per day to $11.15 or 55.7 percent compared with general price increases of 9.7 percent. It would appear the initial impact of insurance was to increase substantially the real inputs to the hospital sector as well as to boost slightly the rate of increase in hospital workers' income status.

In the third phase (1965-71) increasing cost rates began to generate official concern and reaction. Utilization increases were slowing down still more and labor inputs per patient day were nearly static. Nonlabor inputs had risen from $11.15 to $19.76 or 77.2 percent; relative to the general price level increase of 24.2 percent, this amounts to a 42.7 percent increase (compared with 24.1 percent in 1953-59 and 41.9 percent in 1959-65). So it may be that nonlabor inputs are still accelerating. But it may also be that their prices have outstripped the CPI. Actually, we do not know. What is most striking about the 1965-71 period is the dramatic increase in hospital workers' wages per paid hour–96.3 percent or 29.9 percent faster than wages generally. This amounts to a rate of wage status gain of 4.5 percent annually, sustained for six years. On a base of $20.77, 29.9 percent yields $6.21, or 10 percent of total hospital costs and it is due to the relative wage gains of hospital workers during the last six years. Over the whole span, if hospital wages had just kept pace with industry generally, they would have risen to $1.87 per hour.

Of course, whether this is due to national health insurance is another question. Relative wage gains did speed up in the period of introduction of insurance, but became much more rapid in the later period. One could argue that this is a delayed effect of insurance–it took time for employees to absorb the implications of cost-pass-through and unionization for them to apply the lesson. On this argument, insurance shifted the rate of expansion of hospital costs to a new higher trend, and workers learned to exploit this fact. But one could also argue that in an industry with inelastic demand and growing private insurance, cost-pass-through would have been discovered regardless of national insurance. Canadian experience alone cannot answer this question–some U.S. comparisons might be helpful. It is clear, however, that if future cost increases are to be moderated, some way of establishing appropriate relative incomes for hospital workers must be found. If they try to play catch-up with physicians, the cost inflation is only beginning!

It is, of course, true that the above line of argument still has not identified and pinned down the process of hospital expenditure increase in a fully satisfactory manner—there exists the major issue of shifts in labor force composition. It may well be that hospitals respond to insurance, not just by adding more personnel and machines, but by adding more complex and highly trained sorts of personnel. Hence the wage change series might include a significant increase in human capital input rather than merely input price change.

It turns out that this is a remarkably difficult proposition to test, not because of conceptual problems, but because numerous changes in reporting systems and a very detailed but constantly changing specification of the hospital labor force make the reconstruction of a set of consistent historical series a major research project in itself. This project is beyond the bounds of a survey paper such as this one—it cries out to be done as a federal research study.[23] However, a bit of indirect evidence can be brought to bear on the problem.

First of all, despite the attention given to complex diagnostic procedures and highly specialized forms of treatment, nursing services and general support staff (dietary, laundry, administrative) are still the backbone of the hospital. A series of longitudinal studies of particular classes of hospital manpower from 1961 to 1968 shows that the professional and technical classes of employees (radiologists, pathologists, radiology and laboratory technicians, psychologists, social workers, medical record librarians, pharmacists, dietiticians, and physical and occupational therapists) increased their share from 3.44 percent to 4.68 percent of total full-time hospital employment. The percentage increase is large (36 percent increase in an expanding industry) but the absolute numbers are too small to affect total wage movements. Their share in part-time employment also rose, from 5.67 percent to 6.32 percent, but part time employees are only about 10 percent of the total.

In the same period, full time graduate nurses and nursing assistants rose from 6.42 percent and 19 percent to total full-time employment, to 8.90 percent and 21.60 percent, a smaller percentage change (20 percent) but a more significant quantitative shift. Thus a picture emerges of a proportional increase in nursing and nursing assistant staff and a corresponding reduction in relative employment of the unskilled "other" category. It is plausible to argue that, in fact, the human capital input per hour worked did rise somewhat over the period under consideration.

But this change, it turns out, does not appear to explain the wage shift. The reason is that average wages for nursing personnel generally (graduates and assistants) are not markedly different from those of other staff. In the first half of 1971, nurses on short-term units averaged $3.11 per hour and on long-term, $2.86 per hour. These made up 80 percent of all nursing hours in public hospitals. By comparison, averages in general services were: administration \$3.28, dietary \$3.36, medical records \$2.76, housekeeping \$2.21, plant operation and security \$3.28, laundry and linen \$2.19. The pattern of wage differentials is simply not large enough that a major shift in the average could arise from a shift of 10 percent or even 20 percent. We may conclude that shifting personnel mix has had very little to do with the overall pattern of wage inflation.

Two other points deserve comment. Part of the wage increase has clearly been due to the phasing out of the unpaid or almost unpaid workforce of student nurses. In 1953, student nurses, nursing assistants, and interns made up 1.62 out of 9.18 hours worked per patient day. Yet, even if we pulled *all* of these out of the base for computing wage and salary cost in 1953, we divide wage and salary cost per patient day of \$7.20 by 7.56 to arrive at an average wage of 95¢ and an increase in average wages 1953-71 of 232 percent. While substantially below 304 percent, this figure is also well above the approximately 140 percent increase in general wage levels—on the *maximum* possible allowance for the effects of eliminating unpaid or low paid student labor. And, of course, student labor is not yet fully phased out.

One should note that the elimination of student labor has been associated in the latter part of the period with the closure of hospital nursing schools. Consequently, the relative constancy of hours per patient day masks a reduction in education hours and a continued rise in patient care hours. The hospitals have responded to budgetary pressures by shedding functions. Hence the experience of stable hours input during this period may be only a temporary trend break.

A report, *Sources of Increase in Budget Review Hospital Expenditures in Canada, 1961 to 1971*, published in December 1973 by the Health Economics and Statistics Branch of the Department of National Health and Welfare, essentially confirms this picture in the post-insurance period. This report observes that for the 10-year period, total hospital expenditure rose 13.7 percent annually; patient days rose 3.0 percent and costs per day increased 10.3 percent. The report also concludes that outpatient workload shifts were not large enough to affect the pattern of expenditures, and notes that morbidity shifts in patient diagnostic mix may be important but cannot be identified.

Sources of expenditure increase are identified by department, but unfortunately only expenditure on supplies and other nonlabor expense is so allocated. Gross salaries and wages, drugs, and medical and surgical supplies are each treated as aggregates. But the labor cost per patient day is shown to have increased over the period 1961-71 substantially faster than the nonlabor cost, at a rate of 11.2 percent annually against 8.5 percent, and to account for roughly three quarters of the increase in cost per patient day compared with one quarter for nonlabor cost. During this period, paid hours of work per patient day rose 2.1 percent annually and labor cost per paid hour rose 8.7 percent. Thus, wage increase accounts for about seven eighths of labor cost increase per patient day. This source is shown to have accounted for over 50 percent of total expenditure increase in budget-review hospitals, even including effects of population growth and higher utilization. The possible effects of shifts in labor force composition in this process are touched on, and shifts are described in general terms, but the quantitative effects of such shifts are unknown. It is noted that the relative significance of labor cost per hour as a source of expenditure increase over the period is accelerating, but much of this can be accounted for by general inflation in the economy. The rate of *relative* wage gain is, however, somewhat faster in the later period. Hospital hourly wages for the 1961-65 period, as reported in *Sources of Increase,* rose 8.1 percent faster than general industry wages, and 21.3 percent faster during 1965-71. This may be partly a result of the timing of phaseout of nursing education. The impact of the shift away from hospital nursing education and toward more medical education on hospital total costs and average hourly wages has not yet been analyzed. In assessing the response of hospital expenditure to insurance, however, the message of the report parallels that of this paper. Wage inflation in the hospital sector is the main source of increase and the timing does not particularly correspond to the extension of insurance, the expansion of utilization, or even the expansion of employment. The most rapid *relative* wage increases have come in the late 1960's, when paid hours per patient day have been static and both population and utilization increase have slowed down.

Summing up, a picture seems to emerge of rapid increases in hospital capacity and utilization as a precursor to national health insurance. During the pre-insurance period hospital inputs, wages, and costs were rising rapidly, and hospital relative wages also were moving up. Private insurance may have fed this process, but government insurance was more likely a result of it. This would follow to the extent that expenditure increases prior to the national plan increased burdens on the uninsured and further restricted their access. Moreover, provincial and private insurance plans came under increasing fiscal strain. Most of the discussion surrounding the national hospital plan focused on its role as a vehicle for moving more resources into the hospital sector (it worked!); hence the response to increasing expenditure burdens. The initial insurance period saw a jump in hospital expenses, as hospitals appear to have accelerated their expansion of paid hours per patient day. Hospital wages rose at about the same rate as prior to insurance, although their relative status improved faster. The picture does not suggest a strong demand induced wage inflation resulting from expanded employment. Finally, the very rapid expansion in hospital expenditures in the mid-sixties triggered a bureaucratic response which has been fairly successful in containing increases in labor inputs. But the problem of relative hospital wages continues unaffected, as hospital employees seem to be improving their wage status at an accelerating rate. In the absence of a detailed job breakdown in the industry, of course, it is not possible to say whether they are still "catching up"–the industrial composite weekly wage of $137.64 in 1971 divided by 40 yields an "average" hourly wage of $3.44 which is still above the hospital average of $3.14. But neither wage is skill or experience adjusted.

In any case, it is clear that present bargaining and budget-setting procedures in hospitals do not approximate a competitive market process! And it is far from clear that continuation or completion of "catch-up" would have any relevance to future trends. The problem of hospital wage determination is still unresolved.

POLICY RESPONSES TO HOSPITAL COST INFLATION

This leads into the issues surrounding hospital reimbursement and budgetary control. We have argued that the problems of hospital cost inflation in Canada have little to do with utilization, insurance-induced or otherwise, but rather a lot to do with increases in earnings of hospital workers and secondarily with increases in real resource use per patient day (whether "quality" upgrading by managers, pressure for more hands to lighten the load from employees, or demands for further services by physicians). The process of budgetary control has not been notably successful in promoting efficiency and/or containing costs.

As noted above, the initial intention of the Canadian hospital insurance system was to provide a method of paying whatever expenses the hospital system generated. This policy seemed to have an effect of encouraging expenditure increase; the point of a federal program was to mobilize more resources, to lower financial barriers to utilization, and to maintain or increase standards of care. Consequently, the process of budget review did not initially emphasize efficiency or cost control; and when it became apparent in the late 1960's that hospital expenditures were taking an accelerating share of national resources and that "something" should be done, neither the review and reimbursement process nor the statistical framework which surrounded it proved adequate for the task. After more than five years of discussion and study, they still are not.

The budget review process varies in detail from province to province, and, in fact, from year to year in a given province depending on the state of the provincial treasury. For most of the first decade of insurance, provinces employed some variant of a line-item budget approval prior to the budget year combined with a review and settlement at year end.[24] The prospective budget is based on an expected patient-day load, and the ratio of total budget to forecast load creates a synthetic "per diem" which is used as a basis for distributing the hospital's budget over the year, but is not an independent price in the sense that if actual load is above or below forecast, the total budget will not be adjusted proportionately. If significant deviations from forecast occur, partial adjustments may be made at year end. But both agency and hospital are well aware of the difference between average and marginal costs per day, at least in this context.[25]

The patient-day forecast is generally based on the previous year's experience, adjusted for any known special factors in or outside each hospital, and tends to be quite accurate. It is not defined in terms of diagnostic mix, although certain special sub-populations (such as renal dialysis cases) would be forecast separately. For each hospital, expected procedure workloads and input requirements by category are then developed from this forecast; the particular procedure forecasts thus implicitly embody some judgement about diagnostic and severity mix based on the past experience of the hospital. But the judgement never becomes explicit. Once physical requirements, personnel, supplies, and equipment by category, are approved, the final budget will then depend on negotiated wage scales for the positions allowed in each hospital's approved establishment. Formally, these negotiations take place between hospital managements (on a provincial basis) and provincial unions or associations. But since wage costs are usually passed directly to the provincial reimbursing agency, it is not entirely clear what besides public interest stiffens the negotiators for management.[26] This may be one explanation for the unusually rapid wage increases in hospitals.

The review process has required provincial reimbursing agencies to accumulate a great deal of detailed information about each hospital, much of it informal. In Ontario, a commission appoints financial representatives, each responsible for several hospitals. Their task is to work within a hospital during budget preparation, and to act as the hospital's representative in steering its submission through the commission. In British Columbia, the Hospital Insurance Service maintains a budget "model" of each hospital (which is *not* revealed to that hospital) and it uses it in evaluating the submitted budgets.

The problem, however, is that none of this information is organized in a way linking expenditure with output. Since all data are based on inputs neither hospital nor reimbursing agencies know total costs of inpatient care in a given hospital (except for hospitals with no outpatient or educational activity). Direct laundry costs per pound processed, or nursing ward costs per patient day can be calculated, but no allocation of overhead or indirect costs is carried out. If a hospital's diagnostic mix shifts, or if its patient-day load and/or length of stay changes, the reimbursing agency may know in which direction the budget should shift, but never by how much. Thus hospitals are exhorted to lower length of stay. They reply that this would raise their "per diem," and that the paying agency would not approve all the necessary increase. The paying agency says it will approve the *necessary* increase, but no more. Yet no one knows what is necessary. The same problem arises if patient-day forecasts are over- or underrun; no one knows by how much a marginal patient day costs less than average. Arbitrary rules of thumb are used. Comparisons across hospitals cannot be made with any confidence, because "similarity" embodies no adjustment for differences in diagnostic mix. Everyone knows this is important; and this has been shown analytically,[27] but no one is sure what the appropriate adjustment should be. Hence similarity is judged on proxies such as size, location, or educational role. The process of negotiation and budget determination for the largest hospitals in each province is one of the financial responsibilities of senior financial and health officials in the provincial government. It is given appropriate attention and weight; but the data from which the province might determine what it is buying simply do not exist. As long as budgets are based on inputs, and inputs cannot be translated in any comprehensive way to account for outputs—cases treated by type, or students trained, budget makers will fall back on incrementalism, taking last year's budget and adding X percent, plus all requests generated by medical technology and wage demands.

As the inability of budget review to limit cost escalation has become more apparent, public policy has responded along two main lines. Efforts have been made to encourage greater efficiency in hospitals, and to reduce the size of the inpatient hospital sector by substituting other forms of care. Both policies have tended to move the problem out of the hospital sphere and into the realm of medical practice organization; neither has come to grips with the ballooning incomes of hospital workers.

The "management" orientation is reflected in Volume II of the 1969 *Task Force Report, op. cit.,* dealing with hospital services. Much was made of the poor management practices in hospitals, and the recommendations covered the range of training (and even licensing!) of better hospital managers, giving them more scope, and creating incentives for efficiency. Hospital reimbursement has correspondingly moved toward global budgeting. It uses line-item input reports as a guide to setting global amounts but giving administrators more discretion in allocating expenditures within total budgets. Experiments have been tried with fixing annual target budgets and allowing managers to share underruns and use their share for capital expansion or other projects, an incentive reimbursement approach. It seems fair to say, however, that the managerial approach has been relatively unsuccessful for several reasons.

The limited possibilities of comparison across hospitals with existing data make confident identification of "good" and "bad" management impossible. Moreover, detailed analysis suggests there is very little variance across hospitals in *relative* efficiency within each province; the style of medical practice and the pattern of reimbursement jointly determine most of hospital behavior.[28] The administrator may not have much discretion. Even if one could identify desired behavior and if the administrator had enough control over style of care delivery to do what the reimburser desired, creation of incentives is almost impossible. Reimbursement incentives only work if a dollar of "profit" (shared cost underruns) is worth more to management than a dollar of operational expense. In a nonprofit industry whose capital expansion needs are met out of a separate budget on the basis of regional and political needs, this is not so. Direct incentives to managers themselves are likewise ruled out so long as hospitals are nominally controlled by independent boards of trustees. The careers of administrators and their levels of remuneration or both are only indirectly influenced by payment agencies. Rewarding efficiency by "promotion" to a larger hospital is not possible. And finally, everyone knows that hospitals cannot be allowed to go bankrupt. The penalties for inadequate performance can never be absolute; at worst one can fire the administrator. But this weakens any ability he might have to run a tight ship even if he wanted to—the organization itself is never at risk. The focus on improved management has not been abandoned–it is still obviously true that better management can yield more health care for a given budget–but as a technique for overall cost containment it is of less interest.[29]

Consequently, attention shifts to ways of reducing hospital utilization by providing institutional alternatives such as convalescent care, day care surgery, home care; by shifting medical practice away from fee-for-service practice and toward salaried group practice or other arrangements; or by simply closing beds. All of these efforts are currently under way; and although it is too early to give any final judgement as to their success, certain patterns have become apparent.

The institutional alternatives approach has the advantage of being supported by medical as well as economic opinion; the deleterious effects of excessive hospitalization on the patient are well recognized and are often more important than economic objectives in initiating new programs. Particularly in the pediatric area it has been demonstrated that significant medical improvements as well as economic savings can be achieved through day care surgery units or ambulatory medical treatment facilities.[30] The main problems with this approach are twofold: first, the tendency for utilization to rise to match supply insures that unless new facilities are balanced by withdrawal of old ones, total costs will rise. If a home-care program or convalescent beds move less severely ill patients out of acute hospitals, new acute care patients flow in. Moreover, discharge from lower intensity facilities is more difficult. Canadian experience parallels Feldstein's judgement in the U.S.[31] ; provinces with well-developed convalescent care systems, like Alberta, have relatively higher hospital costs per capita.

Second, a problem arises due to the structure of reimbursement. Ambulatory alternatives to inpatient care have tended to be based in hospitals. But hospital budgets are geared to inpaitnet care; and administrators tend to view reduced days of care as threatening reimbursements. A day surgery unit which eliminates a two-day stay minor surgery case is perceived as "costing" the hospital two per diems. The unit price or reimbursement received for an ambulatory case is less than would have been received for a corresponding inpatient. As the hospital's inpatient base shrinks, and its ambulatory load expands, it must negotiate (legitimately) ever higher per diems, and this is not easy to do. Reimbursing agencies see the problem differently. They observe *total* inpatient utilization failing to fall as ambulatory care expands and they are less willing to negotiate higher rates. The crucial aspects of the problem are the responsiveness of utilization to facilities and the inability of either agency or hospital to quantify the full unit costs associated with either inpatient or ambulatory episodes. If episodes could be accurately priced and reimbursed independently of treatment mode, the process of moving patients out of inpatient care would be strongly encouraged.

The utilization response, in Canada as in the United States, has been traced to the mode of organization of medical practice. Evidence exists that physician groups paid on a salary basis use substantially less hospital care for their patients than does the fee-for-service sector.[32] This has led numerous observers and some government study groups to recommend reorganization of medical practice into community health centers (now a very elastic term with features paralleling HMO's) as ways of moderating hospital costs.[33] But there is general agreement that this is a long, slow process. Several provincial governments are committed to the idea in principle; but organized medicine is strongly opposed to modification of the present system.

As for the most simple-minded approach of closing beds, this has been adopted as official or unofficial policy in several provinces. "Standards" of numbers of "needed" acute care beds per thousand population, which never were based on anything very much, are being revised downward, and provincial governments are mounting increased resistance to providing capital for new hospitals or expansion. This tactic is, of course, easiest in provinces such as Ontario and British Columbia with rapidly growing populations. But actual closing of hospitals is politically extremely difficult. (The first province, however, to adopt bed limitation as an official tactic was Quebec after the Castonguay Report which stated that at least a third of the province's beds were unnecessary.) This approach probably holds the greatest promise of cost moderation in the near term, while long-run efforts at control will probably depend on reorganization of medical practice and some improved method of hospital wage determination.

MEDICAL INSURANCE AND MEDICAL EXPENDITURES–CAUSE OR EFFECT?

The question of reorganizing medical practice leads directly to consideration of the impact of Medicare on service supply. Statistical evaluation of this impact is hampered by the fact that the program is recent, and 1971 was the first full year of national coverage for which complete data are available. Moreover, in each of the provinces private nonprofit plans predated the public program and provided a significant degree of insurance coverage.[34] The introduction of insurance is not a clear-cut, point-in-time phenomenon.

Table 5 shows, however, that when data are examined at the provincial level the timing of the public plans is quite apparent. The proportion of personal income in each province spent on physicians' services takes an abrupt jump away from its previous pattern in each province either in the year the public plan was introduced there or immediately after. The Saskatchewan picture is, of course, muddled by the physician strike of 1962 and its aftermath, and Alberta physicians seem to show a degree of anticipation, but elsewhere the change is very systematic. Whether this is a new plateau share of personal income or a new up-trend is too soon to tell (total Canadian personal income was up 10.4 percent in 1971, so the apparent levelling off of the "physician share" may be exogenous). But it is clear that in each province public insurance was associated

TABLE 5
PHYSICIAN EXPENDITURES AS A PERCENTAGE OF PERSONAL INCOME, CANADA AND PROVINCES, 1957-1971

Year	B.C.	Alta.	Sask.	Man.	Ont.	Que.	N.B.	N.S.	P.E.I.	Nfld.	Can.
1957	1.25	1.17	1.40	1.37	1.10	.96	1.10	1.20	1.33	.79	1.11
1958	1.36	1.16	1.35	1.36	1.16	1.04	1.16	1.18	1.44	.86	1.16
1959	1.44	1.18	1.35	1.46	1.18	1.05	1.08	1.22	1.33	.86	1.18
1960	1.48	1.25	1.35	1.33	1.19	1.05	1.19	1.26	1.40	.97	1.20
1961	1.52	1.30	1.69	1.60	1.27	1.15	1.27	1.30	1.34	.95	1.20
1962	1.48	1.31	*1.03*	1.47	1.23	1.16	1.20	1.29	1.19	.93	1.24
1963	1.43	1.27	1.45	1.47	1.31	1.23	1.27	1.25	1.42	1.00	1.30
1964	1.49	1.32	1.65	1.41	1.35	1.21	1.26	1.31	1.29	1.04	1.33
1965	1.44	1.31	1.48	1.46	1.36	1.22	1.25	1.31	1.35	.97	1.33
1966	1.49	1.27	1.41	1.46	1.33	1.23	1.17	1.33	1.29	.95	1.32
1967	1.48	1.45	1.57	1.43	1.39	1.23	1.30	1.27	1.29	.96	1.36
1968	*1.56*	1.67	1.45	1.43	1.45	1.26	1.29	1.41	1.33	1.12	1.42
1969	1.63	*1.62*	1.52	*1.67*	*1.48*	1.28	1.31	*1.51*	1.49	*1.46*	1.46
1970	1.73	1.76	1.75	1.90	1.60	1.24	*1.31*	1.75	*1.33*	1.56	1.55
1971	1.67	1.82	1.58	1.78	1.66	*1.71*	1.48	1.75	1.86	1.51	1.68
% Change											
1957-64	19.2	12.8	17.9	2.9	22.7	26.0	14.6	9.2	-3.0	31.7	19.8
1964-71	12.1	37.9	-4.2	26.2	23.0	41.3	17.5	33.6	44.2	45.2	26.3
1957-71	33.6	55.6	12.9	29.9	50.9	78.1	34.6	45.8	39.9	91.1	51.4

Data of entry to Medicare italicized.

with significant increases in the share of personal income received by physicians. (Table 5 also shows that this increase was superimposed on a general uptrend which may have been levelling off in the mid-sixties.)

Why this was so is less clear. In conventional economics, of course, the answer is obvious. Lower prices to consumers, greater demand, greater utilization, and higher prices charged by suppliers. And undoubtedly some of these changes occurred. But tracing them down is not all that easy. First of all, list prices of physician services did not particularly respond to public insurance. Table 6 reports provincial fee schedule indices (after Medicare the index reports benefits paid by the provincial agency) compiled by the Department of National Health and Welfare since December 1963 and compares these indices with total expenditure and total expenditure per capita.[35] Expenditure data are standardized to the same base as prices in 1964; no average fee level for 1963 is available. The table shows first that both total expenditure and total expenditure per capita rose steadily year by year in each province whether or not list fees rose. Fee increases accelerated the process: their absence did not inhibit it. Of

TABLE 6

INDICES OF FEE/BENEFIT SCHEDULES (ANNUAL AVERAGES), AND CORRESPONDING INDICES OF TOTAL EXPENDITURE AND TOTAL EXPENDITURE PER CAPITA ON PHYSICIANS' SERVICES, CANADA AND PROVINCES, 1963-1973

	B.C.	Alta.	Sask.	Man.	Ont.	N.B.	N.S.	P.E.I.	Nfld.	Can. (Ex.Que)*
Dec. 1963 FB	100	100	100	100	100	100	100	100	100	100
1964										
FB	103.7	101.8	100.0	100.0	100.0	100.0	100.0	112.1	100.0	100.6
TX	103.7	101.8	100.0	100.0	100.0	100.0	100.0	112.1	100.0	100.6
TXPC	103.7	101.8	100.0	100.0	100.0	100.0	100.0	112.1	100.0	100.6
1965										
FB	103.7	104.2	100.0	100.0	105.9	100.0	100.0	112.1	100.0	103.6
TX	111.6	112.5	104.4	110.9	110.9	108.0	107.2	125.6	106.0	109.0
TXPC	108.3	111.0	103.4	110.4	108.5	107.4	107.0	125.6	105.1	107.2
1966										
FB	103.7	107.6	100.0	100.0	107.8	112.7	100.0	112.6	100.0	105.4
TX	130.3	124.8	113.9	119.3	121.8	112.4	120.0	132.5	116.1	120.7
TXPC	121.3	121.9	112.2	119.0	116.2	111.4	119.6	132.5	113.8	116.4
1967										
FB	114.0	116.6	100.9	111.0	117.0	125.4	105.7	112.7	105.5	114.0
TX	143.9	155.0	119.2	130.3	140.9	135.8	126.5	146.8	131.3	137.8
TXPC	129.2	148.5	117.2	129.9	131.2	133.7	125.4	146.8	127.1	130.2
1968										
FB	*114.0*	124.3	113.1	133.1	120.0	125.4	122.7	129.1	116.7	120.1
TX	*165.8*	199.2	124.7	144.1	163.0	149.7	153.4	171.1	169.7	160.1
TXPC	*144.6*	186.7	122.2	142.5	149.0	146.2	150.6	169.5	162.0	148.7
1969										
FB	121.1	*127.2*	124.1	*133.1*	*128.2*	138.5	*122.7*	129.1	*116.7*	126.6
TX	196.9	*217.0*	136.4	*180.8*	*186.2*	167.7	*183.0*	207.0	*243.9*	184.7
TXPC	166.8	*198.8*	134.1	*177.5*	*167.5*	163.4	*177.7*	203.3	*229.2*	168.8
1970										
FB	121.1	131.2	128.1	133.1	130.8	*138.5*	122.7	*147.3*	116.7	128.7
TX	225.5	254.5	146.3	216.9	219.6	*182.4*	230.4	*206.6*	290.1	216.1
TXPC	184.9	228.1	146.6	212.1	193.1	*177.7*	220.9	*204.7*	271.0	194.0
1971										
FB	121.1	135.2	133.9	133.1	134.7	138.5	122.7	147.3	115.1	131.3
TX	247.2	294.0	159.8	226.3	249.8	228.1	248.4	310.1	314.0	243.1
TXPC	197.7	258.3	162.3	219.9	215.4	219.7	237.2	301.7	290.5	214.8
1972										
FB	126.3	135.4	137.8	133.1	136.7	138.5	130.0	151.2	115.3	133.7
1973										
FB	134.6	138.0	143.0	133.1	136.7	138.5	136.2	152.5	124.9	136.9
Dec. 1973										
FB	137.5	143.1	143.0	133.1	136.7	138.5	137.4	152.5	127.3	137.2

*Quebec had no fee schedule for general practitioners prior to Medicare.

course, much of this was due to improving collection ratios over the period, and probably also greater adherence to fee schedules. But this pattern of behavior persisted after Medicare was introduced. The mechanism which drives expenditure clearly does not operate through listed fees alone (or even primarily) and since listed fees are now pegged to actual fees it does not seem to operate through actual fees either. Unfortunately we have no data at all to adjust collection ratios and approximate actual fee movements prior to Medicare.

In Table 7 the same point emerges at the aggregate level. Here the nine-province fee benefit index (weighted by 1964 provincial populations) has been linked to the Consumer Price Index Medical Care Component for earlier years. It shows physicians' fees rising at about the same rate as all prices from 1957 to 1971, faster than the general price level before Medicare but

TABLE 7

PHYSICIAN "PRICE" MOVEMENTS IN CANADA, 1957-1973 (1961 = 100) AND IMPLICIT "QUANTITY" CHANGES

	Physicians' Services* (List Price)	Consumer Price Index	Physicians' Services Expenditure†	Apparent "Quantity" Index††	"Quantity" Per Capita
1957	89.5	94.4	70.0	78.2	85.9
1958	94.4	96.8	77.6	82.2	87.8
1959	97.1	97.9	83.9	86.4	90.1
1960	98.4	99.1	91.4	92.9	94.8
1961	100.0	100.0	100.0	100.0	100.0
1962	103.0	101.2	104.6	101.6	99.7
1963	104.9	102.9	116.8	111.3	107.2
1964	107.1	104.8	127.6	119.1	112.6
1965	110.3	107.4	140.4	127.3	118.2
1966	112.2	111.4	155.9	138.9	126.6
1967	121.4	115.3	176.7	145.6	130.3
1968	127.9	120.1	203.0	158.7	139.8
1969	134.8	125.5	232.1	172.2	149.5
1970	137.0	129.7	265.0	193.4	165.6
1971	139.6	133.4	318.4	228.0	192.8
1972	142.3	139.8			
1973	145.7	150.4			
% Change					
1957-71			354.9%	191.6%	124.4%
1957-73	62.8%	59.3%			
Per Annum	3.1%	3.0%	11.4%	8.0%	5.9%

* Average value of the C.P.I. physicians' fees component, 1957-64, linked in 1965 to the N.H.W. Fee Benefit Index (Table 6).

† Expenditure on Physicians' Services (Table 1), indexed on 1961 = 100.

†† Physicians' Services Expenditure ÷ list price.

substantially slower since. Recalling that actual prices probably moved faster than list in the pre-Medicare years, but not since, it follows that relative price increases in the medical care industry have *slowed down* since insurance went into effect. Yet expenditures go on climbing. If list prices actually reflected actual over this period, one could derive an apparent quantity increase for 1957-71 by dividing expenditure change by price change. This "quantity" estimate increases by 8.0 percent per year. Adjusting for population change brings this rate down to 5.9 percent per year, still a very healthy rate of "real" service input.[36]

These rapid increases in expenditure, whether based on "quantity" or hidden price changes, should show up either as increases in average gross receipts per physician or as increases in the number of physicians available per capita. These data are displayed in Tables 8 and 9. As noted in data sources at the end of this chapter, they apply to fee-practice physicians only; although figures represent only about two thirds of the total physician stock, the remainder are not included in physician expenditure data and neither set nor collect fees. The increase of 28.7 percent in physician stock per capita, combined with an increase of 173.1 percent in gross receipts per physician, yields an increase of 251.5 percent in physician expenditures per capita, and a 29.9 percent increase in population yields the 350 percent increase in physician expenditures of Table 7.[37] Annualizing, population rose 1.9 percent per year, physicians per capita 1.8 percent, gross receipts per physician 7.4 percent, for a total of 11.4 percent.

Several interesting points emerge from these data. First of all, the rise in physician stock has been twice as rapid as that of the population, and has been accelerating. The introduction of Medicare coincides with a significant increase in the rate of additions to the physician stock. Furthermore, gross receipts per physician have gone ahead much more rapidly than list prices. If one accepted the Table 7 list price increase of 56.0 percent from 1957 to 1971, the implicit average increase in real output per physician would be 4.1 percent per year. Yet physician practices are not adding new inputs rapidly; physician practice expenses rose at 5.8 percent per year in 1957-71 compared with general price level increases of 3.2 percent and wage increases of 5.2 percent. Physician net incomes rose steadily relative to the average weekly wage, as shown in the last column of Table 8. What is striking is that average earnings of physicians relative to this industrial composite rose *faster* in the period 1957-64 than in the Medicare period 1964-71. The difference is not large, but it is enough to suggest that the introduction of Medicare did not bring about a change in the longer-run forces which drive the relative incomes of physicians.

So we are left with the observation that Medicare was associated with rapid increases in the numbers of physicians and rates of expenditure on their services, but not with major changes in physician list prices. Physician relative income continued to climb rapidly, but no faster than before Medicare; actual prices and real outputs per physician are unknown. We have, however, some fragmentary data on real outputs. The before-and-after Medicare study of

TABLE 8

INDICES OF AVERAGE GROSS RECEIPTS PER ACTIVE FEE-PRACTICE PHYSICIAN, CANADA AND PROVINCES, 1957-1971
CANADA AVERAGE 1957 ($20,804) = 100

Year	B.C.	Alta.	Sask.	Man.	Ont.	Que.	N.B.	N.S.	P.E.I.	Nfld.	Can.	Can.*	Can.†
1957	114.1	112.3	109.1	113.8	105.8	81.2	88.5	94.4	74.6	109.6	100.0	100.0	3.78
1958	119.7	119.3	113.0	120.3	112.6	87.8	93.9	94.5	85.6	117.0	106.2	107.2	3.91
1959	128.0	121.4	113.9	132.5	116.1	90.0	90.9	102.6	90.6	118.6	110.1	113.5	3.87
1960	134.9	134.7	130.1	123.9	122.7	94.5	108.3	109.6	97.0	137.4	116.7	122.4	4.15
1961	133.9	140.5	130.3	139.7	130.8	106.3	116.4	111.7	96.1	130.7	124.3	128.2	4.21
1962	132.2	149.9	*111.7*	139.4	133.5	112.6	115.3	112.0	94.6	119.3	126.5	132.0	4.21
1963	133.0	148.6	171.4	138.9	147.3	123.8	126.8	112.7	112.5	134.1	137.9	145.4	4.37
1964	146.7	157.1	175.4	139.9	159.6	128.9	133.6	123.7	111.3	147.2	147.0	159.4	4.73
1965	152.3	170.1	180.1	153.4	171.9	139.4	142.4	132.1	123.0	152.0	157.7	171.7	4.85
1966	173.3	182.0	193.0	161.5	183.9	148.5	145.5	144.0	126.3	161.9	169.3	181.0	4.83
1967	185.6	210.6	193.0	176.2	205.3	160.8	172.5	146.1	138.1	175.5	185.9	203.0	5.08
1968	*201.2*	249.4	199.7	192.7	228.0	173.9	187.1	172.2	156.6	207.9	205.6	222.7	5.21
1969	214.9	*251.8*	216.4	*236.8*	*246.0*	187.7	203.6	*197.6*	180.3	*249.8*	222.7	240.1	5.25
1970	235.0	285.8	236.4	280.4	278.1	186.9	*223.0*	234.5	*181.5*	276.5	244.3	267.4	5.42
1971	239.7	298.9	244.7	271.7	296.4	*259.5*	260.5	234.9	246.4	264.8	273.1	305.0	5.70
% Change	110.1	166.2	124.3	138.8	180.2	219.6	194.4	148.8	230.3	141.6	173.1	205.0	50.79
Per annum	5.4	7.2	5.9	6.4	7.6	8.7	8.0	6.7	8.9	6.5	7.4	8.3	3.0

*Canada net receipts (100 = $12,852)

†Canada net relative to average wage (average weekly wage x 50)

Changes in Canada:		1957-64	1964-71
	Average gross	47.0%	85.8%
	Average net	59.4%	91.3%
	Relative net	25.1%	20.5%

TABLE 9

ACTIVE FEE-PRACTICE PHYSICIANS (PER 100,000 POPULATION) CANADA AND PROVINCES, 1957-1971

Year	B.C.	Alta.	Sask.	Man.*	Ont.	Que.	N.B.	N.S.	P.E.I.	Nfld.*	Can.*
1957	94.5	73.3	71.4	72.9	88.1	73.6	58.0	66.8	66.7	22.9	78.0
1958	95.6	73.7	72.8	74.4	89.2	74.8	59.0	67.4	66.0	23.6	79.1
1959	98.4	74.2	73.9	75.6	90.8	76.2	59.8	67.9	66.3	24.0	80.5
1960	100.6	73.7	73.3	76.9	90.8	76.6	59.4	69.9	65.0	26.1	81.0
1961	103.3	73.5	72.9	78.1	91.0	77.0	58.9	71.6	64.8	27.7	81.5
1962	105.8	73.6	72.6	79.5	91.4	77.5	58.5	73.5	64.5	29.5	82.2
1963	106.2	74.1	73.1	80.2	91.8	77.9	59.1	74.0	65.8	30.0	82.7
1964	106.8	74.6	73.7	80.6	92.2	78.4	59.7	74.3	65.1	30.6	83.2
1965	107.5	75.1	74.2	81.0 (86.9)	92.7	78.9	60.2	74.5	66.1	30.9 (50.4)	83.8 (85.9)
1966	105.9	77.2	75.3	83.4 (89.5)	92.9	81.8	61.1	76.6	67.9	31.8 (51.5)	85.1 (85.9)
1967	105.0	81.3	78.5	83.5 (89.8)	93.6	82.5	61.9	79.4	68.8	32.2 (52.2)	86.2 (86.7)
1968	108.2	86.3	79.2	83.9 (90.0)	95.4	83.3	62.5	81.3	70.0	33.9 (54.4)	87.9 (88.7)
1969	117.0	91.0	80.1	85.1 (91.7)	99.1	84.9	64.3	84.2	73.6	38.5 (59.7)	91.4 (92.3)
1970	120.3	94.3	82.6	84.4 (95.3)	102.6	88.4	63.6	87.2	74.5	40.4 (63.8)	94.8 (95.6)
1971	125.8	101.8	88.3	89.7 (101.2)	107.4	95.4	67.2	93.0	81.3	44.3 (69.3)	100.4 (101.5)
% change	33.1	38.9	23.7	23.0	21.9	29.6	15.9	39.2	21.9	93.4	28.7

*Bracketed numbers include salaried practitioners, which are aggregated in other provinces.

physician utilization in Montreal reports that aggregate visit rates did not rise in response to insurance and that physician hours of work did not increase. Instead, physicians reorganized their practice patterns and generated more income from a given number of initial patient contacts.[38] This is supported by data from Trans-Canada Medical Plans showing that in insured populations, rates of physician-generated services per capita tend to rise faster over time and to be more closely associated with physician availability than are rates of patient-generated services.[39] Aggregate data from Quebec for 1971 and 1972, the first two years of insurance, show the same phenomenon, incredible quarter to quarter rates of increase of certain specific physician-generated services as well as a shift across fee schedule items from e.g. "ordinary" to "complete" office examinations.[40]

Rather than having physician expense driven by independent shifts in demand, we seem to be observing a linkage between supply of physicians and the quantity of services they choose to perform to total expense. What we observe, and what generates expense, is not demand in the economist's sense but utilization, and utilization is the outcome of patient demand and physician behavior. This behavior is, at least, partially dependent on the relation between desired and actual physician incomes. The role of national health insurance may simply have been to relax further any market constraints on how physicians manipulate utilization to generate income. Table 8 suggests, however, that these constraints were not very significant before Medicare. Undoubtedly, there was also a once-for-all increase in the ratio of actual to list prices as the plans drove uncollectables to zero in one year. But the primary force driving up physician expenditures in the late 1960's is the increase in physician stock and the changes in physician practice patterns.

This creates a rather puzzling inconsistency. In the time series data, each province shows a clear jump in share of income devoted to medical services when public insurance was introduced; and, as noted above, in most provinces physician incomes rose rapidly in the years spanning the introduction. Yet over the longer period, physician incomes relative to wages and salaries generally have moved up about 3 percent per year and this increase did not accelerate in the 1968-71 period. Of course, wages and salaries do not move with personal income–over this period they have tended to lag behind. But the key question is the difference made by insurance. In the absence of the public plan, would the rapid increase in physicians per capita from 1968 to 1971 (14.2 percent in three years) have driven down average physician incomes? Or would it merely have given rise to price and quantity adjustments in the private market which would have pushed up costs anyway? There is some evidence cross-sectionally in Canada that while *absolute numbers* of physicians per capita have little systematic effect on physician income, *rapid rates of growth* of the stock push down relative incomes. The evidence is not worth much; but we might tentatively suggest that national insurance speeded up physician reactions to an increase in numbers and affected the timing of their income-maintaining responses. Had Medicare not been introduced, the influx of physicians to the market might have held down income increases in the short run; it might have generated pressure for increases in list prices and changes in individual billing practices. Medicare speeded the process up; it shifted actual prices relative to list (hence the slower movement of list prices post-Medicare) and enabled billing practices to shift rapidly without patient backlash (the Enterline findings). Physician influence over the private market, however, seemed to be strong enough, that over the long haul doctors would have been able to absorb the influx and restore their incomes to the long-term upward trend. Of course, this is all hypothetical; we have very little post-Medicare data yet and political variables have now superseded whatever market forces were previously operative.[41]

Table 10 merely provides some corroborative evidence on the role of physician pricing behavior. It shows the variation across provinces in fee levels: British Columbia, Manitoba, Alberta and Ontario tend to be high priced while the eastern provinces are lower. Highest of all is British Columbia. Yet these are also the provinces with the largest number of physicians per capita. British Columbia is the most prominent example, always at or near the top of all provinces in prices; yet far ahead of the others in numbers of physicians (Table 9), and near bottom in physician incomes (Table 8). The inference is that as increases in physician stock spread, the patient load is reduced, and incomes per physician fall. The response is to try to drive *up* prices, and to generate more services or both. Neither tactic has been fully successful in British Columbia, but then the physician stock is abnormally large there, and probably includes a relatively larger number of semiretired practitioners.[42]

If in fact physician behavior is the key to utilization and expenditure behavior, as Canadian insurance experience suggests,[43] it follows that efforts to modify patterns of expenditure by incentives directed at the consumer of care cannot hope to influence overall cost trends. Copayment is pretty much a dead issue in Canada, both because of its distributional effects and because it cannot come to grips with the real problems.[44] Public policy has instead been directed at two approaches–control within the existing structure of medical practice, and modification of that structure.

Control in the existing structure includes negotiation of list fees and could be extended to unilateral determination of such fees by government (although this has not been suggested out loud). The evidence now seems fairly clear that this will not work because billings can be expanded almost indefinitely on a given schedule. Moreover, procedural multiplication can be harmful to the patient's health and can generate substantial external costs in the hospital sector and elsewhere. The "provider profiles" mentioned above merely identify very unusual practitioners. They give no leverage to government over changes in medical practice standards over time. A variety of gimmicks have been suggested or tried. For example, absolute limits on physician earnings (Newfoundland) merely lead to more physician leisure. Prorationing of billings against a fixed pool of reimbursement has been suggested as a short-run measure, but in the

TABLE 10

RELATIVE "PRICES" OF MEDICAL SERVICES ACROSS PROVINCES,* VARIOUS YEARS (ONTARIO = 100)

	1968 All Services	1969 All Services		1973 All Services	
	Fee Schedule (Sept. 1)	Fee Schedule (Sept. 1)	Benefits Paid (Oct. 1)	Benefits All Services†	Paid Visits Only
		General Practitioners			
B.C.	110.9	106.5	106.5	117.25	122.19
Alta.	99.4	106.6	113.2	115.53	121.28
Sask.	104.7	95.2	89.9	92.25	95.14
Man.	127.3	115.5	109.1	103.95	103.30
Ont.	100.0	100.0	100.0	100.00	100.00
Que.*	—	—	—	—	92.72
N.B.	98.3	97.9	92.5	—	86.07
N.S.	110.2	99.1	93.6	—	96.38
P.E.I.	98.7	89.0	98.9	—	85.66
Nfld.	96.6	86.8	86.8	—	85.65
		Specialists			
B.C.	108.9	112.7	112.7	103.64	124.20
Alta.	99.9	99.0	97.4	101.75	104.31
Sask.	103.4	95.4	90.1	87.44	90.34
Man.	112.9	106.1	100.2	92.05	93.02
Ont.	100.0	100.0	100.0	100.00	100.00
Que.	108.1	101.2	101.2	—	91.80
N.B.	95.6	101.4	95.8	—	89.38
N.S.	109.5	101.9	96.2	—	98.14
P.E.I.	104.9	96.5	107.2	—	101.78
Nfld.	100.0	94.1	94.1	—	91.90
		All Physicians			
B.C.	109.6	110.8	110.8	110.33	122.84
Alta.	99.7	102.1	103.4	108.53	115.78
Sask.	103.9	95.3	90.0	89.80	93.58
Man.	118.6	108.7	102.7	97.90	99.96
Ont.	100.0	100.0	100.0	100.00	100.00
Que.*	—	—	—	—	92.42
N.B.	96.2	98.7	93.2	—	87.15
N.S.	109.9	99.2	93.7	—	96.95
P.E.I.	99.8	92.0	102.2	—	90.88
Nfld.	97.8	89.2	89.2	—	87.67

*Quebec general practitioners had no fee schedule in 1968 or 1969.

†Payments for laboratory services in eastern provinces are not on a unit basis.

long run it seems to accentuate the pressures on physicians to multiply procedures by penalizing the "non-multipliers" for the excesses of their colleagues.[45] So far the only sure-fire method of cost-containment appears to be the current suggestion by the Council of Health Ministers that physician immigration be restricted. Fewer doctors, like fewer hospital beds, surely does mean lower costs. Combined with "physician-extender" programs it may not mean fewer services. Thus the escalation of medical costs could be limited to that generated by the income aspirations of current physicians and future Canadian graduates.

Income aspirations of physicians seem to be somewhat muted at present, partly because of large gains in the 1960's, but also because the last five years have seen an outpouring of public and private opinion that "something" should be done about the private practice, fee-for-service mode of medical care delivery. Just as this form of medical care delivery seems to make rationalization of hospital use almost impossible, so it stands in the way of achieving limitations on medical costs. The root of the problem is that while fee-for-service creates incentives for unnecessary care, private practice blocks any information channel which would enable a regulatory agency to determine necessity (or even the accuracy of the billing). The best that can be done is to identify "unusual" patient or provider patterns. Fifty, or 90 percent of tonsillectomies may be unnecessary, but which ones? And who has authority or ability to decide? Attempts to achieve public accountability for medical care delivery fail before the enormous information advantage possessed by the physician. It is exactly the same problem which made the private market useless as a regulatory device.

The recommended solution in Canada is some form of public organization, owning facilities and hiring physicians tied into a much more complete network of patient information. The label attached is usually "Community Health Center" though the name means something different to almost everyone using it. These centers are expected to combine conventional medical practice with a more general social and public health concern; the centers will not be dependent on fee for service, and will be nonprofit. The concept of the community health center is also quite far down the road as a system of medical care delivery, and the road itself is far from clear. Nevertheless, almost every group which has studied the Canadian health insurance system agrees that we cannot stay where we are. Insurance changes only the demand side of health care, the supply side is crucial. The hardest part of the job lies ahead.

FOOTNOTES

1. The federal publication *Health Services in Canada 1973,* Ottawa: Department of National Health and Welfare, 1973, which summarizes the national programs opens its first sentence by referring to the British North America Act. This publication, issued annually in previous years as *Health*

and Welfare Services in Canada is a good overview of the general provisions of the provincial hospital and medical programs as well as the direct service programs of the federal government. In earlier years it also provides a statistical sketch of the hospital system at a point in time, amplifying material in the annual Canada Year Book published by the Dominion Bureau of Statistics.

2. The federal government pays 25 percent of each province's own per capita cost for covered hospital services, plus 25 percent of the national average per capita cost of such services, plus 50 percent of the national average per capita cost of covered medical services, all multiplied by the provincial population.

3. A brief history of the development of health insurance in Canada is provided by Taylor, Malcolm G., The Canadian Health Insurance Program, *Public Administration Review,* Vol. 33, No. 1 (Jan.-Feb., 1973). Other brief descriptions are Hastings, J.E.F., Federal-Provincial Insurance for Hospital and Physician's Care in Canada, *International Journal of Health Services,* Vol. 1, No. 4, 1971; Kohn, R., Medical Care in Canada, in *International Medical Care,* Fry, J. and Farndale, W.A.J., eds.), Medical and Technical Publishing Co., Oxford, 1972; and Ruderman, A. P., The Organization and Financing of Medical Care in Canada in *Health Services Financing,* British Medical Association, London, 1970. Hastings tends to focus relatively more on current administrative questions and on the impact of health insurance on other health and social services and the organization of health personnel; Kohn provides a current snapshot description of health services, insured or uninsured, which tends to cover the "official" features with limited analysis; Ruderman in his description discusses the relatively limited role of price and income effects in the Canadian system and argues that the private market economy approach is not and never was particularly relevant. A more extensive history of the pre-Medicare nonprofit comprehensive insurance plans from which Medicare evolved is Shillington, C. H., *The Road to Medicare in Canada,* Del Graphics, Toronto, 1972. Symposia on the hospital system include the Sept. 16, 1962 issue of *Hospitals,* Vol. 35, No. 18, and *Medical Care,* Vol. 7, No. 6 Supplement (Nov./Dec., 1969). The cornerstones of description in this field are, of course, the *Report of the Royal Commission on Health Services* (Hall Commission), The Queen's Printer, Ottawa, 1964; and supporting studies, the *Report of the Commission d'Enquête sur la Santé et le Bien-Être Social* (Castonguay-Nepveu Commission), Gouvernement de Quebec, Quebec, 1970), and supporting studies; the *Report of the Ontario Committee on the Healing Arts,* The Queen's Printer, Toronto, 1970, and supporting studies; the *Task Force Reports on Costs of Health Care in Canada,* The Queen's Printer, Ottawa, 1969. Someone, somewhere, may have read all this. John

Evans suggests that Canadians spend more time and effort studying health care than most other countries do delivering it. Physicians in a Public Enterprise, *Journal of Medical Education,* Vol. 48, No. 11 (Nov., 1973). The present author strives to uphold that tradition.

4. Taylor, The Canadian Health. . .

5. It must be recalled, of course, that standards of services cannot be measured only by expenditure. The dramatic increases in provider incomes, physicians and hospital workers (see below), which have been the principal quantitative effect of health insurance have tended to even out provincial differentials. Thus health providers have moved faster up the wage structure in poorer provinces, without any observable associated improvement in health status. In medical care, however, much of this behavior predated the federal legislation–see Evans, R. G., *Price Formation in the Market for Physician Services 1957-69,* The Queen's Printer, Ottawa, July, 1972, Ch. 3.

6. These terms are spelled out in more detail in the annual *Health Services in Canada.* The hospital program required participating provinces to sign an agreement with the federal government, detailing licensing, inspection, and supervision requirements and federal audit. These requirements were not imposed in the medical care plan either, as Taylor suggests, because of provincial objections to federal intervention, or because public regulation of physicians is a much more contentious issue than regulation of hospitals!

7. Administrative costs have certainly been held down–in 1971 prepayment and administration of health plans cost Canadians $5.54 per capita compared with $12.83 in the U.S.; total health expenditures per capita are $306.11 and $386.92, *National Health Expenditures in Canada 1960-71,* Canada, Department of National Health and Welfare, Ottawa, 1973. (Both countries, of course, bury compliance costs in provider budgets, but it seems likely that compliance costs are also lower given a uniform national system). The bargain looks a little different, of course, when one discovers that the existing system of administration does not generate data sufficient to understand or control operating expense. But at least the U.S. is no better off.

8. The nub of the problem appears to be the desire of the federal government to turn over tax revenues which will initially yield revenues higher than current health costs but will grow less rapidly (alcohol and tobacco levies). The provinces prefer a larger income tax share, since the income elasticity of this tax will keep pace with past rates of cost increase. The federal authorities note that their plan provides incentives to rationalize delivery at the provincial level, as well as initial resources to support change; the

provinces argue that this scheme imposes all the risks of cost containment on them (as well as the political unpopularity).

9. Moreover, revenues collected in this manner are subtracted from shareable costs, making them "50¢ dollar" revenues from a provincial standpoint.

10. Beck, R. G., *The Demand for Physicians' Services in Saskatchewan,* Doctoral dissertation, University of Alberta, 1971. The charge also lowered use among large families and aged-head families, and was politically unpopular. The liberal government which imposed it was defeated in 1971 and the charge removed by the incoming N.D.P.

11. This is not solidly established, but emerges in several studies, e.g. Beck, *The Demand* . . . in Saskatchewan shows a steady weakening in the relation between income and utilization after Medicare. Enterline, P.E. *et al.,* The Distribution of Medical Services before and after 'Free' Medical Care–The Quebec Experience, *New England Journal of Medicine,* 289:22, Nov. 29, 1973, report a shift in number of visits, up for lower income families, down for upper income families, zero net change. Badgley, R.E. *et al.,* The Impact of Medicare in Wheatville, Saskatchewan, 1960-65, *Canadian Journal of Public Health,* 58:3, March, 1967, show evidence of a similar shift, although less concrete in the absence of visit data.

12. Anne Scitovsky has correctly pointed out that while this paper identifies sources of expenditure increase in insured health care and relates them to increased provider incomes, it does not establish that these developments are a result of national health insurance. In some sense one could never establish this–who knows what would have happened? But it is true that while a short-run expenditure response to national insurance is identifiable in both hospital and medical care, the responses of provider incomes are less clear-cut. The hospital response, if it is that, has a long lag; while the physician response on the contrary may be merely a speeding up of long-run trends which would have happened anyway. If this all sounds a little *ad hoc,* it is. I've also changed some of the hospital wage numbers and their explanation; I regret undercutting Anne's comments but it made a better paper!

13. If is of course true that relative earnings of health care providers rose prior to the public insurance plans as well–to what extent this was due to the spread of private insurance no one knows.

14. A detailed description of the reporting data is available in a pair of booklets published annually by the Dominion Bureau of Statistics and the Department of National Health and Welfare, *Instructions and Definitions*

for the Annual Return of Hospitals Form HS-1 Facilities and Services and *Form HS-2 Financial.*

15. In Quebec the medical association collects additional data from each practitioner on auxiliary personnel employed, hours of work, and distribution by activity of hours of work. Analysis of the relationships between practice characteristics, physician characteristics, and pattern of workload is now being carried out by Contandriopoulos, A. P., and Lance, J. M., Modele de Prévision de la Main-D'Oeuvre Medicale Document de Travail No. 8, McGill University, May, 1974. The authors express some reservations about the quality of the practice characteristic data.

16. Some efforts have been made to carry out such estimates, e.g. Evans, R. G., "Behavioral Cost Functions for Hospitals," *Canadian Journal of Economics,* Vol. IV, No. 2, May, 1971 and Evans, R. G. and Walker, H. D., Information Theory and the Analysis of Hospital Cost Structure, *Canadian Journal of Economics,* Vol. V, No. 3, August, 1972.

17. This view was still being urged in 1969, see Canada, Department of National Health and Welfare, *Task Force Reports on the Costs of Health Services in Canada,* Vol. III, pp. 170-182. That particular report, on Medical Prices, seemed more concerned with physician autonomy.

18. Thus in 1970 the British Columbia Medical Association promulgated a new fee schedule. The province declared it too high, and said that the plan would not pay it. The profession replied that its members would collect the increase from patients. The government advised patients not to pay, and published (by name) each physician's gross receipts from the plan in the newspapers. The profession thereupon lowered its schedule and a compromise was adopted; but it worked to defeat the government at the next election. In nost provinces the process is less open.

19. This is an implication of empirical research in British Columbia, Evans, R.G. *et al.,* Medical Productivity, Scale Effects, and Demand Generation, *Canadian Journal of Economics,* Vol. VI, No. 3, August, 1973. It has also been commented on by informed observers, e.g. John Evans, "Physicians in . . . "

20. This was expressed as a positive goal in the Hall Commission Health Charter for Canada, "Based on freedom of choice, and upon free and self-governing professions," Report of the Royal Commission . . . pp. 11-12.

21. These comparisons also illustrate the dangers of interpreting share movements. 1961 was a recession year, so personal income was down and

the jump in hospital share was accentuated. The long boom of the early sixties held the physician share nearly constant from 1961 to 1966; only when the growth of the economy slowed did physicians' share move up again.

22. Canadian hospital accounts do not include employee benefits in gross salaries and wages but classify these as "supplies and other expense." These amount to about 9 percent of the total budget in recent years. (Note that hospital budgets include little or no capital expense.) In 1969, radiologist and pathologist remuneration was transferred from "supplies and expense" to "gross salaries and wages"; this amounts to about 2.5 percent of total budget and has been transferred back to supplies and expense in this paper for consistency. The 1971 data also reflect an exclusion from hours worked of intern and resident time and classroom hours, thus biasing downward the change in hours per patient day from 1965 to 1971. The effect appears, however, to be quantitatively insignificant (of the order of .2 to .3 hours per patient day).

23. One study has been conducted which attempts to examine wage change by employment category within the hospital labor force and relate such changes to wages in similar occupations elsewhere in the economy: Canada, Department of National Health and Welfare Research and Statistics Memo, *Salaries and Wages in Canadian Hospitals 1962 to 1970* Ottawa, n.d. (1971). This source draws on data from the Department of Labor as well as D.B.S. and N.H.W. Unfortunately the longest data span assembled is 1962 to 1969, and in this case the 1969 data are contaminated by failure to include a major subsequent retroactive agreement in Quebec in 1970. The report is carefully documented and extremely honest about its limitations; it does show that by 1969 hospital employees in such service trade occupations as cooks, laundry workers, maids, and seamstresses were paid well above their private industry counterparts. But its coverage both cross-sectionally and over time is far too limited to support any general conclusions.

24. Saskatchewan, typically, tried out a variety of innovative approaches in the 1940's long before anyone else had considered the problem. See Roth, B. *et al.* The Saskatchewan Experience in Payment for Hospital Care, *American Journal of Public Health,* Vol. 43, No. 6, June, 1953.

25. Although in calculating, e.g. savings to be achieved by reduced utilization of acute inpatient facilities, this distinction may be forgotten by exponents of alternative programs.

26. On one occasion, however, the Minister of Health in British Columbia simply refused to pay all of negotiated wage increases and forced hospitals

to find the differential by cutting staff or using their own revenue sources (e.g., the preferred accommodation differential). The policy was monumentally unpopular, and it is asserted that hospitals merely ran up their lengths of stay, but there is some evidence that it slowed cost trends.

In Quebec the provincial government has participated directly in wage negotiations since 1966.

27. Evans, "Behavioural" Cost Functions . . . and Evans and Walker, "Information Theory. . . .

28. *Ibid.* These findings relate to aggregate hospital budgets. Some provinces, notably Quebec, are using cross-hospital sub-indices, such as dollars per pound of laundry processed, as control devices to identify and place administrative pressure on hospitals which are above average on these direct departmental costs. This may simply lead back to standardizing the internal structure of hospital budgets–uniform inefficiency again.

29. A cynic might fear that better managers in the existing structure might make the problem worse–they'll simply negotiate better for more money!

30. Evans, R. G., and Robinson, G. C., *An Evaluation of the Economic Implications of a Day Care Surgery Unit,* Final Report, N.H.W. Grant #610-21-14, Vancouver, October 1973.

31. Feldstein, M., An Econometric Model of the Medicare System, *Quarterly Journal of Economics,* Vol. 85, No. 1, February, 1971, reports that extended care facilities raise costs per hospital *episode*–what is saved on lower acute care stays is lost in long extended care stays.

32. McPhee, J. L., *Community Health Association Clinics,* Saskatchewan Department of Public Health, Regina; August 1973, and Hastings, J.E.F. *et al.* Prepaid Group Practice in Sault Ste. Marie, Ontario: Part I," *Medical Care,* March-April, 1973.

33. The *locus classicus* is the *Rapport du Commission d'Enquête . . .* (Castonguay Commission). The federal equivalent was the Community Health Center Project, directed by J.E.F. Hastings, which reported to the Council of Health Ministers in July of 1972 and supported the C.H.C. concept strongly. More recently the Report of the British Columbia Health Security Program Project (Victoria: December, 1973) also endorsed the C.H.C. idea.

34. The nonprofits on which the national program was modelled, provincially

based but affiliated as Trans Canada Medical Plans, covered 30 percent of the population in 1967 (adding in the population of Saskatchewan which had a universal public plan since 1962). Coverage was, however, proportionally much higher in the western provinces. Moreover most of the population had *some* medical coverage, although private insurance plans were more likely to limit coverage to inhospital care and/or impose copayment features. With reference to the role of insurance in expanding demand for care, the TCMP plans had an average cost per insured of $34.95 in 1967, compared with a national average of $33.63 for medical expenditures of all Canadians. Moreover, TCMP subscribers were concentrated in high-cost provinces. See Evans, *Price Formation* . . . Ch. 2, or Trans Canada Medical Plans, *Annual Enrollment Experience and Annual Financial and Statistical Experience Report, 1967 Year* (mimeo), July 1968.

35. The indices are current-weighted composites derived from a sample of key items in each provincial fee schedule, with the size of the sample growing over time. By contrast the C.P.I. Component (discontinued after Medicare) was a base-weighted index of prices of four procedures performed by general practitioners in urban areas, measured by telephone survey. For further discussion, see Evans, R.G., *Price Formation* . . . Ch. 1 and appendix 1-2, where it is also shown that although the proportion of specialists in Canada rose from 35 percent in 1957 to just over 50 percent, the impact of this change on measured prices is almost certainly less than 10 percent over all.

36. The table suggests that this "quantity" increase has accelerated since Medicare, but the 1971 increase is distorted by the massive effects of the introduction of the Quebec program. In that province average gross incomes of physicians jumped 38.9 percent, 1971 over 1970, and net incomes were up 50.1 percent. Expenses of practice rose 8.6 percent on average. This leads to the suspicion that there was substantial under-reporting of income in Quebec prior to 1971.

37. There are a few conceptual discrepancies in moving from physicians to physician services. See *Earnings of Physicians . . . 1961-71.*

38. Enterline, P. E. *et al.* The Distribution of Medical Services . . . and also MacDonald, A. D. *et al.* Physician Service in Montreal Before Universal Health Insurance, *Medical Care,* Vol. XI, No. 4, July-August 1973.

39. Evans, *Price Formation* . . . Ch. 4.

40. Regie de l'Assurance-Maladie du Quebec, *Annual Statistics 1972,* Quebec: n.d.

41. This whole paragraph is in response to Anne Scitovsky's comment that this paper really says more about the forces driving expenditure increase than about the role of health insurance, and that its treatment of the impact of insurance on physician incomes was inconsistent. I have attempted to rationalize the inconsistency; but I confess I do not know the answer.

42. Within British Columbia, however, the effects of differing physician density across regions on regional provider incomes seem to have been almost entirely (about 85 percent) wiped out by variations in practice patterns; Evans *et al.* "Medical Productivity, Scale Effects . . ."

43. This is, of course, a growing view in the U.S., Fuchs, V. and Kramer, M., *Determinants of Expenditures for Physicians' Services in the United States 1948-1968,* N.B.E.R. Occasional Paper #117, D.H.E.W. Pub. (HSM) 73-3013, Washington; December 1972, being perhaps its leading exponents. The discretionary behavior of the physician and his influence over demand emerges also in the work of M. Feldstein, U. Reinhardt, J. Newhouse, often by default.

44. Moreover, if copayment were to become large enough to reduce demand and utilization, private insurance would return . . . for the good risks.

45. Rivard, J.-Y. *La Rémuneration du Corps Médical,* Annexe 13 to the Castonguay Report, also Ch. 5 of Evans, *Price Formation . . .*

DATA SOURCES FOR TEXT TABLES

The most comprehensive data on health care costs in Canada are prepared by the Health Economics and Statistics Directorate of the Department of National Health and Welfare, Government of Canada. Their personal health care concept, generally speaking, covers all health care expenditures which are, or prior to the public medical and hospital plans were, made by persons from family budgets, payments to hospitals, physicians, dentists and for prescription drugs. It excludes public health, research, and educational expenditures on health care, but does include governmental expenditures on special category hospitals. Research charged to a hospital budget is included in PHC, but only operating costs are included, not capital expenditures.

The Personal Health Care (PHC) concept also excludes health expenditures not directed by the health care provider "establishment," such as nonprescription drugs, eyeglasses and appliances, services of health professionals outside hospitals other than physicians and dentists, and nursing home care. The line between nursing homes (excluded) and private convalescent hospitals (included) becomes a little fuzzy, but is drawn on the basis of administrative arrangements. Private hospitals contracting with the provincial agency and providing insured care for all or part of their patients are included with respect to their expenditure on insured patients. The amounts involved are trivial.

Annual PHC data for Canada and provinces are published irregularly, the latest being Canada, Department of National Health and Welfare, *Expenditure on Personal Health Care in Canada,* 1960-71, Ottawa, n.d. This is the basis for Table I; pre-1960 data are from Canada, Department of National Health and Welfare, *Expenditures on Personal Health Care in Canada, 1953-61,* Health Care Series Memorandum #16, Ottawa, March, 1963. In 1960 and earlier, expenditure in hospitals run by the Department of National Defense (like private hospitals, a very small part of the Canadian hospital industry) are excluded. The earlier prescription drug series also fails to include prescribed drugs sold outside retail pharmacies–the inclusive series can be pushed back to 1957 by earlier "occasional memoranda" from Health and Welfare but the series breaks there.

A more inclusive definition of the health care industry is the basis for a new data series, recently released as Canada, Department of National Health and Welfare, *National Health Expenditures in Canada 1960-71,* Ottawa, October, 1973 (including comparative U.S. data). It adds to PHC nursing home care, nonprescription drugs, eyeglasses and other appliances, services of other health professionals outside institutions, costs of prepayment administration, voluntary organizations, research, new-facility construction, and public health activity. Some specific exclusions are made (such as Government of Canada hospital facility construction) but these are quantitatively trivial. This comprehensive series indicates that total health expenditures per capita in Canada rose from $113.50 in 1960 to $306.11 in 1971, compared with $80.53 and $236.61 for PHC. Thus the PHC percentage has risen from 71.0 percent to 77.3 percent, indicating the faster growth of the hospital and physician sectors.

Data on the physician stock and physician incomes are generated along with the health care expenditure series, and are reported in Canada, Department of National Health and Welfare, *Earnings of Physicians in Canada, 1961-1971,* Health Care Series #30, Ottawa, n.d. Earlier data are from *Earnings of Physicians in Canada 1957-1965,* Health Care Series #21, Ottawa, April, 1967. This series covers "active fee practice" physicians, those "whose main employment is in the provision of personal medical care services" and "whose professional income is mainly in the form of fees for services rendered." It thus excludes all salaried physicians providing medical care, whether in a private group practice, on a hospital staff, or in public service. In fact, however, prior to 1970 a small number of salaried physicians working in group practices were included; only those in Manitoba and Newfoundland where salaried service was quantitatively important were excluded. In 1970 all salaried group practitioners were excluded, so that the reported increase in manpower 1971 over 1970 is remarkably low. In this chapter we have added back the salaried physicians outside Manitoba and Newfoundland for 1970 and 1971 to keep the series consistent. The bracketed figures in the text tables show the effects of adding back salaried practitioners in those two provinces as well.

As a measure of the availability of physician services, the fee-practice physician is somewhat unsatisfactory. To compare service availability in e.g. Newfoundland with the national average by looking at fee practitioners only is grossly inaccurate. Similarly it appears that some of the discrepancy between Quebec and Ontario in physicians *per capita* is made up by larger teaching programs in Quebec with more hospital staff, interns, and residents supplying medical services but appearing in hospital budgets (Quebec, Commission d'Enquète sur la Santé et le Bien-etre Social *Analyse Comparative des Coûts de l'Hôspitalization au Quebec et en Ontario,* Annexe I du Rapport, Gouvernement de Quebec, Sept. 1967). Total active civilian physicians in Canada in 1971 are reported as 32,625 (Canada, Department of National Health and Welfare, *Health Manpower Inventory 1972* (Ottawa, October, 1972) but this includes administration, teaching, part-time practitioners, etc. This source, which also includes stock estimates back to 1963, merely references the Canadian Medical Directory. But another federal publication, *Health Services in Canada 1973,* produces the same figure and refers to it as prepared by the Ministry of National Health and Welfare based on data from Medical Marketing Systems Ltd. (Seccombe House) (formerly Canadian Mailings Ltd.) maintains records for the drug detail men and other medical suppliers. The Health Manpower Inventory divides this total of 32,625 into 12,566 general practitioners, 13,616 specialists, 1,257 "not in private practice" and 5,186 interns and residents, yet this implies 26,182 active practitioners or 20 percent more than the 21,895 active fee practice physicians in 1971 reported in *Earnings of Physicians*. . . when all reporting salaried practitioners are added in. No "reconciliation statement" is prepared. Moreover, no documentation is provided as to the methodology employed in the tabulation. Thus the primary official source of data on the physician stock is effectively undocumented (in contrast, e.g. to the detailed methodology available in *Earnings of Physicians* . . .). For further discussion of alternative estimates prior to the manpower inventory, see Evans, R.G., *Price Formation in the Market for Physician Services in Canada, 1957-1969,* Ottawa, 1973, esp. Ch. III and Appendix III-3.

The active fee practice series is, however, preferable as a basis for analyzing market behavior since this group sets fees and receives them, and is the provider of almost all insured care under the Medicare plan. The income series associated with this group and reported in the text has certain problems as well. It includes part-time physicians who are semi-retired, or who entered practice part way through the year. This is partly corrected by focusing on the physicians with net incomes above some arbitrary minimum. In 1971 this minimum was $15,000. Any self-employed practitioner netting less than $15,000 *cannot* be fully employed! In 1971 average gross and net incomes for this group were $61,516 and $42,624 compared with $45,824 and $39,203 for all fee practice physicians. Thus $42,624 would be a better estimate of the net earnings of a "representative" fully employed practitioner. Unfortunately, a time series of this sort is not very meaningful since it would move with the (arbitrary) choice of full-time cut-off. There are also problems in the gross income and expenses of practice data due to disentangling group practices with salaried physicians; and the investment earnings component of nonprofessional income is almost certainly understated since all data are drawn from tax returns which do not include capital gains prior to 1972. Physicians tend to invest in assets (such as medical arts buildings) yielding high capital gain but low income, and it is hard to believe that the average physician in fee practice earned only $798 from all nonfee sources in 1971, including incidental wages and salaries, given one's fragmentary knowledge of physician-owned real estate holding companies! Some of this may be picked up in 1972 and after, as half of capital gain must now be reported as income (when realized). The same sort of problem arises with expenses of practice, some of which of course reemerge as investment income. Still, it is doubtful if these factors influence trends over time to any great degree.

The physician price series for earlier years is the Consumer Price Index, physicians' fees component, prepared by the Dominion Bureau of Statistics and reported in Canada, Department of National Health and Welfare, Research and Statistics Memo, *Health Care Price Movements,* Ottawa, April 1968. The overall CPI is from Canada, Dominion Bureau of Statistics, *Canadian Statistical Review: Historical Summary 1970,* Ottawa, August 1972. Updating of statistics in this issue was from the February 1974 issue of the *Canadian Statistical Review* (monthly). All population data (June first annual data) and average weekly and hourly wage data are drawn from these sources.

The Consumer Price Index had relatively limited coverage, fees for office visits, home visits, an obstetrical confinement, and an appendectomy as reported by six general practitioners in each metropolitan area to a semiannual telephone survey. It was phased out city by city as Medicare spread across the provinces. The Department of National Health and Welfare also prepares an index of provincial fee schedules, starting in December 1963, which in earlier years might differ substantially from fees charged to uninsured patients. As each province entered Medicare, this index was shifted from a listed fees to a benefits paid basis (since many provinces pay less than 100 percent of the schedule or impose administrative limitations). These data are unpublished, but were generously supplied by the Health Economics and Statistics Division, Health Programs Branch, National Health and Welfare. A compound index was constructed using the CPI index to 1964, the N.H.W. fee schedule index to 1968 or whenever each province entered Medicare, and the N.H.W. benefits paid index thereafter. The 1965 overlap between CPI and NHW was used to link these two series (the CPI is Laspeyres, the NHW Paasche) and the second point of linkage was implicit in the N.H.W. procedure which reports only month, year, and size of percentage increase in fee or benefit schedule from December 1963 to the present by province. Until 1970, however, when Quebec entered Medicare, Quebec general practitioners had no fee schedule. Hence the Canada average fee benefit schedule is a weighted average of the nine other provinces. An index of total expenditure on physicians' services can then be derived from the personal health care data and compared to changes in listed prices or benefits to indicate the extent to which listed fees account for changes in total expenditure. A similar sort of comparison can be made between list prices and physician gross receipts.

The primary source of hospital data is the set of *Hospital Statistics* volumes published annually by the Dominion Bureau of Statistics. Hospital reporting by D.B.S. began in 1932 but in 1952 a new and more extensive reporting system was introduced and the reports expanded to two volumes. Since then, the structure and content of the reports has changed, but the volume of data collected has steadily expanded. Until now seven volumes have been published annually in addition to Mental and Tuberculosis Hospital statistics and numerous occasional studies on manpower and salaries.

In dealing with the text data, a number of points must be kept in mind. First of all, "general and allied special hospitals" in the D.B.S. data excludes all private hospitals since these do not report the same detailed federal returns. In the total personal health care expenditure, however, National Health and Welfare includes any private hospital providing care under contract with a provincial agency. The discrepancy is not large, but is just enough to keep the numbers inconsistent! Data on number of hospitals and number of beds in the text are taken from Canada, D.B.S., *Hospital Statistics Vol. I–Hospital Beds 1971*, Ottawa, November, 1973, historical data pp. 46-50. Patient days are adult and child only, and include chronic, convalescent, rehabilitation and other specialty. Patient days per thousand population were calculated by taking the reported average daily number of patients for each year, multiplying by 365 (or 366) and dividing by national population. Admissions per thousand population were calculated by dividing reported total admissions by population. The ratio of the two does not equal reported mean stay per separation (discharge or death), presumably because in an expanding hospital sector, admissions systematically outran separations in every year.

This may not be the whole explanation; a number of small arithmetic discrepancies turn up in this vast array of data; particularly in earlier years. As noted in the text, total hospital beds in general and allied special hospitals seem to be undercounted in 1961. Data on p. 33 of *Hospital Beds, 1971* suggest that in 1961 about 1800 chronic, convalescent, and rehabilitation beds were shifted to mental, and "restored" the following year.

Costs per patient day in the text always refer to total expenditures per adult and child patient day, excluding newborns. Earlier data sources often include newborns, whole- or part-weighted. Cost per day back to 1956 is reported on pp. 28-30 of Canada, D.B.S., *Hospital Statistics Vol. VI: Hospital Expenditures 1971*, Ottawa, October, 1973. For the earlier years, data were taken from *Hospital Statistics, Vol. II Expenditure* for each year. Reconstructing these data, however, must take into account that prior to 1956 *net* expenditure per patient day was reported, excluding courtesy rebates to staff and revenue from nurses' board. Reported patient-day costs from, e.g., p. 89, Col. 5 of the

1953 publication ($11.95) have been adjuted up by the ratio of gross to net (p. 105), and similarly in 1954 and 1955. The 1953 total was then allocated by class of expenditure using the proportions in *Hospital Statistics, Vol. II,* p. 88; wages and salaries, drugs, etc. No allocation by department was possible since throughout the 1950's reporting procedures permitted a very large "undistributed expenditure" component which was nearly a fifth of the total. The breakdown in 1971 used data reported in Tables 30-33 of Canada, D.B.S., *Hospital Statistics, Vol. VII: Hospital Indicators 1971,* Ottawa, August, 1973; Table 18 provided paid hours data to compare with the hours data in Table 31 of *Hospital Statistics Vol. I, 1953.* Historical length of stay and occupancy data came from *Hospital Statistics Vol. I: 1971,* while all 1953 and 1971 disaggregated expenditure data came from *Hospital Statistics, Vol. VI, 1971, and Vol. II, 1953.*

Data for the subperiods between 1953 and 1971 are much less comprehensive than one would like, because reporting categories and definitions kept changing so as to make the construction of long and consistent series on the internal expenditure components of hospitals rather difficult. Gross salaries and wages and paid hours are drawn from the 1953 *Hospital Statistics Vol. II.* For 1959, 1965, and 1971 gross salaries and wages are drawn from *Hospital Statistics Vol. VI.* Expenditures and paid hours derive from *Hospital Statistics Vol. VII, Indicators.* Data on numbers and wages of professional and technical employees for 1961-68 are taken from a series of twelve occasional papers published by D.B.S. *Health Manpower in Hospitals 1961-68,* first *general* and then covering each of eleven specific occupations and reporting *inter alia* the share of total hospital budgets made up by their wages. Wages per paid hour by occupation in 1971 are from Canada, Dominion Bureau of Statistics, *Hospital Indicators January, June 1971,* Ottawa, October 1971. This was based on the quarterly survey but not reproduced in the annual volume.

The general principles followed in data preparation were first to emphasize construction of consistent series over time, and second to choose data concepts as closely as possible related to potential insurance responses or behavior. There is a huge quantity of statistical data on hospitals which could be used to show the responses of detailed hospital budgets, where shifts took place after the insurance programs were introduced; but such a project was well beyond the resources available for this paper. The Department of National Health and Welfare has made a good beginning with its *Sources of Increase in Budget Review Hospital Expenditures in Canada 1961 to 1971,* Ottawa, December, 1973; it is to be hoped that this will be pushed back to pre-insurance days and expanded in detail. It would also be helpful if federal statisticians could spend some time on indicating the appropriate reconciliation of sources, where possible. So far, generating the numbers has tended to outrun either documentation or reconciliation, but the trends appear favorable.

Acknowledgment

This paper owes a great deal to initial discussions with Uve Reinhardt, and was initially presented in a slightly different form at the conference on the role of health insurance in the health services sector held at Rochester, New York, May 31 and June 1, 1974. At the conference the discussants, Herbert Klarman and Anne Scitovsky, were both very helpful as were Victor Fuchs, Lee Soderstrom, and other participants. Their improving influence should be obvious; the rest is mine.

DISCUSSION

PETER J. BANKS: First, I would like to underline a statement made by Dr. Maurice LeClair in the first chapter. In his retrospective analysis he states that, "more participation in decision-making by those affected by the decision, such as the providers of health insurance and the consumers, would have prevented many problems." The provision of a suitable system of health care insurance needs the cooperation of the providers. Administrators tend to administer by fiat. It is essential that a *consultative partnership* be developed between the providers and the administrators at an early stage so that both can understand each other's viewpoint in providing the common goal of the high standards of care at a reasonable cost to the people. Where this essential partnership has broken down in Canada we have experienced serious troubles up to the withdrawal of professional services. In these disastrous confrontations neither side emerges the winner and, even if it takes months of negotiating, it is essential that they be avoided.

At the present time in Canada we have evolved a system of health care insurance for all the people. Obviously, it needs improvement. The doctors are not convinced that it needs the radical surgery that some would advocate, but the problems are obvious to all and we are anxious for the right answers.

Professor Robert Evans' chapter is an excellent economic commentary and it is refreshing that, on several occasions in it, he acknowledges he has no answers. This is a change from many economic commentators who, to use his own words, "proceed to give the data a vigorous massage" so that they fit with their own preconceived ideas. The problems, however, are too profound for dogmatism and it is through discussion that constructive solutions are more likely to emerge. To quote Hippocrates, "Life is short and the art long, the occasion fleeting, experience fallacious and judgment difficult."

Dr. Evans starts by saying we really don't have a national health service because of the British North America Act, which gives the provinces autonomy in the health field. I believe this is excellent. In a big country like Canada and like the United States, differences in local needs are profound, as are the local resources to meet those needs. In Canada the decentralization of the federally funded system into 10 separate administrative approaches, gives us 10 separate ways of solving the problems. This ongoing experiment is especially important as we do not know all the answers to the best administrative approach. Our biggest problem, as Dr. Evans has pointed out in his essay, is one of escalating costs (Table 1).

TABLE 1
EXPENDITURE PER PERSON ON PERSONAL HEALTH CARE

	1960 ($)	Annual Increase (%)	1970 ($)
Hospitals	47.18	10.7	130.21
Physicians	19.82	9.3	48.09
Dentists	6.12	7.5	12.57
Prescribed Drugs	7.32	6.8	14.07
TOTAL	$80.44	9.8%	$204.94

The questions he asks are: a) How did this come about? b) Is it justified? c) How are we going to pay these costs? d) Can we evolve a better system?

How did it come about? Evans justly criticizes the statistics available from Canadian hospitals. I am certain these could be improved. But figures, however complete, never tell the whole truth. I am reminded of the economist who arrived at a river and was told that the average depth was 2.9 feet. He walked across and was drowned. Not necessarily a bad thing, but in this sphere Dr. Evans' conclusions are correct. First, he proves that the labor force composition within hospitals has changed dramatically. This is not surprising because in Canada at that time we saw the development within hospitals of coronary care units, intensive care units, units for renal dialysis, and open heart surgery, while the whole field of arteriography blossomed. This will get worse. Medicine will become more costly and more complicated, both in and out of hospitals, and escalating costs in both fields are inevitable.

Secondly, Dr. Evans is at some pains to show that hospital workers' wages went up faster than wages in other fields. This is undoubtedly true. The starting baseline was low. There was without doubt a change in attitude as government assumed responsibility for payment. This could be seen very clearly in one of the hospitals in which I work, which used to be owned by religious Sisters. The change from "The Sisters can't afford it" to "The Government has plenty of money to pay us a fair wage" was very striking. In addition, unionization of hospital workers has proceeded apace. Unions were first developed to obtain for workers a fair share in the open marketplace. They were very necessary and have achieved tremendous social gains. But the underlying assumption was that if workers obtained too much, the enterprise for which they worked might become bankrupt. When institutions become nationalized, the situation changes dramatically. Essential institutions such as hospitals cannot be allowed to go bankrupt. Administrators and politicians always have to settle and as they prefer peace, they tend to settle high. We have seen this in Canada on many occasions with seaway workers, airline workers, grain handlers, in addition to hospital workers. As everybody knows, the situation in the nationalized industries of Great Britain was such as to bring the government down. I believe that the problem of union demands in essential industries which are payrolled by governments, is one of the great social problems that the twentieth century has still to solve, and we can certainly see the results of this problem in the hospital cost figures.

Is it justified? I would comment with Robert Evans that the escalation of costs is not justified. As we have pointed out in Canada, we made a mistake of bringing in hospital insurance before medical costs were covered. This had the effect of making doctors and patients concentrate too much on hospitals. The patients were often admitted merely for investigation and we have had some difficulty in reversing this tendency. Second, in Canada we experienced, as you have in the United States, the effects of local pride which tends to construct too many beds. This was particularly seen in the Province of Quebec. Some beds have been closed or reallocated to less acute modes of care. Third, we had no alternative accommodation that was jointly funded by federal-provincial sharing. This includes home care programs, ambulatory care units and chronic care hospitals. This is slowly being corrected. Fourth, we suffered, as the United States has suffered, from the duplication of facilities. The concept of regionalization is accepted, but it means sacrifice by institutions that are to give up facilities, and this is sometimes very difficult to obtain without confrontation. There is also the possibility of abuse of hospital facilities by doctors. To offset this, we have developed across Canada The Specialist Register of the Royal College of Physicians and Surgeons of Canada, which covers all specialty fields. Credentials committees are set up in all the large hospitals to make certain that only those qualified can do the specialist work. However, this tends to break down in smaller, rural hospitals where there is a necessity for emergency work. Tissue committees and record committees are common all across Canada but the difficulty here is that what is on the piece of paper, often bears little relationship to what is going on in bed.

We have in various parts of Canada, entered into an extensive program of PAS Review. The problem here is that statistics must be translated from figures into something readable by the medical staff. We have found it necessary to develop systems of bed review by the staff of hospitals. The way this usually works is that the admitted patients are given a predicted day stay depending on the admitting diagnosis. Should this be exceeded, the nursing staff informs the rotating duty doctor who contacts the attending doctors to find out why the case is being held in hospital. This procedure is time consuming but very well worthwhile and it is very educative for the staff to do it for themselves. It is also much more acceptable than if it were done by some nonclinical administrator.

Finally, in Canada we have a system of hospital accreditation which demands certain standards but again, this breaks down in smaller hospitals where there are only a handful of doctors who are unable to form all the necessary committees of supervision realistically among themselves.

I would also state that it is very hard for a doctor to discipline his colleagues when he is working with those colleagues on a day-to-day basis. However altruistic he is, these difficulties are compounded when the doctors to be disciplined are also those that are likely to refer him cases.

How are we going to pay these costs? Dr. Evans in his essay calls premiums a retrogressive poll tax. I would suggest that you do not throw them away too readily. In British Columbia a very reasonable premium provides 52 percent of the costs of our plan and in Ontario, to quote the Mustard Report, "Premiums generate $520,000,000 a year. It is unlikely that they will be discontinued." Our experience with premiums is that group collections at the source of payment often as part of union agreements is a very effective way of raising funds. The difficulty of premiums falling more heavily on the poor can easily be overcome without any cumbersome means of testing. In British Columbia those paying no income tax merely sign the back of a card. Then their premiums are paid for them by the government, up to 90 percent. In an era of computer consciousness, it is surprising how little dishonesty is encountered in this simple device. Should all the costs be taken out of general revenue, they can only come from corporation taxes and income taxes which will be passed back to the people as an increase in their cost of living. This is the problem of inflation and surely the poor are hit harder by inflation than they are by subsidized premiums.

Deterrents: Both Dr. LeClair and Dr. Evans have stated that deterrent fees are a dead issue in Canada. Following the Saskatchewan experience this is true at the present time, but it is my feeling that in the decades ahead they will be brought back as an attempt to hold down costs. But they will always be politically unpopular. *I would, therefore, suggest very strongly that if the United States is going to put in any deterrent or responsibility or cost-sharing mechanisms into a future national health insurance scheme, it should do it at the start.* To do it as a remedy for cost control, is politically difficult and likely to become a political football kicked out of bounds by succeeding administrations and legislators looking for popularity.

Can we evolve a better system? To consider this question properly, we must, with Dr. Evans, leave the hospital field and consider the whole arena of medical care. Several times in his essay he states that the doctors have a naive medico-technical view of disease. We have been telling people for years not to smoke, not to eat too much, not to drink too much, to wear seat belts, to take exercise and to choose the right grandparents. We, the doctors, will go on advising people to do this, but I am glad that I am not in the position to order people to do this as I would be if I were a part of the government bureaucracy. Anybody who has visited the People's Republic of China and seen the compulsory exercise programs, must be impressed by their medical advantages but appalled by the utter disregard of the individual's freedom of choice to participate or not. Dr. Evans' essay, on several occasions, points an accusing finger at the physicians as though they are responsible for the escalating health costs. As Dr. LeClair has already pointed out, the utilization figures show that doctors are in fact being responsible and that patient utilization is falling per active physician. Obviously, the overall costs are increasing at their usual rate because of newer techniques, newer specialties and more doctors moving into the field. Let us then look at the income figures for doctors in Canada.

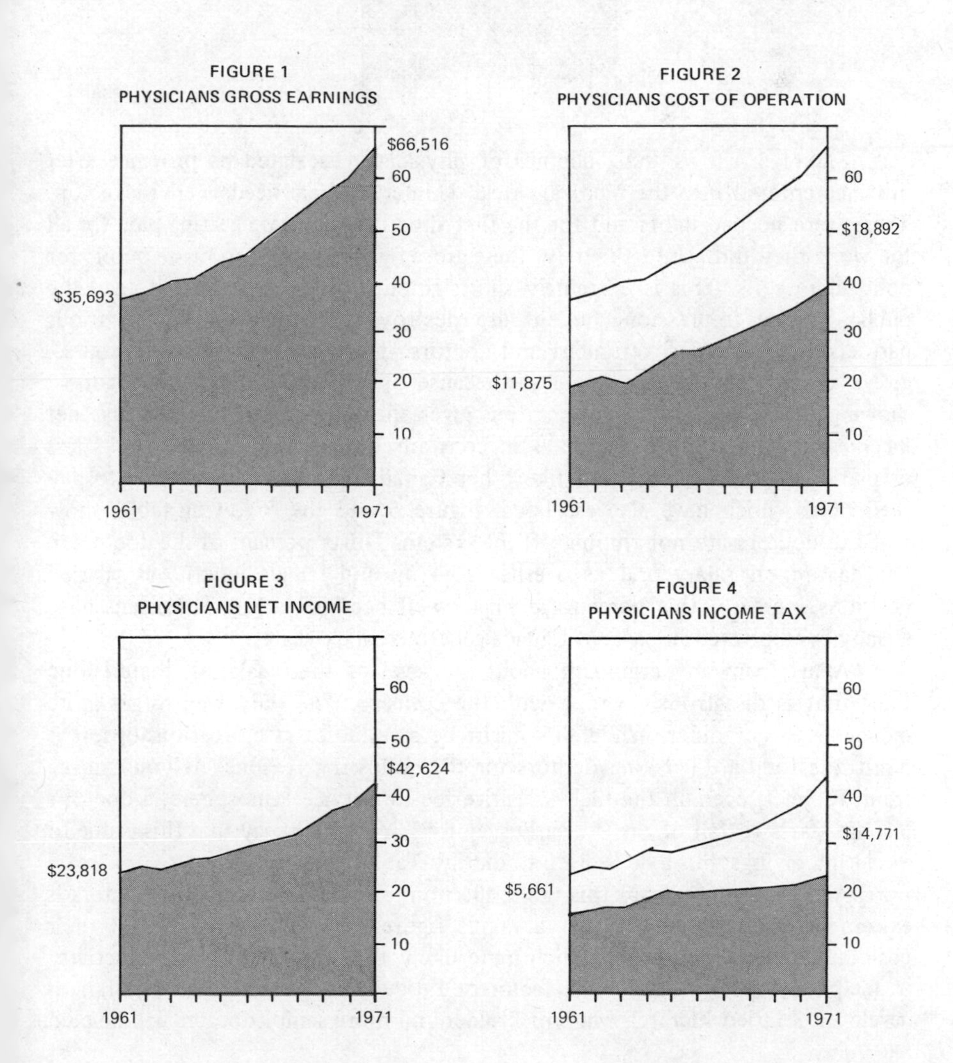

FIGURE 5
PHYSICIANS NET INCOME
IN CONSTANT 1961 DOLLARS

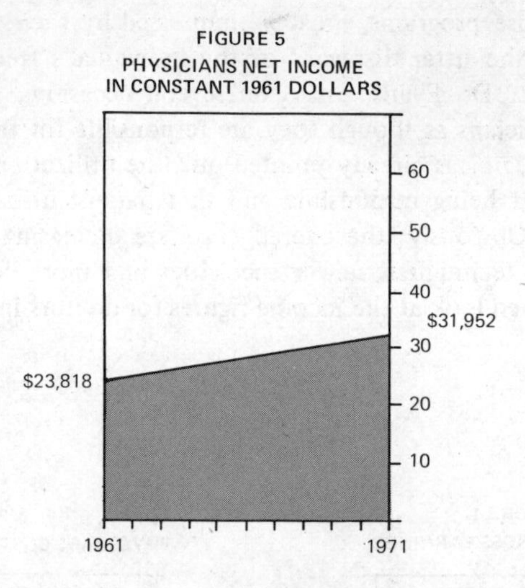

Figure 1 shows that incomes of physicians escalated as province after province entered into the Medicare field. Unmet medical needs were picked up. There were no bad debts and for the first time doctors were getting paid for all the work they did. Unfortunately, these gross figures have been made public for political reasons. This is extremely shortsighted, not only because it gives the public a false impression, but it also destroys the trust in the precarious partnership between government and doctors. Those gross incomes, of course, give a completely fallacious picture because of increasing overhead. Figure 2 showing physicians' cost of operation gives the impression of a healthy, net income increase, but in Figure 3 in constant dollars this increase looks less dramatic. Figure 4 shows that like other Canadians doctors are proud to pay their taxes which have also escalated. Figure 5 and the following tables show that the doctors are not ripping off the system. Thirty percent of the doctors in Canada are on salary and as overheads go up and fringe benefits in salaried positions increase, this percentage might well become larger. Physicians have already been offered in parts of Canada generous salary scales.

Apart from any argument about the level of these salaries, there is one thing that is disastrously wrong with the concept. The only way to get more money is to get older. While this might be a suitable system for bishops, it is disastrous for hard-working doctors for the following reasons. As you can see from Table 3, even in the high incentive fee-for-service atmosphere, a doctor's income starts to fall off at the early age of 42. You might say that this is due to escalating savings, but a lie is given to that by Table 4.

As you can see from this table, the nonprofessional income of doctors is extremely small. Often it is at a minus figure as they are paying for their postgraduate education. It is much more likely that the fall-off in productivity of fee-paying doctors reflects a factor of fatigue. But it is obviously unfair to develop a salaried hierarchy in which older and more senior doctors will be paid

TABLE 2
SUGGESTED SALARIES FOR BC PHYSICIANS
(The Foulkes Report)*

Years of Internship	Since Residency	Average Age	Annual Salary	
			GP's	Specialists
1		27	$28,000	$
2		28	30,000	
3		29	32,000	
4		30	34,000	
5	1	31	36,000	36,000
10	5	36	37,000	38,000
15	10	41	38,000	40,000
20	15	46	39,000	42,000
25	20	51	40,000	44,000
30	25	56	41,000	45,000
35	30	61	41,000	46,000
40	35	66	41,000	46,000

*Excerpted from the Foulkes Report of British Columbia.

TABLE 3
PHYSICIANS PROFESSIONAL EARNINGS BY AGE GROUP

1971	
< 35 years	$28,282
35-44	43,599
45-54	43,476
55-64	38,132
> 65	21,190

TABLE 4
PHYSICIANS NONPROFESSIONAL EARNINGS

1971		
< 35 years	+	$137.
35-44	-	354.
45-54	+	426.
55-64	+	2751.
> 65	+	5535.

more when our figures show without a doubt that it is the younger doctors who are doing most of the work.

The main problem with a salaried payment in the field of medicine is that the workload is variable. One is either paying too much for too little, or too little for too much; the latter can only lead to increased waiting lists and dissatisfaction which can be clearly illustrated in the British National Health Service at the present time. Efforts by the workers to increase their establishment after the fact of an increasing workload are usually frustrated by committees comprised of administrators all of whom are interested primarily in keeping the establishment and the resulting costs down.

The fee-for-service system, on the other hand, is a system of high incentive. The doctors are interested in doing the work that the patients are interested in having done. Their interests are parallel. In addition, it is a nonrigid system and its elasticity allows part-time workers, such as married women and doctors who are slowing down because of sickness or age, to be rewarded fairly. In Canada, two recent reports on Ontario–The Pickering Report and the Mustard Report–have both come to the realization that fee-for-service, in spite of its many disadvantages, is at the present time the only fair way of rewarding the profession.

There are, however, disadvantages. In the words of Kenneth Galbraith, doctors tend to be "self-exploitive." We have in Canada set up quality committees to see that doctors are not performing too much work in too little time so that standards fall. Profiles are developed on all physicians and are compared with their peer group. This is in contrast to the Professional Standards Review Organizations (PSRO) system in the United States which develops set patterns of health care. It must be admitted, however, that it is hard to draw a line between good, careful medical care, and abuse, and that profiles tend to hide a lot of bad doctors who are working within the average. Nevertheless, the mere fact that there is a surveillance system, can be compared with the presence of the traffic police; everybody slows down. A further disadvantage from the doctors' viewpoint of the fee-for-service system is that it is a treadmill. There is no security and no comfortable fringe benefits. If you are not working, you are not getting paid. Further, some sections of the profession are getting paid more than others. There is an obvious reason for this. Our professionally accepted fee schedules were set in the days when insurance was not universal. Many bad debts were likely to be encountered, particularly in the high cost surgical fields. Surgical fees were, therefore, set high to justify this. Now we have 100 percent coverage, some fields in medicine are earning much more than others and this cannot be justified.

Table 5 shows the results of our attempts to adjust fee schedules to make earnings more equitable between specialties. We have only been partially successful. A tentative further approach is to estimate lifetime earnings (Table 6).

Table 6 contains the only figures that are not accurate government figures

TABLE 5

INDICES—AVERAGE NET PROFESSIONAL INCOME

	1966	1971	new placing
General practice	100	100	
Orthopedics	185.2	158.1	(1)
Neurosurgery	183.8	148.1	(4)
Otology	171.9	152.7	(3)
Radiology	166.6	141.1	(9)
Plastic surgery	156.7	155.2	(2)
Urology	155.5	141.6	(7)
Ophthalmology	155.5	141.4	(8)
Thoracic surgery	150.4	144.5	(6)
General surgery	138.5	127.5	(12)
Dermatology	135.7	133.4	(10)
Obstetrics-gynecology	133.5	146.0	(5)
Pathology	129.6	131.2	(11)
Anesthesiology	119.9	111.9	(13)
Internal medicine	113.0	106.4	(15)
Psychiatry	108.1	95.4	(16)
Pediatrics	107.6	106.9	(14)
All specialists	134.5	126.7	

TABLE 6

LIFETIME EARNINGS OF PHYSICIANS

General practice	$ 950,000
Medical specialties	986,000
Surgical specialties	1,086,000
Radiology and pathology	1,373,000

and they are only approximations. I do not believe that all doctors should have the same lifetime earnings and I certainly believe that my surgical colleagues should earn more than I do as a physician. The stress of their life is greater and their period of work expectancy is shorter. But some adjustments must be made on a continuous basis. The Relative Value Fee Schedule suitably adjusted with cross bars between the surgical, the nonsurgical and the investigative groups should still be looked into and developed as a logical approach. As Dr. LeClair pointed out in Chapter 1, doctors' incomes depend on the concentration of doctors in the area. This shows clearly in our provincial averages (Table 7). Tables 8 and 9 merely illustrate what has already been pointed out—namely the falling utilization once Medicare is established.

Tables 10 and 11, developed by Dr. Robert Armstrong of the Federal Government, tend to show that as the concentration of neurosurgeons and

TABLE 7

PHYSICIANS AVERAGE INCOME BY PROVINCE, 1971

Quebec	$45,445
Alberta	44,283
Ontario	44,065
New Brunswick	43,608
Newfoundland	42,397
Manitoba	42,128
Prince Edward Island	41,380
Nova Scotia	40,087
Saskatchewan	37,026
British Columbia	33,675
Territories	32,406

TABLE 8

UTILIZATION CHANGES—NEWFOUNDLAND

	1969-70			1971-72		
	S.P.	Spec.	Total	S.P.	Spec.	Total
Services/M patients	+17.0	+3.5	+11.2	+6.4	+0.9	+4.2
Services/Physician	+ 1.7	+2.6	+ 4.3	- 1.5	- 5.6	- 3.0

TABLE 9

PHYSICIANS SERVICES UTILIZATION CHANGES 1970-71

Province	A	B	C	D	E	F	Total
Services/M patients	+4.2	+4.2	+3.4	+5.2	+0.87	+2.8	+3.0
Services/Physician	- 3.0	- 0.05	- 1.0	+0.2	- 5.7	- 1	- 2.0

TABLE 10
SERVICE SATURATION—1970

	Per 1000 Patients		Indices	
Province	Neurosurgeon	Services	Neurosurgeons	Services
A	0.0019	0.8 (maj. surg.) 7.8 (other serv.)	100	100
B	0.0063	0.9 8.0	331.6	102.6
C	0.0067	0.9 13.4	352.6	171.8
D	0.0077	1.1 9.1	405.3	116.7

TABLE 11
SERVICE SATURATION POINT—1970

	Per 1000 Patients		Indices	
Province	Neurologists	Services	Neurologists	Services
A	0.0044	12.7	100	100
B	0.0055	14.1	125	111.0
C	0.0067	15	152.3	118.1
D	0.0082	13.9	186.4	109.4

neurologists increases between Province A to Province D, the amount of work they do also increases, but there comes a point of medical saturation after which the amount of work they do will fall. This is shown in Province D. It is this state of affairs that will tend to direct those specialists to Province A where there is a low concentration of competitors. However, I am not happy about statistics of this nature because I feel that in such fields as primary health care, psychiatry, pediatrics, geriatrics, there is, in fact, no saturation level. Work will increase in direct proportion to the number of doctors. It is, therefore, in these fields that we are, in Canada, looking for cheaper substitutes to help the doctors. Where you are using Medex, we are tending to develop nurse practitioners. Dr. Evans' statistics do, however, show that more doctors means more public expenditure and, therefore, our politicians are now looking at the development of quotas of doctors in various areas and various specialties. The profession is cautious about this approach as it will modify the free competition of which we are so proud. However, some quota system will probably be necessary in the future.

What we have established is that it is quite possible to budget a fee-for-service system of health care. Table 12 shows this very clearly.

TABLE 12

MEDICARE BUDGETING, BY PROVINCE

		Estimate	Actual
Newfoundland	1969-72	$ 44,106,695	$ 42,994,891
Prince Edward Island	1970-72	4,581,410	4,901,367
Nova Scotia	1969-72	87,443,132	84,857,179
New Brunswick	1970-72	26,876,051	23,244,823
Quebec	1970-72	418,135,966	370,318,884
Ontario	1969-72	1,033,291,256	1,045,236,757
Manitoba	1969-72	149,266,477	147,422,397
Saskatchewan	1968-72	126,208,281	123,262,701
Alberta	1969-72	214,451,976	210,912,204
British Columbia	1968-72	411,095,230	411,324,505

As you can see, the difference between the estimated costs and the actual cost was usually small, and usually cheaper than the estimate. As an ex-commissioner it is with some pride that I point to the British Columbia figures of $411,000,000 estimated and spent. Costs, however, will inevitably increase and regardless of how we readjust the system, the following figures (Table 13) must give rise to disquiet.

TABLE 13

HEALTH CARE EXPENDITURE, 1957-80

Year	GNP	Income	Disposable Income
1957	3.4%	4.7%	5.1%
1966	4.8	6.5	7.3
1970	6.0	7.8	9.0
1980	9.1	11.3	13.3

You will note that by 1980 young Canadians will be expected to pay 13.3 percent of their disposable net income to care for an increasingly larger percentage of old people. Political pressures will inevitably build up. We are, therefore, looking for cheaper modes of delivery. Community health clinics are the present suggestion.

Unfortunately in Canada, our experience of these clinics has been poor. We have found that there is certainly no cost saving and there is a good deal of unnecessary lay interference which makes them extremely unpopular. Nevertheless, we are experimenting with more of these clinics and one can only hope that the statistics derived from them will be interpreted altruistically rather than by those trying to prove a point of view on one side or the other.

In recent years we have also heard the term Global Budgeting. This is a euphemism for a rationing scheme. In Canada, in my view, we made a mistake in that we *promised everything for everybody.* This is impossible. It would take the whole medical profession merely to provide adequate annual checkups. *The lesson we have learned is that once you have promised everything for everybody, it is extremely hard to take anything away.* It is, therefore, my suggestion that in the United States you should keep your options open in the realization that global budgeting is incompatible with global aspirations.

In Canada there has been some tendency to cut down on the funding of research. This surely is a disastrously shortsighted attitude because it is only by research programs that true savings can come. To cite the successful treatment of polio, tuberculosis and mental illness is not to overlook the fact that much of our treatment of the diseases of degeneration is at the present time in the expensive middle period, before research has given us the final and hopefully cheaper answers.

Doctors are quite conscious that savings are likely to be attempted by reducing their fee-for-service incomes by proration of fees. It is because of this that in province after province the doctors' associations have written agreements with governments as to how they should be paid and how the fee schedules should be changed up or down. These agreements are interesting; they are changing from year to year and they would repay attention. In British Columbia at the present time, for instance, fees can only go up according to an index derived from arriving at a mean figure between the provincial wages and salaries and the index of provincial cost of living increase. This figure is then reduced by half the corrected increase in the utilization of established medical services, thus bringing part of the responsibility for increased utilization back on the shoulders of the doctors. These agreements also cover the problems of extra billing and usually protect the patients, either by forbidding this altogether or allowing it only with prior written agreement from the patients.

Regardless of the attempted ways that we try to reduce costs by trying to adjust our health care delivery system, the contemporary evidence points only too clearly to escalating costs. It is, therefore, essential that in both Canada and the United States we try to muster the wisdom and judgment, to develop a system of medical priorities. We have to decide in which fields we will spend our limited resources. This will require judgment of the highest order and I have grave doubts whether our political system is such that these choices can be made.

Finally, I would make one further point. In Canada we have developed a system which keeps the profession relatively independent. It is of crucial importance that this professional independence be maintained. This is not so that the doctors can protect a possible vested interest, but so that they keep working for their patients, responsive to their patients' needs, advisors to, and not dictators of those who are sick. The fee-for-service system keeps the patient in the driving seat. If we were on salary we would be working for somebody else, and were that somebody a government, the interests of the government in saving money could be in direct conflict to the interests of our patients who wish money to be spent on their care.

The doctors must always be able to react against the system and to criticize on behalf of their patients. This they cannot do if they are built into the bureaucracy. And should the standards of that system degenerate to unacceptable levels, the doctors must be free to opt out of the system entirely.

As you can see, in Canada we have many problems; we have many unanswered questions but by a cooperative effort of those who administer and those who perform, all the people in Canada at the present time have their hospital and medical costs covered for very reasonable outlays of money.

CHAPTER 4 • STUART H. ALTMAN

Health Care Spending in the U.S. and Canada

National health insurance is an idea nearing birth as a program in the United States. But since we have no real experience with national health insurance within our own borders, it is extremely helpful to look elsewhere to study the experience of other countries. In this connection, I found my review of cost and expenditure trends of the Canadian health system very informative, especially when compared with the United States. In particular, Professor Robert Evans' analysis of expenditure and cost trends in Canada before and after the introduction of a national insurance system is quite revealing.

As a gross generalization, the cross-country comparison seems to suggest that major health expenditure and cost trends in Canada and the United States during the 1960s and early 1970s exhibited a very high degree of similarity. But when we go beyond the first level of comparisons, we discern significant and interesting differences in the experiences of the two countries.

Trends in expenditures

In Canada and the United States health expenditures increased rapidly and by very similar amounts during the 1960s. Between 1960 and 1971, national health expenditures in Canada rose at an annual rate of 11.8 percent; in the United States the annual increase was 11.1 percent.[1] By 1971 health care expenditures accounted for 7.1 percent of Canadian Gross National Product (GNP), while they accounted for 7.6 percent of GNP in the United States. After adjusting for the amount of nonpersonal health expenditures in the two countries, both the United States and Canada spent about 6.3 percent of their GNP on personal health care services.

*The author is currently deputy assistant secretary for health planning and evaluation, U.S. Department of Health, Education and Welfare. The views expressed here are his and do not necessarily represent the views of HEW.

The distribution of the health care dollars in the two countries, however, differs somewhat. In 1971, hospital care accounted for about 51 percent of personal health care expenditures in Canada, whereas it represented only about 42 percent of personal health care expenses in the United States. The Canadian health care system has consistently emphasized hospital care more than the United States. With the introduction of the Canadian hospital insurance program in 1958, hospital care increased as a proportion of total hospital and physician care reaching a level of 51 percent by 1968. Since 1968, with the introduction of national medical insurance and the rapid increase in spending for physician services, the hospital share declined slightly to about 50 percent.

In the United States, the largest single expansion of health insurance coverage came with the introduction of Medicare and Medicaid in 1966. Such coverage, while providing protection for both inpatient and outpatient services, tended to stress hospital care. For example, under Medicare there is both a deductible and coinsurance for physician services but only a small deductible for hospital care. This has, as might be expected, shifted United States spending more in favor of hospital care. Hospital care accounted for about 40 percent of health spending for the elderly before 1966. Once Medicare was introduced, the hospital share grew to 48 percent by 1973.

If the Canadian and Medicare experience is repeated for the entire U.S. system, the introduction of national health insurance in the United States should have a smaller effect on spending for hospital services than for ambulatory care. Currently, over 90 percent of all hospital expenditures are paid by some third party, while only 57 percent of physician services are reimbursed in such a manner (Table 1). With national health insurance, much greater third-party coverage will be available for physician services leading to more spending for

TABLE 1
DISTRIBUTION OF U.S. PERSONAL HEALTH CARE SPENDING BY SOURCE OF FUNDS AND TYPE OF EXPENDITURE FISCAL YEAR 1973

	Hospitals	Physicians	Dentists	Drugs	Other Services
Direct Payments	10%	42%	87%	87%	39%
Private Health Insurance	36	35	8	5	3
Government	53	22	5	8	6
Philanthropy	1	1	0	0	52
	100%	100%	100%	100%	100%

SOURCE: *National Health Expenditures, 1929-73,* Cooper, Worthington, Piro, Social Security Bulletin, February 1974.

such services. Even greater increases will occur for dental services and drugs if they are included in the plan finally adopted.

Physician expenditures

Expenditures for physician services have been growing more rapidly in Canada than in the United States. Currently, both countries spend about 20 percent of their total health expenditures on such care. In the U.S. total expenditures for physician services increased 97.1 percent between 1965-72. In Canada they increased 126.8 percent between 1965 and 1971.[2] Canadians have also more rapidly increased the share of personal income spent on physician services—a 45 percent increase between 1959-71, compared to 28 percent in the U.S.[3]

Table 2 shows the relative growth in spending for professional services in

TABLE 2
NATIONAL HEALTH EXPENDITURES ON PROFESSIONAL SERVICES BY TYPE OF PROFESSION, CANADA AND THE UNITED STATES

	Average annual change (percent)							
	Canada				United States			
	1960-1971	1965-1971	1969-1971	1970-1971	1960-1971	1965-1971	1969-1971	1970-1971
Physicians' services	13.0	15.0	17.4	20.1	10.2	11.0	11.4	10.0
Dentists' services	10.0	11.2	11.8	14.0	9.1	9.9	9.6	10.0
Other health professionals	8.2	9.8	7.4	5.9	6.3	7.5	10.7	9.8
All health professionals	11.9	13.8	15.5	17.9	9.7	10.5	10.9	10.0

SOURCE: *National Health Expenditures in Canada, 1960-71 with Comparative Data for the United States,* Health Program Branch, Ottawa, October 1973, Table 12.

both the U.S. and Canada. In Canada, physician services have grown the fastest of any professional service, both before and after the enactment of Medicare. The growth in expenditures for all types of professional health services in the U.S. has been more uniform. Expenditures for physician services in Canada rose 15 percent annually between 1965-71, compared to 11.2 percent for dentists and 9.8 percent for "others." In the U.S. the comparable growth rates were 11.0 percent for physicians, 9.9 percent for dentists and 7.5 percent for "others." The differences in spending for physician services as opposed to other health professions seem to be widening over time in Canada, while in the U.S. they appear to be narrowing. These are the results one would expect given the introduction of Canadian Medicare in 1968 (without the coverage of dental services), and the recent trends in the U.S. increasing expenditures for dental services and the use of allied health professionals.

One might have expected a sizable portion of the increased spending for physician services that accompanied the introduction of Canadian Medicare would have resulted from price rationing of a fixed stock of available services. This was not true, however. As shown in Table 3, physician fees did not increase markedly after the introduction of Medicare. In fact, the rates of increase were

TABLE 3
PRICE INDICES FOR PHYSICIANS' SERVICES, UNITED STATES AND CANADA
1957-1972 (1963 = 100)

	United States		Canada	
Year	Physicians' Fees Index	Physicians' Fees Index as Percent of Consumer Price Index	Physicians' Fees Index	Physicians' Fees Index as Percent of Consumer Price Index
1957	84.6	92.0	85.3	93.0
1958	87.5	92.5	90.0	95.7
1959	90.5	95.0	92.6	97.4
1960	92.7	95.8	93.8	97.4
1961	95.1	97.3	95.3	98.1
1962	97.8	99.0	98.2	99.9
1963	100.0	100.0	100.0	100.0
1964	102.5	101.2	102.1	100.3
1965	106.3	103.1	105.1	100.8
1966	112.4	105.9	107.0	98.8
1967	120.3	110.3	115.7	103.3
1968	127.1	111.9	121.9	104.5
1969	135.8	113.4	128.5	105.4
1970	146.1	115.2	130.6	103.6
1971	156.2	118.0	133.1	102.6
1972	161.0	117.9	135.7	99.9

SOURCE: Reinhardt and Branson, "Preliminary Tabulation of Selected Comparative Statistics on the Canadian and U.S. Health Care Systems," August 1974, Mimeograph.

lower than just before Medicare. Between 1969-72, physician fees rose less than 2 percent annually. The rates of increase immediately before Medicare were in excess of 5 percent. Similarly, the ratio of the physician fee index to the Consumer Price Index remained relatively constant over time, although it rose briefly just after the introduction of Medicare.

In contrast, Table 3 shows that the U.S. experienced significantly higher rates of increase of physician fees with the introduction of its Medicare program in 1966, with these fee increases rising faster than the U.S. Consumer Price Index. Between 1966-72, American medical fees rose 43 percent, 11.3 percent faster than the CPI. In Canada the fee increase for the same period was 27 percent, only one percent faster than their CPI. Although Medicare covers only those over 65 in the U.S., the principles of reimbursement are based on the fees charged all patients, and do not allow discrimination in the form of higher than stated fees for insured patients. Thus, it is not unreasonable to use the introduction of American Medicare as a comparison to Canadian Medicare.

Clearly, Canadian Medicare did not produce the same price response from physicians as did American Medicare. Evans argues that one reason why price increases did not occur after Medicare in Canada was that bad debts were substantially reduced. Physicians thus managed to maintain the prior rates of increase in their incomes without such fee increases even though the supply of physicians grew rapidly. Evans points to this very rapid increase in the number of physicians in Canada as the major factor explaining the rapid increase in spending for physician services. In 1968, when Canadian Medicare began, Canada had 130 physicians per 100,000 population (Table 4). By 1972, the physician/population ratio had grown to 158 with 59 GPs per 100,000 population versus 54 in 1968.[4] This compares to a much slower rate of growth of per capita physician supply in the U.S.--131 practicing physicians per

TABLE 4
ACTIVE PHYSICIANS AND GENERAL PRACTITIONERS IN THE UNITED STATES AND CANADA, 1968-1972

	United States			Canada		
Year	Physicians Per 100,000 Population	General Practitioners Per 100,000 Population	General Practitioners As Percent of Physicians	Physicians Per 100,000 Population	General Practitioners Per 100,000 Population	General Practitioners As Percent of Physicians
1968	131	30	23.0	130	54	41.7
1969	134	29	21.4	141	57	40.2
1970	137	28	20.4	146	57	39.1
1971	139	27	19.2	151	58	38.5
1972	140	26	18.7	158	59	37.0

SOURCE: Reinhardt and Branson, "Preliminary Tabulation of Selected Comparative Statistics on the Canadian and U.S. Health Care Systems," August 1974, Mimeograph.

100,000 population in 1968 to 140 per 100,000 population in 1972.

The limited evidence that exists suggests to Evans that, had Medicare not been introduced, the influx of physicians to the market might have held down physician income increases *in the short run,* but that "physician influence over the private market seemed to be strong enough, however, that over the long haul they would have been able to absorb the influx and restore their incomes to the long-term upward trend."

Obviously, a good understanding of the interrelationship between increased physician supply, the introduction of national medical insurance, expenditures for physician services and the fees charged by physicians is of keen importance to the U.S. There is now considerable debate going on about what impact national health insurance will have on the cost of medical care and whether the U.S. should increase further its supply of health professionals. According to the Evans hypothesis, national health insurance will have little impact on medical costs, physician fees or expenditures, for medical care unless it is associated with an increase in physician supply.

I'm afraid I have trouble believing Evans completely. There is little doubt that physicians have great control over the level of the fees they charge and to a large extent the amount of services they provide. But what kept Canadian physicians from raising their fees as fast as those of U.S. doctors? Would they have accepted as readily the provisional fee schedules if there was a serious shortage of physicians? While the evidence is inconclusive either way, it appears to me that the rapid increase in physician supply in Canada did have a moderating influence on the fees of Canadian physicians. It is also clear that this increase in supply contributed significantly to the rapid increase in expenditures for physician services by permitting greater access to such services.

Hospital expenditures

The largest component of the health care dollar in both Canada and the U.S. is for hospital care. But whereas hospital care is the fastest growing component in the American system, in Canada it has been growing at about the same rate as physician services during the last seven years, and a bit slower than physician care since Medicare began in 1968.

The Canadian people use hospitals much more than do Americans. Table 5 shows that Canadian admissions per 1,000 population have been consistently above the U.S. In 1960, the U.S. had 128.5 admissions per 1,000 population to Canada's 146.1, and in 1971 the two rates had grown to 146.6 and 164.9

TABLE 5

HOSPITAL UTILIZATION IN THE UNITED STATES AND CANADA, 1960-1972

	United States			Canada		
	Admissions Per Bed	Admissions Per 1000 Population	Average Length of Stay (days)	Admissions Per Bed	Admissions Per 1000 Population	Average Length of Stay (days)
1960	32.7	128.5	8.5	25.8	146.1	11.2
1961	32.2	128.6	8.5	26.5	145.9	11.2
1962	32.6	131.7	8.5	26.1	149.7	11.5
1963	32.9	134.8	8.5	25.7	151.1	11.6
1964	33.1	136.8	8.5	25.7	152.8	11.5
1965	33.0	137.6	8.5	25.5	152.2	11.7
1966	32.4	138.8	8.7	24.9	152.0	11.8
1967	31.3	137.5	9.1	24.5	151.6	11.9
1968	31.4	137.5	9.1	24.8	155.1	11.9
1969	31.9	140.8	9.0	24.9	156.4	11.9
1970	32.4	144.2	8.8	25.3	161.1	11.7
1971	32.8	146.6	8.6	25.7	164.9	11.5
1972	32.9	148.3	8.4			

SOURCE: Reinhardt and Branson, "Preliminary Tabulation of Selected Comparative Statistics on the Canadian and U.S. Health Care Systems," August 1974, Mimeograph.

respectively (a constant difference of about 16 admissions per 1,000 population). One reason for this difference could be the higher proportion of rural communities in Canada, and the lack of alternatives to institutional care.

Added to the higher hospital admissions rates, each Canadian admission lasts longer, with length of stay ranging from 11.2 days in 1960 to 11.5 days in 1971 (it had risen to as high as 11.9 days in 1967-69). Length of stay in American hospitals exhibited the same directional movement during this period, although at lower levels. Length of stay was 8.5 days in 1960 and 8.4 days in 1972. Longer lengths of stay also occurred in 1967-68 in the U.S., immediately after the introduction of Medicare, but the American system responded faster than the Canadian in reducing length of stay following its Medicare bulge.

With both admissions and lengths of stay higher, the Canadians managed to keep the occupancy rate in their hospitals higher than in the U.S. In comparison to the often cited optimal occupancy rate of 85 percent, the Canadians appear to do a better job in properly using their hospitals. In 1953 their hospital occupancy rate was 81.2 percent, and in 1971 it was 81.3 percent.[7] In contrast, the current rate in the U.S. is about 75 percent.[8]

In part, the better utilization of hospital facilities leads to hospital expenses per patient day which are significantly lower in Canada than they are in the U.S. The rates of change, though, are remarkably similar. Table 6 shows that between 1963-71 they increased by 12 percent annually in the U.S., while they

TABLE 6

INDICES OF HOSPITAL EXPENSES IN THE UNITED STATES AND CANADA, 1961-1972 (1963 = 100)

United States			Canada		
Total Hospital Expense Per Patient Day	Hospital Payroll Expense Per Patient Day	Payroll as a Percent of Total Hospital Expense	Total Hospital Expense Per Patient Day	Hospital Payroll Expense Per Patient Day	Payroll as a Percent of Total Hospital Expense
89.6	89.4	99.8	86.0	87.1	101.4
94.3	94.6	100.3	92.4	94.5	102.3
100.0	100.0	100.0	100.0	100.0	100.0
107.7	107.9	100.0	108.6	109.7	101.1
115.6	115.6	100.0	118.8	121.1	102.0
125.1	123.7	98.9	134.2	138.0	102.7
139.0	135.3	97.3	150.3	156.9	104.4
160.4	154.9	96.6	167.5	175.7	104.8
183.4	175.5	95.7	188.6	200.7	106.4
213.1	201.3	94.4	209.3	223.6	106.8
243.1	229.3	94.4	229.2	243.8	106.4
277.2	255.0	91.9			

SOURCE: Reinhardt and Branson, "Preliminary Tabulation of Selected Comparative Statistics on the Canadian and U.S. Health Care Systems," August 1974, Mimeograph.

increased 11 percent annually in Canada. The cost of an average patient day in Canada was $62 in 1971 compared to a rate of $92 in the U.S.[9] There has been a difference in the rate of investment in medical facility construction between Canada and the U.S. Investment in medical facility construction increased 12.5 percent annually in the U.S. between 1960-71, and only 5.3 percent annually in Canada.[10] There was, however, a tremendous increase in Canadian construction expenditures between 1970-71 (16.7 percent) which is highly atypical for the entire period.

Another significant difference between Canadian and U.S. hospitals is the relative importance of labor costs. In the U.S. payroll accounted for 62 percent of hospital cost per day in 1961, and fell to 57.1 percent of costs in 1971.[11] In Canada, on the other hand, payroll was 67 percent of cost in 1961, and rose to 70.3 percent in 1971. The relatively low labor intensity in U.S. hospitals is due to a number of factors. After the introduction of American Medicare, the number of institutions offering more complex services increased rapidly. Also, as stated before, the U.S. expanded greatly its investment in new and much more expensive hospital facilities. But part of the difference is also due to the accelerated increase in the earnings of Canadian hospital workers following the introduction of their national hospital financing system.

Although hospital costs and expenditures rose faster during the 1950s and early 1960s than general prices or even incomes in the U.S., the real pressure came after 1966. Admissions per population rose 7 percent in the U.S. from 1960-68, but then rose 7.8 percent between 1968-72 (Table 4). During 1960-68, while admissions were rising marginally, the stock of beds increased faster leading to a decrease of about 4 percent in admissions per bed. Canada experienced similar trends before 1968. Since 1968, Canada has increased admissions per bed and admissions per 1,000 population at about the same rate as the U.S., although length of stay in Canada has been falling only about half as fast as in the U.S.

The key point to be made concerning Canada is that there does not seem to have been a great increase in demand for hospitalization during the first years of the hospital insurance program. Evans points this out but cites the fact that several provinces already had insurance programs prior to 1958. But there was a slight increase in hospital admission rates after the introduction of Medicare. This appears to be consistent with the hypothesis that increased coverage for ambulatory care is more likely to lead to an increase in hospital care than a decrease. That is, such services actually are more complements than substitutes for institutionalization. Increased encounters with physicians can increase diagnosis of disease and hence the rate of institutionalization. But it is still unclear whether this is not simply a short-term catch-up phenomenon; and that in the long run, ambulatory care is more of a substitute for hospital care.

Discussions of hospital cost increases and the American problem of hospital cost inflation always move rapidly from gross expenditure and utilization data to an analysis of hospital cost per day and the factors that cause it to increase. Table 7 shows what has happened to hospital cost per day in the U.S. between 1951-73. Using a 60-40 payroll/nonpayroll division, the contribution to per diem cost increases is calculated for wages and prices and for additions to labor and nonlabor inputs.

Whereas wages of hospital employees rose about 5 percent annually between 1950-67, when Medicare and Medicaid were introduced in the U.S. in 1967, wages began to rise 10 percent annually. During most of the 1950-71

TABLE 7

COMPONENTS OF INCREASES IN HOSPITAL CARE PER PATIENT DAY IN U.S. COMMUNITY HOSPITALS

Item	Average annual percentage increase					
	1951-60	1960-65	1965-67	1967-69	1969-71	1971-73
Total increase	7.5	6.7	10.3	13.8	14.8	11.5
Increase in wages and prices	3.8	3.5	4.1	8.0	8.2	5.9
Wages	5.2	4.7	4.7	9.9	10.0	6.6
Prices	1.5	1.3	2.9	4.8	5.1	4.9
Changes in services	3.7	3.2	6.2	5.8	6.6	5.6
Labor	3.1	1.7	3.8	2.8	3.7	2.3
Other	4.6	5.6	9.6	9.8	10.3	10.0
Percent of total increase due to:						
Wages and prices	50.0	51.5	39.7	58.2	55.3	51.3
Changes in services	50.0	48.5	60.3	41.8	44.7	48.7

SOURCE: Price data are from the *Consumer Price Index*, Bureau of Labor Statistics. All other data are from *Hospitals*, Guide Issues, August 1, various years, and *Hospital Statistics* 1973, American Hospital Association, 1974.

period, hospitals were also increasing their labor input about 3 percent annually. However, increases in nonlabor inputs far exceeded increases in the hospital labor force throughout the period.

Evans provides rough data for the 1953-71 period which contrast significantly with the American trends. In the U.S., increased labor and nonlabor inputs per day accounted for about 50 percent of the added cost. In Canada, however, increased wages was the largest item, accounting for 58 percent of all increases in per diem cost. Together with price increases they represented fully two thirds of all per diem cost increases. Wage increases have continuously accelerated throughout the 18-year period (8.6 percent annually in 1953-59, 10.0 percent annually in 1959-65, and 12.5 percent annually in 1965-72). Additional labor inputs, on the other hand, increased only 0.4 percent annually in 1965-72. Clearly, U.S. hospitals have added more inputs to the day of hospital care, both labor and nonlabor (at least in dollar terms). The relative impact of these added resources on actual health status, however, is still unclear.

Evans suggests that the inflation experienced in Canada in the second half of the 1960s was more a supply response than a demand response. That is, increased spending occurred more from the relative availability of physicians and hospital beds than from the fact that a national financing system was put in operation. The U.S. has experienced similar growth in bed supply and yet we tend to think more of increased demand than supply as the first stage of our inflation cycle. In both countries the supply of beds rose faster in the early and mid-1960s than in the latter part of the decade. Similarly, admissions per 1,000 population were relatively stable before 1968 compared to after 1968. More curious is Evans' comment in the light of his decomposition of cost increases over the 1953-71 period–of the 13.2 percent annual increase in Canadian hospital expenditures, 2.1 percent was due to population, 1.4 percent inpatient utilization and 9.3 percent in expense per day. These proportions are not terribly different than those for the U.S.

To Evans, the relatively low increase in utilization under health insurance is evidence of the supply basis for the inflation. Clearly, the largest component in the cost increase is the wages of hospital workers. In fact, of the 1971 expense per day, 25.8 percent was due to the higher wage increases granted hospital workers *relative to the average weekly wage.* It may be that some of this increase is due to catch-up from the old days of charity care (as in the U.S.) but the rates of increase of hospital wages in Canada relative to wages of nonhospital workers far exceeds those in the U.S. But I have the same question here about the Evans explanation as I had with respect to his explanation of the increase in expenditures for physician services. Would the beds have been built or the wages increased without the financing system to pay for them? In both situations, I think Evans has skipped the first link in the causality chain–the existence of new money generated by the national insurance system. Instead he has jumped to the second stage–increased supply–as the key factor explaining increased expenditures.

To really compare Canadian and U.S. hospitals, it is necessary to analyze the relative size and geographic distribution of institutions as well as the geographic distribution of population. Smaller, rural American hospitals tend to be less expensive and less capital intensive than are larger/urban hospitals. Much of the difference in the relative growth of factor inputs in the U.S. vs. Canada may be accounted for by asking ourselves the following questions:

1) To what extent have the increases in Canadian hospital costs been due to the introduction of national health insurance?

2. What can we learn from the Canadian experience to avoid unnecessary cost inflation with the advent of national health insurance?

Evans discusses the first question and concludes that extension of health insurance in Canada has not caused any great increase in demand for or utilization of services. Increases in expenditures have been generated by the increase in supply of physicians. Similarly, there has been no great price increase pressure in the health sector that was not accompanied by inflationary pressures at least as great in the general economy.

Evans suggests that perhaps the accelerating increases in wages in the later years under consideration were the result of the realization by workers that they were in a cost pass through industry. Evans looks to the U.S. for guidance in determining if this realization was the effect of national health insurance or if it is a function of the industry itself.

Evans himself points out the relative ease with which the physician stock of Canada can and has been changed. He also points out the fortuitous stressing of investment in hospital beds before hospital insurance began and the increases in physician stock when Medicare began. Can it really all be coincidence? Trends in total spending for hospital and physician services have taken remarkably similar turns in Canada and the U.S. in the last 20 years. Yet what is really remarkable is that spending patterns have been similar even though the two systems stress different inputs in the provision of care.

After reviewing these many diverse trends, the Canadian experience suggests to me that:

1. A national health financing system will not radically expand the demand for health service.
2. Much of the increased expenditures for health services result from the increased availability of resources to supply such services. Tight constraints on the growth of such resources, e.g., hospital beds or physician supply, can be a major deterrent to increased expenditures.
3. A physician fee schedule can work in a fee-for-service system although it is unlikely to unduly constrain physician incomes.
4. Hospital workers and other health workers are likely to be key beneficiaries of a national health financing system.
5. Sharply rising medical costs are an international problem with no immediate solution evident from either the Canadian or U.S. experience; that is, at least up until the U.S. experiment with its

Economic Stabilization Program (1971-1973). (Information about the Canadian experience after 1971 is not yet available.)

FOOTNOTES

1. See Reinhardt and Branson, Preliminary Tabulation of Selected, Comparative Statistics on the Canadian and U.S. Health Care Systems, August 1974, Mimeograph.

2. See Reinhardt and Branson, *op. cit.,* for U.S. data and Evans, Beyond the Medical Marketplace: Expenditure, Utilization and Pricing of Insured Health Care in Canada, Table 1.

3. Reinhardt, Branson for U.S. data and Evans for Canadian.

4. See Reinhardt, Branson, *op. cit.*

5. See Evans, *op. cit.,* p. 49.

6. *Ibid.*

7. Evans, *op. cit.,* p. 24.

8. *Hospital Statistics, 1974 Edition,* American Hospital Association, Table 1, p. 20.

9. Evans, *op. cit.,* Table 4 and *Medical Care Expenditures, Prices and Costs: Background Book,* U.S. Department of Health, Education and Welfare, Social Security Administration, Office of Research and Statistics, September 1973, p. 38.

10. See *National Health Expenditures in Canada, 1960-71 with Comparative Data for the United States,* Health Program Branch, Ottawa, October 1973, Table 18, p. 24.

11. See Reinhardt and Branson, *op. cit.*

III THE PUBLIC INTEREST AND THE PROFESSION

CHAPTER 5 • HORACE KREVER

National Health Insurance and Problems of Quality

The introduction of national health insurance has profound implications for society, government, the health professions and the institutional providers of health services. Consequently, one would expect that the first concern of a nation contemplating such a system is to anticipate its effects on the quality of health services. It is reasonable to expect that the architects of an original plan of national health insurance would prepare an inventory of anticipated problems of quality and incorporate solutions or measures to alleviate them. As a generalization, and with one important qualification to be mentioned later, it is fair to say that, in Canada this approach was not taken. Why it was not taken is a matter of speculation, but it may be of interest to suggest some of the reasons.

Most of the problems of quality were of long standing so their existence was not felt to justify delaying the introduction of a plan which for some time the major political parties had supported. The stereotype of the Harley Street physician overcharging the dear old patient suffering from no pathological condition, overutilizing a scarce service, or paying a chemist an unconscionable sum of money for a colorful placebo, was part of the popular and professional culture. Canadians are essentially a pragmatic people and a way would be worked out to handle problems. Though capable of being ignored in a laissez-faire era, the problems became everyone's business and government's obligation under a system in which all members of society were paying for a service they now had a right to receive. That working out process was recognized to be a job for government and, although Canadians are as fond as any people of the absence of governmental restraints, they do not distrust government and indeed have looked upon their governments as a mechanism to implement social policy. It is difficult to find fault with the comparisons made by Robert Presthus in his recent analysis of the differences between interest group lobbying in Canada and the United States:

> ". . . Canada inherited from Britain an organic, corporatist social philosophy in which the role of private groups is equally legitimate as that of government and equally essential to wise policy making. From Confederation onward, the often invidious dichotomy which Americans have made between government and society, has rarely appeared. Government has obviously been put to the service of private groups in both systems, but in Canada the process has been more positively legitimated.
>
> Essentially collectivist, corporatism is a conception of society in which government freely delegates many of its functions, and much of its largesse, to private groups which enjoy both normative and functional legitimacy in the political system. In this appreciation, collective goals are usually seen as prior to those of any discrete individual or interest. Government is not regarded as some alien apparatus requiring constant surveillance by outsiders, but instead the usual expectation is that political elites will generally act in the larger community interests. Because interest groups and their agents are integral parts of the system, lobbying is not required to ensure that government does its duty. Instead, political elites enjoy a legitimacy and autonomy rarely experienced in the individualistic, American milieu where a historic fear of government and a highly pragmatic ethic have meant that groups are expected to compete in advancing their disparate interests. In Canada citizens tend to believe in a transcendental public interest, while in the United States, this honorific condition is defined as the outcome of the clash among opposing private interests."[1]

It may be added that political labels play no part in the attitude of Canadians in general toward their government. A fuller appreciation of this important fact in the weighing of Canadian experience may be gained by considering that, even in the extremely sensitive field of the dissemination of news and opinion, it was a conservative government in Canada that caused Parliament to enact The Canadian Radio Broadcasting Act of 1932.[2] This empowered a government-appointed commission to take over all broadcasting in Canada, to own and operate radio stations across the country, recommend the issue, suspension or cancellation of private broadcasting licenses, and prohibit the organization or operation of networks of private radio stations.

The absence of techniques for solving problems relating to quality when the national health insurance scheme was introduced, reflects another facet of Canadian-style pragmatism. The exigencies of the legislative process, both nationally and provincially, despite the relative weakness of formalized lobbying practices, are such that the more controversial a proposed legislative measure is, the more the bill is likely to suffer amendments from the original blueprint. Recent examples of this process in Ontario may be found in the handling of difficulties relating to quality in the treatment of denturists or dental technicians and acupuncture. It may be, at least in the Canadian context, a waste of precious time to postpone the introduction of a necessary plan until the conceptual solution to the concomitant problems is found, when there is reason to believe the actual solution may be far different from the conceptual one. It may be preferable to resist anticipating the problems, wait until they arise in practice, and then seek acceptable solutions to them.

This is not to say that no concern was expressed and no attention paid to the likelihood or certainty of quality problems which would arise in the future. During the gestation of the Medical Care Act[3] many of the interest groups quite clearly expressed their fears and gave warnings about the threat to quality that a compulsory government-controlled plan would involve. Some of the risks warned against were based on logical premises which, though reasonably foreseeable, did not in fact occur. These included the fear that because medical services would become accessible to more people, the system could not function unless available manpower was drastically augmented before the plan was put into effect. Although health professionals were subsequently trained in larger numbers to increase supply, the beginning of the plan did not await the increase in the supply of professional services and the system did not break down. Indeed, the theory that demands for essential medical service are insatiable has not been proven. Today it is generally accepted that our concern, largely economic in nature, should be not with a shortage of physicians, but with a surplus and that attention should now be directed to the question of distribution of physicians, both geographically and by specialty. Other fears expressed were based on professional ideology, not widely shared by persons outside the professions, and without any firm foundation in Canadian experience. Apart from the professional fear of government and central administration, the principal warning in this connection was that good medicine depended on a sound physician-patient relationship which was certain to be impaired by third-party intervention for the purpose of payment (unless the third party were a physician-controlled paymaster). There is no evidence of a significant deterioration in the physician-patient relationship in Canada, and if the incidence of malpractice litigation is any criterion at all, which is not an unreasonable assumption, this relationship is much healthier in the Canadian system than in the American.[5]

Hall Commission Report

It was not only in the expression of professional interests that concern was exhibited for the implications of a national plan on quality. They included the reports of publicly appointed bodies, of which certainly the most influential was the Report of the Royal Commission on Health Services, the "Hall Commission Report."[6] One obvious implication for quality in a national scheme that would have the effect of eliminating the traditional "charity patient" was a possible threat to the availability of "teaching material." At the very beginning of this influential report, which became the inspiration, if not the blueprint of The

Medical Care Act of 1966, we find this recognition:

> "One other aspect of the education of health professions demands comment. It is the anomaly that the training of our most essential health workers–the front-line medical practitioner–has depended upon there being a low-income or indigent group in our society to provide the essential clinical experience in 'public wards' and 'outpatient' clinics. We have not yet abolished poverty or indigency but the training of society's essential professions can no longer rest on this limited, indigent base. It is now a *public* responsibility in the sense that every member of the public must accept the obligation, when hospitalized in teaching hospitals, to serve in the education process."[7]

Indeed, the Hall Commission Report was keenly conscious of the quality implications of its recommendations because it saw its purpose as suggesting the means of creating a system whose goal was the "achievement of the highest possible health standards for all our people."[8] Quality, the report stated at the beginning of Volume II, "depends primarily on the supply, availability, knowledge, skill and dedication of professionally qualified personnel; secondly, on the facilities at their disposal and, thirdly, on the organization of the services."[9] Considerable attention was directed to the issue of quality throughout the report,[10] but, as suggested earlier, no thoroughly articulated proposals for the solution to the apprehended problems were provided or thought necessary. Similarly, to turn to a provincial example, the monumental Report of the Commission of Inquiry on Health and Social Welfare known as the Castonguay-Nepveu Report, which set the scene for Quebec's entry in November 1970 into the scheme created by the federal Medical Care Act, was much concerned throughout its commentary and recommendations with problems of quality. "The health plan must assure the distribution of quality care on the scientific, human and social levels."[12] A concise statement of the need for the "evaluation of the quality of care and of the efficiency of health organization" may be found in the report[13] and need not be summarized here. But, as contrasted with the Hall Commission Report, the Castonguay-Nepveu Report did spell out, with much particularity, measures for the solution of problems which would become impossible to ignore after the plan began to operate. The case of Quebec, therefore, requires a qualification of the earlier statement that, by and large, the creators of the plans of health insurance in Canada did not incorporate solutions to the anticipated problems of quality. It should be added that Quebec was exceptional in one other aspect of the implementation of health insurance plans. The first chairman of the Castonguay-Nepveu Commission, Claude Castonguay, resigned from the commission before it had fully reported to become Minister of Social Affairs in the Quebec Cabinet, with the responsibility of implementing that Province's plan.

Approaches to quality

The creation of health insurance plans in the provinces[14] did not generally await the conceptual solutions to the problems with which this chapter is concerned. But with participation in the scheme or, in some cases, with recognition of the inevitability of participation, governments and agencies across the country began to give serious study to the health system. Out of these studies,[15] which have not finished and will never finish, have come tentative and suggested answers to the difficult issue of balancing economy and quality. The remainder of this chapter considers some of the approaches taken or recommended in connection with the maintenance or improvement of the quality of health care. Because of greater familiarity with the jurisdiction of Ontario and its problems that province is the focus of the review.

Whether one is concerned with quality of care from the viewpoint of the consumer, the provider, the service institutions, government or society at large, at the heart of that concern lies the "supply, availability, knowledge, skill, and dedication of professionally qualified personnel"–to repeat the language of the Hall Report. Regulation of the professions in the health field, given their traditional individualism and relative freedom from interference by the public or government acting on behalf of the public, is a delicate undertaking. But it is necessary if one is determined to provide high quality health care universally at a cost society can afford. For in the final analysis in a society which calls itself democratic it must be the government which determines priorities in the allocation of expenditures for public programs. But history shows that the cooperation of the professions in the reordering that occurs when government acknowledges its responsibility for health services is also essential. And experience teaches that, if the professions are approached the right way and without unnecessary haste, their cooperation and acceptance of the new order will be forthcoming. All parties in Canada have learned much from the experience of the regrettable physicians' strike in Saskatchewan in 1962, resulting from the enactment of the Saskatchewan Medical Care Insurance Act, 1961.[16] In Canada, regulation of the professions, for constitutional purposes, is reserved to the 10 provincial legislatures and a word about professional organization is helpful at this point.

Clearly, the medical profession is the key in the regulation of the other health professions though only indirectly as will become evident later. It is a pluralistic profession consisting of a regulatory body, a voluntary association which is a part of a national voluntary association, a university educational institution and, indeed many other groups including specialty associations, a mutual protective association and a national specialty accrediting body. In Ontario,[17] by an Act of the Legislature,[18] only a member of the College of Physicians and Surgeons of Ontario, a corporate body created by legislation, may practice medicine, surgery or midwifery. The College is governed by a council. Its members, until recently, with the exception of the Minister of

Health who need not be a physician but serves as an ex officio member, are members of the medical profession who either represent the five medical schools in the province or are elected by the members of the profession in the province. The Council is a licensing body in the true sense of the term and has jurisdiction over education, by virtue of its right to determine educational qualifications of applicants for admission, as well as to discipline (partly through a Discipline Committee). The committee has the power to reprimand, suspend and erase from the register for professional misconduct, conduct unbecoming a medical practitioner or incompetence. Despite the College's nominal control over education, university medical schools are, in fact, the educational authority and suffer no interference from the College. About 75 percent of the profession belong to the provincial medical association which in Ontario is entirely voluntary. The association is a provincial branch of the Canadian Medical Association and a mechanism for asserting the interests of the profession.

Professional vs. public interest

One of the most important measures designed to ensure quality in the provision of health care is a deliberate policy adopted recently restricting the College of Physicians and Surgeons to its proper role–namely, protecting the public as opposed to the professional interest. It is now firmly recognized that the sole purpose of conferring on the College the power to give its members a monopoly to practice medicine is the protection of the public. This conclusion, a proposition fundamental to the Report of the Committee on the Healing Arts in Ontario, was also reached by the Castonguay-Nepveu Commission in Quebec, which put it this way: "We believe it necessary to distinguish between the professional organization charged with defending an occupation (scientific or technical) and playing, in this respect, the role of mandatory of society, from those which exist to defend their members."[19] Until recently it was not always possible for physicians, elected to the council by colleagues, to see that there might occur a conflict between public and professional interests and, to put it crudely, on such occasions the function of the Council was to protect the public against those who elected it. Recent legislative developments have seen increased use of the College as an instrument for implementing health policy and some of these developments must be mentioned. Before doing so, however, one small illustration may indicate how important to public policy, and hence to quality, a clear distinction among the roles of the various parts of the profession can be. At a public hearing of the Ontario Committee on the Healing Arts in 1967, a spokesman for the Ontario Medical Association, the voluntary professional interest group, took the position, in answer to a hypothetical* question that it would be acceptable professional conduct for doctors collectively to withhold

*The question was hypothetical in the Ontario context, but it had occurred in Saskatchewan when doctors went on strike a few years earlier.

their services when they disagree with a statute enacted by the legislature establishing a new method of paying physicians. At a hearing attended by members of the council, the registrar of the College said he would prepare a list of the offenders and send it to the College's Complaint Committee if such conduct should occur. The immediate past President of the College, a distinguished practicing physician, added:

> "Mr. Chairman, may I say that it is the belief of the College that modern medicine has a major social responsibility to the community and it also has a major responsibility to go along and direct change in terms of the distribution of medical care in bringing the benefits of medical care to the community. But I would hope that this hypothetical situation that has been posed would never occur. It is inconceivable to me that it would, but if it did, I don't think that the College would have any choice but to discharge its responsibilities. I think I can assure you that it would."[20]

It is safe to say that use of professional licensing authorities in self-governing professions as an instrument of public policy would not have been recognized as legitimate by most members of the profession before the advent of national hospital and health insurance. This trend has been accelerated by other developments. Legislation has been enacted to place on the councils of self-governing professional colleges lay representatives. New professional legislation, partially enacted in Ontario, will make such representation numerically more significant for all professions.[21] Perhaps even more significant are two legislative innovations which underline clearly the obligations of public accountability of the professional regulatory bodies. They stipulate that in the future the health professions must cease to function as though the interests of the consumer were secondary to those of the providers of health care, and that the professions were discrete entities rather than a single group, and as such they must work cooperatively. The first provision is the creation of an exclusively lay body to be known as the Health Disciplines Board. Its chief functions when it receives a complaint are to inquire into the disposition of a case made by the complaint committee of a professional college, to make recommendations, and to review in a similar way the refusal of a registration committee of a college to admit an applicant to medical practice.[22]

The second legislative change is a recognition of the executive branch of government, in this case the Minister of Health, as the watchdog of the public interest, who must supervise the legislature's delegation of the governing powers to professional colleges. In the words of the statute his function is "to ensure that the activities of health disciplines are effectively regulated and coordinated in the public interest, to have appropriate standards of practice developed . . . and to ensure that the rights of individuals to the services provided by health disciplines of their choice are maintained."[23]

New look at regulation

With universal acceptance of government's responsibility to make health services of high quality available to everyone, and with the shift of the burden to pay for those services to everyone in society, either by premiums or taxes, it is widely conceded that as society can no longer afford to squander its human resources, greater reliance must be placed on all the skills and competence in the health professions and occupations. This concession has necessitated a new look at regulation of the professions.

Our traditional methods of regulating the health professions have placed emphasis not on the actual but on the legal competence of the worker. The assumption here was that the physician was omnicompetent. In many instances, deciding when a nonphysician health worker, say a nurse or a hospital technician, was capable of performing a procedure thought to be a medical act was the job of the physicians' regulatory body. Its members had a monopoly to practice medicine, surgery, and midwifery,* and had the right and duty to prosecute any nonphysician who practiced these skills regardless of his actual competence to do so. What has emerged from the identification of these problems has been a reorganization of the regulation of all the professions and occupations. It involves a rational and careful reassessment of those who need state licensing, those who require only state certification, and those who require neither licensing nor certification except, perhaps, at the educational level.

At the same time conscious efforts are made to provide the available skills to the public. It is being accomplished by encouraging slowly and under acceptable conditions the training and use of nurse practitioners and nurse midwives. Equally important is the creation of a climate among the professions and the public in which traditional patterns of professional practice can change from those characterized by independence of the practitioner to interdependence of practitioners. Such a move may have the combined effect of making full use of all available skills in a cooperative work setting and removing a significant portion of care from general hospitals in which care is expensive and relationships among health workers are determined by the rigid and hierarchical nature of hospital organization. With the exception of Quebec, Manitoba and Saskatchewan, the provinces have not yet committed themselves to the implementation of the recommendations made by the 1972 Report of the Community Health Centre Project. This report, commissioned by the conference of federal and provincial health ministers, attempted to provide guidelines for a change of this sort.

> "The Committee sees a community health centre as a facility, or intimately linked group of facilities, enabling individuals and families to obtain initial and continuing health care of high quality. Such care must be provided in an acceptable manner through a team of

---

*These terms are either left undefined in some provinces including Ontario, or are badly defined in other provinces.

health professionals and other personnel working in an accessible and well-managed setting. The community health centre must form part of a responsive and accountable health services system. In turn, the health services must be closely and effectively coordinated with the social and related services to help individuals, families, and communities deal with the many-sided problems of living."[24]

The report called for legislative changes that would give community health centers corporate or collective responsibility for the professional actions of all personnel whatever their status in law may be, e.g. irrespective of their position as independent contractor or employee. In terms that echoed the expressed concerns of other groups and studies pointing the way to the economical provision of high quality health care, the report said:

> "Corporate responsibility would give persons cared for through a health centre redress against the centre for professional negligence on the part of team members, encourage physicians and other professionals to delegate tasks which can safely be carried out by other health workers by removing the basis for their continually expressed belief that responsibility for quality of care resides in them alone, and, finally, would enable professions and other health workers to enter into contracts of service with the centre and thus give them a sense of security.
>
> ... At this point ... it should, however, be noted that precise and rigid fixing of roles, responsibilities and functions of professionals and institutions through statute or licensing regulations would constitute a serious obstacle to the development of effective programs, true teamwork, and innovation. There are, for instance, real disadvantages and practical problems in trying to distinguish a 'medical act' from a 'nursing act' in a situation where changing and flexible roles are necessary.
>
> Professional licensing legislation will also require review and modification to the extent that statutes currently in force may prevent some prospective members of the health team from becoming true colleagues of other members who are not members of the same profession."[25]

Acceptance by the government of the responsibility to oversee the self-regulation of the professions in the interests of a workable system may help bring to an end jurisdictional disputes among professions and occupations. It may end unilateral actions by a senior profession vis-a-vis a traditionally subservient one which may appear, and often with good reason, to be economic protectionism. It is interesting, however, that even in the face of this governmental acceptance of responsibility, one still finds that well-considered advice on the issue of quality and safety falls to the forces of the pragmatic legislative process. Two recent examples in Ontario serve to illustrate the point.

In Ontario, dental technicians who manufactured prosthetic devices such as plates and bridges have traditionally worked on the prescription of a dentist; they are prohibited by law from serving customers directly. From time to time the government was asked to amend the legislation to permit direct access by the public to dental technicians, now called "denturists," so that the cost of their product can be more reasonable. Several advisory committees have recommended against completely free access because of the danger of pathological conditions going undetected by persons untrained to identify pathology. Legislation was enacted[26] on the basis of these recommendations authorizing suitably trained "denture therapists" to practice intra-oral procedures in a dentist's office or elsewhere under the direct supervision of a dentist. Within months of the enactment, a large and expensive campaign was undertaken by the technicians who appealed to the public by newspaper advertisements, and engaged in open defiance of the law calculated to attract news media attention. Yielding to the political exigencies, the government caused the legislature to pass new legislation,[27] permitting some intra-oral procedures to be performed by denture therapists without the intervention of a dentist.

Perhaps a better example of the power of political reality to minimize the effect of expert advice with regard to quality is the more recent development concerning acupuncture. As in other parts of North America, Ontario experienced the discovery by the West of the ancient practice of acupuncture. This occurred when it was reported that wise and respected North American physicians, including a president of the Canadian Medical Association and other well-known Canadian practitioners of scientific medicine, had visited China and had become persuaded that acupuncture was a valid form of anesthesia for some types of surgery. The danger was apparent to all that before long the public would demand the end of the medical "conspiracy" that prevented access to practitioners of acupuncture. With deliberate speed, an advisory group was set to work to inquire into the matter. It soon recommended that acupuncture research and service take place in the controlled environment of health science centers so that in due course a body of knowledge and experience could be resorted to for the creation of guidelines. Perceived public impatience, however, caused the minister of health to announce in the legislature that the government would make grants for research in acupuncture and that until the therapeutic values of acupuncture had been established the government would not include these services as insured benefits under the health insurance plan. In what might reasonably be construed as an abdication of decision making, the minister also welcomed the apparently unilateral decision of the College of Physicians and Surgeons to designate acupuncture as a medical act and to take steps to control its practice. This step was taken despite the proliferation of unlicensed and unsupervised acupuncture clinics and the knowledge that many patients may delay getting proper medical care in the absence of a differential diagnosis. It is clear that the manner in which decisions of this sort are made in the posthealth insurance system is inappropriate.

Quality control and hospitals

In Canada, hospital insurance has had a longer history as a responsibility of government than medical or health insurance. The effect of hospital insurance was to erode the historic autonomy of the voluntary hospitals by making them more responsive to governmental policy. All hospitals can be expected to have bylaws which meet the requirements of a government department or commission. These provide the framework for the maintenance of quality such as tissue committees, admission committees and continuing reviews of length of hospital stay and so on. Clearly, however, the strongest tool for striving for a balance between economy and quality is the control over hospital budgets. Such control has been used to eliminate unnecessary duplication of services among hospitals. In many instances, this method of control has created difficult problems which have impeded progress. Many hospitals, for example, have been owned and operated by religious orders to which many communities are morally indebted. For government to decide that in a given community the nonsectarian hospital will have the pediatric service for the community, and the other hospital owned by a religious order will have the obstetrical and gynecological service is certain to cause misgivings in an era when abortion and sterilization procedures are increasingly common. Similar political problems result when a decision is made to deprive a community hospital of the right to purchase sophisticated equipment such as a heart-lung machine for sophisticated surgery, because the latter should only be permitted to be carried out in a medical center associated with a medical school.

In the Canadian provinces, despite the recognition that hospital association is a force for the continuing education of the physician, physicians do not have a right to hospital privileges by virtue of their license to practice. In this respect at least, hospitals remain fully autonomous. But it is somewhat anomalous that although a person has been certified by the duly constituted authority as fit to practice medicine, he can be effectively prevented from doing so by a hospital's refusal to grant him privileges. As a result, appeal mechanisms have been created in some provinces and may be considered another erosion of autonomy, for the appeal body can force a hospital to accept a physician it has rejected. In Saskatchewan, the creation of this new mechanism was directly associated with the introduction of a medicare plan.[28] In Ontario it was not.[29] It may be appropriate to comment on one aspect of the report which led to the creation of the Hospital Appeal Board in Ontario. The report pointed out that The Public Hospitals Act, the statute enacted by the legislature for the regulation of public hospitals, provided that a hospital could not turn away a patient requiring active treatment. But in conflict with this statutory duty of a hospital was subordinate legislation providing that no patient could be admitted to a hospital without authorization by a physician on the hospital staff. The report recommended that this conflict be resolved. The government complied promptly by abolishing the previously existing duty to admit a person in need of active treatment to a hospital![30]

Another example of modern legislation, which reflects the new role of the hospital as a direct provider of high quality care as distinguished from a physician's office, is a provision which did not result from national health insurance. Moreover, it serves as an example of the extent to which the state is prepared to interfere with strongly held beliefs of a profession, in this case the almost sacred nature of the physician-patient relationship, when such beliefs are inconsistent with high quality. The measure[31] simply empowers hospitals to pass bylaws which would have the effect of requiring the chief of service to replace the attending physician if the care fails to meet quality standards, and to become responsible for the care himself without the patient's consent.

When one turns to the problem of abuses of the system such as overservicing by physicians, overutilization by patients, overcharging and so on, it becomes impossible to state with any degree of confidence the real magnitude of the problem. That abuses have occurred is known, but if there is any evidence that they have occurred on a large scale, the evidence is not available. On the other hand, without safeguards the opportunity for abuse on any scale clearly exists and cannot be denied. There are safeguards, however, which can be employed. Some are in use and others have been proposed.

Preventing abuse of the system

For the purposes of this review, the Ontario plan is used as a model. But it is fair to say that many of these issues surfaced first in Saskatchewan in the early 1930's and the techniques for handling them were in part developed there. The Ontario Health Insurance Plan (OHIP) pays physicians on a fee-for-service basis at the rate of 90 percent of the fee found in the tariff of services established by the Ontario Medical Association. A physician may bill the plan directly for the performance of insured services and payment is made directly to him. He may not submit any bill for any amount to the patient. The reimbursement by the plan constitutes payment in full.[33] It is conservatively estimated that over 90 percent of Ontario physicians accept the plan's reimbursement as payment in full, despite the fact that in 1971 when the legislation designed to discourage extra billing of patients was passed, it was strongly opposed by members of the profession. Tollefson succinctly states the nature of the problems in his discussion of the earlier Saskatchewan plan:

> "In any medical care insurance plan billing procedures must be constantly watched to prevent strain on the economic capacity of the plan through fraudulent billing, excessive billing or the rendering of unnecessary services . . .
>
> A more complex facet of the problem is whether the insured services for which the claim has been submitted ought properly to

have been given. Here the physician's professional judgment is being questioned. Any restriction upon the type of medical procedures he may employ constitutes a restriction upon his professional independence . . .

[The practice of paying a given proportion of the fee established by the voluntary association] in effect gives the [profession] a blank cheque drawn on the provincial treasury–a privilege which is not accorded to any other group in our society. Furthermore, . . . it removes one of the essential limits of the cost of the plan, thereby placing the whole plan in jeopardy."[34]

The approach taken to these questions involves the cooperation of the medical profession through both the regulatory body, the College of Physicians and Surgeons of Ontario, and the voluntary one, the Ontario Medical Association. In the case of both, unlike the earlier experience of Saskatchewan, and at least partly because of the experience of Saskatchewan, that cooperation has been forthcoming. Under the plan the general manager, a civil servant, is given the duty of approving and assessing claims for insured services, determining the amounts and authorizing payment.[35] But if he has reasonable grounds to suspect that all or part of the insured services were not in fact rendered, all or part of such services were not medically necessary, all or part of such services were not provided in accordance with accepted professional standards and practice, or that the nature of the services is misrepresented,* the general manager must refer the matter to the Medical Review Committee.[36] Established under the Health Insurance Act of 1972, the committee is composed of the College of Physicians and Surgeons, none of whom may be a government employee.[37] The committee may recommend to the general manager that he pay, refuse or reduce payment of the amount otherwise payable, and subject to appeal the general manager must carry out the committee's recommendations.[38] The consequence of mechanisms of this sort has been not only the rejection or reduction of a physician's bill, but disciplinary proceedings by the provincial colleges across the country[39] and prosecutions in the ordinary criminal courts for fraud.[40]

On the question of the relationship between the plan's benefits and the tariff of fees set by the Ontario Medical Association, the theoretical possibility that a unilateral decision by the voluntary association to increase fees could irreparably damage the solvency of the plan has been eliminated. It was accomplished by the creation in 1973, of a joint Committee on Physicians' Compensation with the result that there is now, if not true collective bargaining, at least negotiation between the association and government. This machinery will have the additional benefit of enhancing quality by giving the public,

---

*The general manager may act on information obtained from random or periodic examination of physicians' computerized profiles or other appropriate computer services.

through the government members of the committee, the opportunity to develop a policy as to the validity of the respective claims of the various specialties in the setting of fees. Furthermore, the committee's existence facilitates the exploration of alternatives to the prevailing fee-for-service method of remunerating physicians.

Certainly more controversial than the techniques just described, because of the perceived threat they pose to the individual judgment of physicians and popular conceptions, are proposed forms of intervention which may well be introduced in the near future. These proposals are the result of the deliberations of the Primary Advisory Group on Medical Care Insurance Review, composed overwhelmingly of physicians and created by the Ontario Council of Health at the request of the minister of health. The recommendations in the report,[41] submitted to the minister in February 1973, include the following:

1) That the current method of dealing with abuses by physicians through the Medical Review Committee of the College of Physicians and Surgeons of Ontario, though a satisfactory method, be intensified and more effective techniques for screening be developed, and that a similar arrangement be established for consumer review;
2) That a mechanism be established to allow for review of apparent abuses by other health professionals similar to the procedures of the Medical Review Committee;
3) That a consumer review committee be established to deal with apparent aberrant utilization by patients. Initially, persons might be singled out for an educational experience and, if not successful, penalties should be imposed;
4) (i) That plan payments for primary care provided by physicians be at general practitioner rates. When a patient chooses to go to a specialist for primary care the patient must be responsible for any additional charges;
   (ii) That payments at specialist rates only be accepted where there has been a definite referral and the conditions of referral are clearly set out;
5) That a mechanism be developed to permit patients to verify the services and the costs of the services rendered to them;
6) That rather than attempting to impose a patient participation fee under OHIP the entire question of funding of OHIP be studied with a view of establishing a premium level so that at least one third of the entire cost is met through premium revenue;
7) That heart transplants and similar experimental procedures be excluded from the plan;
8) That the plan only pay for diagnostic tests and procedures which are relevant and pertinent to the patient's condition;
9) That a "Patient Bill of Rights" be established and publicized.

Perhaps the most controversial of all is the last example to be given:

10) (i) That periodic health examinations for plan purposes be restricted to the following: during the first five years of life there should be approximately seven routine health examinations to be programmed at the discretion of the physician; between the ages of 5 and 44, routine examinations should be carried out approximately every ten years (e.g. at age 14, 24, 34 and 44); beyond age 44, examinations should be carried out every five years (e.g. at age 49, 54, 59, 64 and 74), and
(ii) That routine Papanicolaou tests be carried out no more often than once every two years after age 20.

For the public and physicians conditioned to believe in the virtue of "preventive medicine" through annual physical examinations, and for women accustomed to annual "pap smears," this advice may appear to be concerned more with economy than with the maintenance of health. But recent epidemiological studies have persuaded many thinking physicians that the value of some of these traditional practices is without solid foundation.[42]

Unfortunately, space does not permit more than a brief mention of two other recent important proposals which unquestionably have serious implications for quality of health care or simply health. The first is the Report of the Health Planning Task Force,[43] the "Mustard Report," which lays out a detailed plan for decentralization or "regionalization" of health care services placing the responsibility for decision making about needs and resources at a regional and district level. This would include decisions about the number and location of facilities and the number and mix of health professionals. Perhaps this approach might help bring within soluble range the thorny problem of physician manpower and make possible resort to a utilization basis rather than to the licensing mechanism for the threat in some of the provinces of an imminent surplus of physicians. The second is a "working document" entitled *A New Perspective on the Health of Canadians*[44] by the Hon. Marc Lalonde, the minister of national health and welfare. It suggests that the federal government, with the concurrence of the provincial ministers of health, will place great emphasis or funds on concerns of the "health field," a broader concept which includes all matters affecting health than just the "health care system." The thrust of the document is to take what may be called a "macro-health" view by concentrating on factors that cannot avoid being of direct influence on personal health, namely human biology, environment and lifestyle. To the extent that improving the conditions of health improves health itself, the provincial health insurance plans will be affected in terms of both cost and quality of care.

In summary, a variety of techniques designed to ensure quality and quality control of health care services in an era when governments accept the responsibility for making health care available to all residents of the country have been brought into existence. They were, generally speaking, not devised before national health and hospital insurance was introduced but were often *ad hoc* answers to a discrete problem. Some of the measures elicited initial professional hostility which, in most cases, if one excludes the exceptional crises in Saskatchewan and later in Quebec, evaporated in time and was replaced by a responsible spirit of cooperation. A national health insurance plan for services of high quality requires, as an essential precondition of its satisfactory operation, acceptance by the health professions. There is no reason to believe that the professions, if dealt with sensibly and sensitively, will not respond responsibly to the demonstrated need for change. There is equally no reason to believe that the search for solutions will ever cease.

FOOTNOTES

1. Presthus, Robert, Interest Group Lobbying: Canada and the United States, 413 *The Annals of the American Academy of Political and Social Science,* 44, pp. 45-46 (May 1974).

2. Statutes of Canada 1932, chapter 51. For an excellent study of this extraordinary example of collectivism see Peers, F. W., *The Politics of Canadian Broadcasting 1920-1952,* University of Toronto Press, Toronto, 1969, especially chapter 4.

3. Statutes of Canada, 1966, chapter 64.

4. Helpful discussions of this point may be found in Blishen, B. R., *Doctors & Doctrines,* University of Toronto Press, Toronto, 1969. (Professor Blishen was research director for the Royal Commission on Health Services, better known as the Hall Commission), and the as yet unpublished Ph.D. thesis of Prof. Carolyn Joy Tuohy of the University of Toronto, "The Political Attitudes of Ontario Physicians: A Skill Group Perspective," Yale University, 1974.

5. Unfortunately, 1967 was the last year for which statistics, the validity of which the author has checked, are available. In that year, although there were approximately 24,000 licensed medical doctors in Canada, there were fewer than 65 malpractice actions commenced. See Report of the Committee on the Healing Arts, The Queen's Printer, Toronto, 1970, Vol. 3, pp. 70-71 and 72-73. It is known that in the intervening years the incidence of this type of litigation has increased by a number which, as a percentage of the 1967 figure, may seem large but which, in absolute terms compared with the incidence in the U.S., is not significant.

6. Ottawa, Queen's Printer, Vol. I, 1964, Vol. II, 1965.

7. Hall Commission Report, *op. cit.,* Vol. I, p. 8.

8. These are the opening words of the Health Charter for Canadians, the Commission's suggested objective of national policy for Canada. See the Report, *op. cit.,* Vol. I, pp. 10-12.

9. *Ibid.* Vol. II, p. 1.

10. See particularly Vol. II, pp. 1-10.

11. Vol. I, Quebec Official Publisher, Quebec, 1967. The other volumes were not fully completed until 1970.

12. Castonguay-Nepveu Report, *op. cit.,* Vol. IV, Tome II, Second Title, The Health Plan, p. 20.

13. Vol. IV, Tome III, Second Title, The Health Plan (continuation), pp. 107-138.

14. The date of entry of the 10 provincial plans into the scheme created by the federal Medical Care Act were as follows: British Columbia and Saskatchewan, July 1, 1968; Manitoba, Newfoundland and Nova Scotia, April 1, 1969; Alberta, July 1, 1969; Ontario, October 1, 1969; Quebec, November 1, 1970; Prince Edward Island, December 1, 1970; and New Brunswick, January 1, 1971.

15. The list, which is not exhaustive, includes the Task Force Reports on the Costs of Health Services in Canada, Information Canada, Ottawa, 1969, submitted to Conference of Ministers of Health; the Report of the Community Health Centre Project to the Conference of Ministers of Health (the "Hastings Report"), Information Canada, Ottawa, 1972; Robertson, Rocke H., Health Care in Canada: a Commentary, a background study for the Science Council of Canada, Information Canada, Ottawa, 1973; the Report of the Committee on the Healing Arts (Ontario), *op. cit.*; the Report of the Commission of Inquiry on Health and Social Welfare (Quebec), *op. cit.*; J. T. McLeod Research Associates Ltd., Consumer Participation, Regulation of the Professions, Decentralization of Health Services, a Report Submitted to the Minister of Public Health, Saskatchewan, Saskatoon, Department of Public Health, 1973; Pickering, E. A., Report of the Special Study regarding the Medical Profession in Ontario (the "Pickering Report"), Ontario Medical Association, Toronto, 1973; Report of the Health Planning Task Force (the "Mustard Report"), Queen's Printer, Toronto, 1974; and the many Reports of the Ontario Council of Health and its task forces.

16. Statutes of Saskatchewan, 1961 (second session), chapter 1. See Tollefson, E. A., *Bitter Medicine,* Modern Press, Saskatoon, 1963; Tollefson, E. A.,

The Aftermath of the Medicare Dispute in Saskatchewan, 72 Queen's Quarterly, 452-465 (August 1965), and Badgley, R. F. and Wolfe, S., *Doctors' Strike: Medical Care and Conflict in Saskatchewan,* Macmillan, Toronto, 1967.

17. For a full description of the organization of the profession in Ontario see Grove, J. W., Organized Medicine in Ontario, A Study for the Committee on the Healing Arts, Queen's Printer, Toronto, 1969.

18. The Medical Act, R.S.O. 1970, chapter 268 as amended by 1973, chapter 129 (soon to be superseded by The Health Disciplines Act, 1974, not, at the date of writing, yet proclaimed in force).

19. Castonguay-Nepveu Report, Vol. VII, Tome I, The Professions and Society, p. 32.

20. Transcript of the hearings of the Committee on the Healing Arts, July 5, 1967, p. 5790.

21. Statutes of Ontario, chapter 129, which provides that the Council of the College of Physicians and Surgeons of Ontario shall contain three lay members to be appointed by the government. The new legislation, The Health Disciplines Act, 1974, provides that for all the colleges dealt with in the Act, i.e. dentists, physicians, nurses, optometrists and pharmacists, the councils shall include not fewer than four and not more than six lay members.

22. The Health Disciplines Act, 1974, sections 6-11, not yet proclaimed in force.

23. *Ibid.*, section 3.

24. The Community Health Centre in Canada, Information Canada, 1972, p. 1.

25. *Ibid.*, pp. 23-24.

26. The Denture Therapists Act, Statutes of Ontario, 1972, Chapter 163.

27. The Denture Therapists Act, Statutes of Ontario, 1974, chapter 34.

28. See Tollefson, E. A., The Aftermath of the Medicare Dispute in Saskatchewan, *op. cit.,* pp. 462-465. The repeal of the provision, when a new government came to power replacing the government that brought in the plan, was followed by the restoration of the appeal mechanism by an

amendment to The Hospital Standards Act, Revised Statutes of Saskatchewan 1965, chapter 265, by 1972, chapter 52.

29. The Ontario legislation was the implementation of one of the recommendations of the Report of the Minister's Committee of Inquiry into Hospital Privileges in Ontario (the "Grange Report"), Queen's Printer, Toronto, 1972, and was enacted by 1972 chapter 90, section 23, amended in 1973 by chapter 164, section 1. So far, in Ontario, unsuccessful applicants for hospital privileges have not fared well before the Appeal Board with the exception of one surgeon whose successful result before the Board was reversed, on the Hospital's appeal to the Divisional Court, in *Board of Governors of the Scarborough General Hospital and Schiller,* June 4, 1974, not yet reported.

30. Section 17(1) of The Public Hospitals Act, R.S.O. 1970, chapter 378 provided, in part, that ". . . no hospital receiving provincial aid . . . shall refuse to admit as a patient any person who from sickness, disease or injury or otherwise is in need of active treatment." This section was repealed and replaced by the following provision by 1972, chapter 90, section 11: "Where (a) a person has been admitted to hospital by a physician pursuant to the regulations, and (b) such person requires the level and type of hospital care for which the hospital is approved by the regulations, the hospital shall accept such person as a patient."

31. Section 41 of The Public Hospitals Act, R.S.O. 1970, chapter 378, which was enacted by Statutes of Ontario 1966 chapter 126, section 4.

32. See the very clear discussion of the question in Tollefson, E.A., The Aftermath of the Medicare Dispute in Saskatchewan, *op. cit.*, pp. 458-462.

33. The Health Insurance Act, 1972, Statutes of Ontario 1972, chapter 91, section 20.

34. Tollefson, *op. cit.*, footnote 32, pp. 458-460.

35. The Health Insurance Act, 1972, section 22(1).

36. *Ibid.*, section 22(2).

37. *Ibid.*, section 5.

38. *Ibid.*, section 22.

39. For example, in British Columbia, the case of *Ahmad and the College of*

Physicians and Surgeons, [1973] 6 W.W.R. 412 and [1974] 3 W.W.R. 673 (British Columbia Supreme Court dismissing a physician's appeal from a decision of the Council of the College finding him guilty of infamous and unprofessional conduct in overservicing patients for his own undue financial benefit) and in Ontario, the case of *Casullo and College of Physicians and Surgeons of Ontario,* (1973) 42 D.L.R. (3d) 43, (Ontario Court of Appeal ordering a rehearing before the College's Discipline Committee which had found a physician guilty of professional misconduct in that, for his own personal gain, he ordered tests to be performed for certain of his patients in a laboratory in which he had a financial interest, which tests were unreasonable and excessive).

40. For example, *Regina v. Sanghi* (1971), 6 C.C.C. 123 and *Regina v. Sanghi,* (1973) 11 C.C.C. 265, (Nova Scotia Supreme Court, Appeal Division which in both cases, on the evidence, set aside the physician's conviction for defrauding the government medical care plan).

41. Found in A Review of the Ontario Health Insurance Plan, a report of the Ontario Council of Health, Toronto, 1973.

42. See, for example, Sackett, D. L., Can screening programs for serious diseases improve health?, *Science Forum,* Vol. 3, No. 3, p. 9 (June 1970). Reference may also be made to Cytological Services in Ontario, Toronto, Ontario Council of Health, 1973, a report of an expert group on cytological services. On page 7 the following sentence appears: "With reference to gynecologic cytology, the probability of significant cellular abnormalities becoming evident within 2-3 years after an adequate double negative baseline and laboratory evaluation is so minimal that it is difficult to justify repeat screening smears during such an interval."

43. Report of the Health Planning Task Force, Queen's Printer, Toronto, 1974.

44. Lalonde, Marc, *A New Perspective on the Health of Canadians,* a working document, Ottawa, 1974.

DISCUSSION

JOAN HOLLOBON: Consumer interest in health services has risen in Canada since introduction of health insurance schemes across the country, partly because of a coincidental rise in consumer consciousness over the past few years; partly because a public system provides a focus for criticism; partly because any system using a large proportion of tax dollars is constantly center-stage in public and political discussions.

As Prof. Horace Krever has noted, Canadians do not distrust government in any basic sense, although they dislike "red tape" and suspect "bureaucracy" frequently entails administrative bumbling. Indeed, Canadians display greater distrust of the professions, which are perceived as intrinsically self-serving and usually secretive. Government is often regarded as a protection against powerful sub-groups, whose members (armed with their esoteric knowledge) are considered to stand shoulder-to-shoulder against the common man.

Because of the complexity of the health sciences, the quality of health care is difficult for the public to control or even to analyze. Surveys show the public to be ambivalent: people take for granted that doctors and other professionals "must be" competent ("how would they be allowed to practice otherwise?"); yet, simultaneously, they suspect that professional control is inadequate ("doctors all stick together").

Quality in health care is also defined differently by lay and professional people. As a Toronto orthopedic surgeon commented, "A patient who waits two hours for good advice gets good care; if he waits five minutes for poor advice, he's getting poor care." A survey of specialists' attitudes some years ago revealed that many surgeons felt meticulous surgery was all that could be required of them: rapport with the patient was unimportant or even irrelevant.

Lay people see it differently: communication with doctors and other health workers, as well as the organization that produces tiresome waits, is considered an important and inseparable part of quality of care.

Several studies in Canada have revealed these attitudes. An independent study of the medical profession commissioned by the Ontario Medical Association showed that while nearly 90 percent of people were reasonably satisfied with the medical care they were getting, more than three quarters complained about doctors–generally their poor "human relations." Nearly one half put human relations ahead of competence in what they require of a doctor.

Public agencies controlling quality in a public system must take these wishes into account, as also should the educators of health workers. Doctors, for example, are taught little if anything about how to communicate or how to organize their offices efficiently for their patients' convenience as well as their own.

A publicly funded health system will ultimately face the question of priorities. Whether this reduces quality of care depends also on definition, as well as on aims. Does quality depend on technologically advanced treatment to benefit the relatively few, or refer to a high standard of simpler, less expensive care for the many? Sir MacFarlane Burnet said once that a major medical requirement at world level is provision of good, 1955 standard preventive and curative medicine to 99 percent of the world's population who need it now. This may apply also to more people even on this wealthy continent than is willingly admitted.

If this is rationing, then, as others at the Health Forum pointed out, rationing has always existed, but until now on an individual basis, enforced by each individual's own "cost control" problem through his personal pocketbook. A public system must face the task of redistributing what is available by other criteria than individual wealth. As a Canadian internist Dr. D. D. Gellman noted some years ago, "heartbreakingly difficult" decisions are inevitable as medical technology advances, and "The time may soon come when society may formally and according to a plan (as it does now informally and haphazardly) deny expensive treatment to some individuals in order that less expensive treatment may be made available to a larger number of individuals."

Advances in medical technology make it inevitable that more and more such "heartbreakingly difficult decisions" will have to be made on some basis, private or public. A public system has at least the potential for establishing priorities rationally and distributing the best available to the greatest number equitably.

IV IMPLICATIONS FOR THE UNITED STATES

CHAPTER 6 • THEODORE R. MARMOR

Can the U.S. Learn from Canada?

Concern about problems of health care and interest in issues of national health insurance are salient features of American politics today. Within the larger public there is a broadly diffused sense of unease, particularly about the potential costs of illness and the convenience and reliability of access to care. Politically, there is visible attention to the details of competing national health insurance proposals and some searching about what they would realistically do about the problems of cost, quality and access. Were it not for impeachment, the summer of 1974 might well have been one of sustained debate over America's road to national health insurance. Turning to Canada in this context is a timely effort to learn from the experiences of a broadly comparable nation.

The case for American scrutiny of Canadian national health insurance experience rests on at least two propositions. First, the health care concerns of the two societies are strikingly similar.[1] Worry about the increased proportion of national resources going to medical care is widespread and some uncertainty about the marginal efficacy of increased expenditures is visible among the public officials of both nations. Beyond costs, there is concern about equal access, socially, geographically, and financially. Among a relatively small but vocal public there is substantial interest in questions of quality and organization of care and ferment about regulating health care providers. Second, after many years of focus on expansion of medical care facilities and personnel, there is widespread interest in reducing the use of expensive hospital services and carefully monitoring any efforts to increase the number of hospital beds.

If Canada and the United States share health policy worries, they also have enough other similar features to make the cross-national study of public programs and their effects promising. To put it simply, Canada is enough like the United States to make the effects of Canadian health policies rather like a large natural demonstration or experiment. Most of the industrial countries of the

West share similar health concerns. But major political, social, economic, or cultural differences raise questions whether public policies on health care in those countries would be applicable to the United States. The differences are far less marked with Canada. Politically, while the parliamentary system is an obvious difference, Canada has extensive decentralization of authority, with a tradition of dispute over federal authority that is analogous, though by no means identical to American federalism. In health the structure of the professions, the hospitals, and the history of voluntary health insurance reveals striking similarities as contrasted with, for example, France or Great Britain. America and Canada have medical care industries characterized by voluntary hospitals not owned by the state, a medical care profession under largely fee-for-service remuneration, and a pattern of partial adjustment to the intervention of insurance, mainly nonpublic at first, but in the postwar period incrementally more public in character.[2] It is well to point out that Canadian public involvement came incrementally through benefits (national hospitalization insurance first) rather than beneficiaries (the aged and the poor) as in the United States. But the claim is not that Canada and the United States are identical. Rather, they share enough similarities to make Canadian experience with policy instruments a valuable source of conditional predictions for the United States, even if the proper names have to be changed of both the institutions and the actors.

This paper addresses the implications of Canadian experience with problems of cost, access, and quality of care. One set of implications has to do with how we regard these problems, their causes, character, and level. The second set–and the most relevant from a policy standpoint–follows from the efficacy of Canadian efforts to cope with these problems. It is perhaps appropriate here to mention a serious difficulty in translating Canadian experience into current American debate over national health insurance. The most directly relevant Canadian experience is with particular policy instruments for the control of costs, the fairer distribution of health care access, and regulation of poor quality care. Canadian information may make our appraisal of similar instrumentalities* in American proposals more realistic and informed than usual. But Canada does not constitute a laboratory for the full range of health insurance programs. Without extensive coinsurance or deductibles, Canada does not allow us a test of such a national scheme in practice, though her reluctance to employ such policies is relevant to the discussion. Further, the reputed advantages of prepaid group practices cannot be tested from Canadian experience nor can the way be seen for using national health insurance as a prod for their expansion. They have been, quite simply, too small a part of that

*As one conference participant, Robert Sigmond, later commented, it is the provinces and not the Canadian federal government that deal most fully with particular policy instrumentalities affecting cost, access and regulation. He points out that policy instruments vary greatly among and within provinces, a pattern of administrative decentralization that the reader should keep in mind.

experience for exportation of lessons. It should thus be kept in mind that Canadian experience bears most directly on those proposals in the United States which would follow Canadian example.

COSTS AND COST CONTROL

Discussions of health care costs, prices, and expenditures are possible at many levels of sophistication. The experts have arcane qualifications that can paralyze the unwary. But, broadly speaking, the striking fact about cross-national cost comparisons between Canada and the United States are the parallel findings. The movements of prices, use, and expenditures are similar, particularly for hospital care, and the proportion of national resources or personal income being spent on health is almost identical.[3] As a result by the late 1960's there was a sense of inflationary crisis in both countries and a common preoccupation with ways to contain that inflation.[4] For clarity of discussion it is best to consider Canadian cost experience with hospitals and separately from physicians.*

Hospitals

What are the implications of the growth of Canadian hospital expenditures and efforts to restrain it? It should be noted that Canada and the United States proceeded in the postwar period from somewhat different starting points as to number and costs of beds. Those differences have persisted. Canada remains more generously supplied with hospital beds per capita and has experienced higher rates of hospital admissions and patient days of care.[5] Canada has been and continues to be a heavier spender in the hospital sector. But one must be careful about attributing expenditure increases to national hospital insurance.

American interpreters of Canada must confront two contentions: national health insurance, in and of itself does not seem to have caused rapidly increasing use of hospitals in Canada. But it did bring relatively more rapid increases in expenditures for hospital services.[6] Postwar Canadian experience does not support the interpretation that hospital insurance drives expenditures up through markedly increased utilization. Most of the postwar increases in hospital expenditures in both America and Canada are accounted for by growth in expenses per patient day, not increased per capita utilization. From 1953 to 1971 Canadian hospital expenditures per capita increased 436 percent while hospital patient days per capita only increased 29 percent.[7] Thus, increased utilization accounted for less than 7 percent of the growth in hospital expenditures per capita. The introduction of universal insurance in Canada did not produce a marked increase in admission rates. Indeed, as Andersen and Hull point out, "although these rates continued to increase in the first seven years following the

*This separate treatment may confuse as well as clarify unless the connections between doctors and hospitals are borne in mind. The most obvious is that hospitals directly employ a significant number of doctors. Moreover, physician decisions determine hospital expenditures to a very large extent.

passage of the act, they increased much more slowly than in the period immediately preceding its passage."[8]

Hospital costs thus went up sharply, but not utilization. As Robert G. Evans suggests, this supports the view that hospital admission is not very sensitive to price; and the reduction in point-of-service costs of care did not lead to a large increase in demand. On this view, it follows that copayment mechanisms designed to reduce costs by directing incentives at patients will have little effect on utilization, will redistribute costs to the ill, and in hospitals will not restrain increasing costs.[9] For purposes of American discussion this interpretation of Canadian hospital inflation raises doubts about some of the cost-sharing provisions of a number of current national health insurance proposals.

The fact that Canadian hospital cost increases were dramatic in the late 1960's has serious implications for proposed methods of restraining hospital expenditures in the United States: detailed budget review, incentive reimbursements schemes with global budgeting,* and bed control. As Evans argues:

> . . . wage inflation in the hospital sector is the main source of increase [64 percent] and the timing does not particularly correspond to the extension of insurance, the expansion of utilization, or even the expansion of employment. The most rapid relative wage increases have come in the late 1960's, when paid hours per patient day have been static and both population and utilization increases have slowed down.[10]

If one accepts Evans' view, it suggests limited governmental capacity to restrain hospital expenditures through either detailed budget review or incentive reimbursement schemes. Canada has employed detailed budget review for more than a decade, and while useful for detecting fraud, it has apparently not been thought a successful expenditure restraint and has been partially replaced in some provinces with global budgets and special incentives.[11] Indeed, it appears fair to conclude that Canadian officials have adopted a bed supply strategy of hospital expenditure control. The cutting off of national grants for hospital construction in 1969 parallels the interest in the United States in controlling hospital inflation by reducing the number of hospital beds or at least halting any increase in them. Both the use of supply controls and the concern for better

*The concept of global budgeting confused many symposium participants. Global budgeting with respect to hospitals refers to overall expenditure limits for each hospital either retrospectively or prospectively. Used in this sense, global budgeting is contrasted with line-by-line budgeting in which the lines include pencils, paper, etc. Canadians use global budgeting in another sense as well. They refer to prospective federal expenditure limits as the global amounts available to individual provinces by use of a global budget for health based on last year's expenditures with some adjustment for inflation. Used in this sense, global budgeting is prospective and in contrast to retrospective reimbursement for some portion of provincial health expenditures.

incentive reimbursement schemes can be understood as responses to the failure of detailed review as a major cost-control measure.

Faced with the inability of budget review to limit cost escalation, Canadian officials experimented in the late 1960's with incentive reimbursement approaches to hospitals. The governmental task forces on the costs of medical care made much of the increases in efficiency which were available to the hospital sector. But, according to two of the Canadian authors in this volume, better management as a technique of overall cost containment does not seem as powerful as making hospital beds more scarce. This interpretation ought to be viewed in light of the faith so many American economists have in devising a reimbursement method which would make the hospital sector largely self-regulating.

The full reasons that sensible incentive reimbursement schemes do not seem very powerful are too complicated for this discussion. But the fact that there are serious limitations is of great import. Some American policy commentators firmly believe that "reimbursement patterns must be changed so that hospitals are no longer guaranteed that revenues will equal costs regardless of their productivity." They hold out the hope for an

> . . . incentive reimbursement system . . . advocated to promote hospital efficiency and rationalize capital expenditures. Hospitals would be reimbursed on a case basis, taking account of the case mix of the hospital and its teaching program, the system would be based on a formula that assured the hospital of average efficiency recovery of operating and capital costs. Deficits would force inefficient hospitals to improve their management, change the nature of their operations, or shut down.[12]

Our Canadian interpreters provide evidence that such a system, however appealing theoretically, is very hard to implement. Any one of a number of actual conditions constrain the operation of a self-regulating reimbursement scheme. Poorly managed hospitals are not allowed politically to fail, capital funds are supplied separately, case mix adjustments are not well worked out, or managers of hospitals do not seek "profits" as strongly as increased expenditures. Whatever the reason, the Canadian turn toward supply constraints rather than relying on fine-tuned management incentives is revealing.

National health insurance in the United States has been presented by some as the remedy to cost inflation and by others as further cause of disaster. But in the debate over the causes, character, and appropriate remedies for hospital inflation, a common thread has been the belief that hospitals are used inappropriately and that savings are possible through the more sensible use of this very expensive health institution. This can be thought of as the "hospital substitute" theory, the view that insurance programs should have very wide benefits so as to discourage the use of hospitals for pecuniary rather than medical reasons. This rests, in turn, on the view that excessive hospitalization does take place, that it is dangerous as well as costly, and that alternatives–whether nursing homes or outpatient clinics–would save money. Yet, according to Robert G. Evans, "unless new facilities are balanced by withdrawal of the old, total costs rise." He cites Alberta's experience as evidence that well-developed out-of-hospital convalescent systems do not necessarily reduce hospital costs per capita and explains why "reimbursing agencies [may] fear . . . that attempts at partial efficiency may raise overall health costs"[13]:

> If inpatient care by class of illness of days of stay is unknown, how can one tell if home care, for example, is cheaper or more expensive than institutional care? Proponents of home care note that *average* costs per patient day are much lower than *average* inpatient costs. Everyone knows that the comparison is illegitimate, but no one knows what the cost of convalescent care in acute hospitals really is. So one cannot be sure that home care is really cheaper. Moreover, any acute care beds freed by home care are likely to lead to more admissions, thus raising total hospital costs as well as home care costs. Once again, incomplete information makes identification of efficient strategies difficult. . . .

One can see, without understanding the full complexity of medical economics, why some infer that limiting the supply of hospital beds is a more effective constraint than relying on the alternative institutions strategy (through more comprehensive benefits) to deal with the problem of unwarranted hospitalization. But the diagnosis that Canada has had too "many general hospital beds" which cost them a "great deal of money" (according to the deputy minister of health and welfare), must confront the equally striking fact that "once a modern hospital is built, it is politically very difficult to close."[14]

Making hospital beds more scarce than at present is a cost-control strategy which has advocates in the United States. For the short term at least, it appears that crude measures are likely to be more effective than subtle management methods of theoretical force for which there are few examples of success in the health sector. If there is parallelism on this issue between the United States and Canada, there is a seemingly greater difference in the degree of close budgetary control and review of hospitals thought efficacious. Many Canadian interpreters judge detailed budget review a time-consuming, conflictual, and relatively inefficient method for restraining hospital expenditure increases. They seem to find global budgeting appealing because even if it does not substantially restrain inflation, it will not do worse than previous methods. It is thought to be less conflictual to administer, and at least permits more creative use of hospital resources. By moving from one appealing but disappointing reimbursement system to another, Canada might be said to have provided a demonstration lesson for the United States.

Physicians

There are at least three important topics in the American health care debate for which Canadian experience with medical insurance is strikingly relevant: complaints about the fees and incomes of physicians, the impact of their practices on the total costs of health care, and the controversy over the costs and benefits of different strategies to redistribute physician services by location and by specialty.

The complaint in the United States is that we have too few doctors in the places or specialties of greatest need and that not only are fees and incomes quite high, but physicians contribute to the escalation of health care costs in a number of indirect ways. One strategy that has been advanced in the United States—and is embodied in the fee schedule provisions of several National Health Insurance bills—is detailed specification of fees and peer review of the pattern of services as well as of the appropriateness of the price per unit of service. What can we learn from reported Canadian experience on the likely implications of such a strategy?

The use of explicit fee schedules as currently conceived, will not have nearly the expected force of restraint on physician incomes that its most ardent backers have suggested. This should not be construed as implying that open-ended fee reimbursement systems are superior, or even acceptable; rather it points out the fact that sufficient attention was not paid to the mechanisms by which average net physician incomes would rise markedly under the Canadian Medicare program. Planners there sought to implement physician reimbursement at 85 or 90 percent of established fee schedules. At this they largely succeeded. But percentage reimbursement on an artificial basis of a fee schedule rather than on an estimate of actual fees received per service provides the mechanism by which large-scale increases in physician earnings are guaranteed. Thus, Canada's experience with Medicare, as pointed out by LeClair,[15] has meant "for most physicians . . . a sizeable increase in earnings; in some provinces a 50 percent jump in net earnings occurred in one year." Table 12 of his paper presents the annual percentage change in physician net earnings by province for the 1958-71 period. The marked impact of medical insurance during the year of its implementation and in some cases the following year as well is clear in each province. Evidence on the sources of this increase suggests that increased utilization cannot explain the change.

Participants in the discussion of fee-for-service reimbursement under national health insurance should grasp clearly the indirect mechanisms by which net physician earnings are likely to increase. There are at least two mechanisms of importance. The first and simplest illustration is the reduction of bad debts under National Health Insurance. There has been in Canada some useful and realistic discussion of the relationship between bad debt reduction and percentage increases in net and gross earnings. Consider a physician who collects his standard fee from only 90 percent of his patients, where the payers are subsidizing the nonpayers. Assume that costs per patient are 30 percent of the standard fee. Then the average earnings of the physician can be calculated as follows: assuming 100 patient visits in a given period and \$10/visit as the fee, gross receipts are $900 if 10 percent of the visits are not paid for. Costs are $333, or 1/3 the standard fee times the number of visits. Net earnings then are $567, or gross receipts ($900) minus costs ($333). The average net income per visit is $5.67.

National health insurance presumably does away with bad debts completely. The net earnings calculation is thus 100 visits at $10/visit, or $1000 minus costs of $333, equal to net earnings of $667, or average net income per visit of $6.67. Under these assumptions, the eradication of 10 percent bad debts increases net earnings by 16.5 percent if reimbursement is set at 100 percent of the standard fee. The actual impact of bad debt reduction varies with two factors: the percent of bad debts and the expenses per patient service.

The second mechanism by which incomes will rise is closely akin to the first. It is assumed that physicians vary their fees somewhat in relation to income and insurance coverage. Physicians try to establish their highest rates as the customary fee, even though that is not necessarily either the average fee received or even the most frequently asked fee. If national health insurance reimburses at the highest rate, net earnings will increase just as with bad debt reduction and not show up in official fee increases.

What is at issue is the appropriate standard for fee-for-service remuneration under national health insurance. It seems clear that the appropriate standard should proceed from average fees received, not stated customary charges. But that standard is not operable unless detailed information on the actual fees and costs of physicians are known, and in turn broken down by specialty and region.

Further, we should anticipate from Canadian experience that physician incomes will be a contentious public issue, not simply between the profession and the government, but involving considerable public clamor. Though published material on Canada, such as the papers for this volume, do not regularly provide the details of public debate, disputes over physician incomes in British Columbia, Ontario, and Quebec among others have been among the most conspicuous of the postenactment politics of health care. Of equal interest is the concern of physicians like Bolton of British Columbia to try to explain a) why incomes rose faster than fees in the post-Medicare period and b) how efforts are being made to police the small proportion of Canadian doctors who are engaging in questionable and highly lucrative reimbursement practices.[16] All American discussants are prepared for controversy over the level of fees in a national health insurance program, over whether direct or assignment billing will be mandated, over variation in fees by education or location. But few, in my experience, have extensively considered how fees should be adjusted when a government program removes the issue of bad debts and "reduced" fees completely. A substantial jump in the incomes of American doctors took place through the Medicare program and it is arguable whether reduced fees or bad debts are as significant in the United States now as were in Canada at the outset of their Medicare program. What appears unarguable is that Canadian experience highlights an issue which our policymakers will want to consider as payment methods and levels are debated.

A related implication involves professional review of the "patterns of service." "Peer review" is already a heated issue among American physicians; Canadian concern about patterns of costly service which do not show up in extra billing, but in extra servicing, is parallel. One lesson apparently drawn in Canada is that a claims review works well for the egregious cases of excessive and inappropriate claims but that the fee-for-service system's tendency toward multiplying units of care and altering the mix of procedures is very hard to control. It is worth noting at this point a paradox concerning the insistence on fee-for-service payment in societies like Canada and the United States and the increased threats to professional independence which the governmental review of such a payment method entails. Brian Abel-Smith suggests elsewhere that,

> . . . world experience has shown, as the United States experience is also beginning to show, the paradox underlying attempts to preserve the free and independent practice of medicine. At first sight, fee-for-service payment enables private free-market medicine to be readily combined with health insurance. In practice, it is not long before interference with medical practice becomes much greater than occurs or needs to occur when physicians are salaried employees in government service. Physicians are made answerable for each of their acts. Because there are incentives for abuse, restrictive and punitive safeguards are established to prevent abuse from occurring. Sometimes the punishment falls on the physicians, but sometimes it falls on the patient.[17]

Whatever world experience has shown about the problems of fee-for-service payment, Canadian experience suggests for America that fee-for-service payment will predominate in the postnational health insurance world. Indeed, it is the problems of making fee-for-service regulation appropriate without its being excessively punitive that should occupy the attention of planners more than imagining general shifts from present fee-for-service methods to other forms like capitation and salary.[18] Concern for wholesale transformation may drive out discussion of marginal improvements in the present dominant method of payment or of ways to adjust national health insurance to other less traditional remuneration methods. Making prepaid group practices financially attractive to either patients or medical care providers is under Canadian Medicare apparently a continuing problem.

For some American health care discussants increasing the supply of physicians is a strategy for improving both the distribution of physicians and for restraining through competition the fees doctors can charge. That strategy appears, from Canadian experience and commentary, to lack promise on either count. And, to the extent physicians determine the use of other medical care facilities, it presents additional inflationary problems as well. The common sense view that increasing the supply of physicians will improve matters greatly—what

John Evans has referred to as the "spillover" theory–is challenged now by a number of Canadian commentators and the national government publicly expresses concern that a "saturation point for certain specialties is very close or has been reached in a number of provinces."[19] While there appears to be some improvement in supplying physicians to underdoctored areas, dramatic increases in physician numbers do not apparently restrain fees through competition. British Columbia, as Robert G. Evans points out, is typically near the top in the levels of fees and near bottom in average physician incomes, despite being the province with the largest number of physicians per capita. It may well be that the role of "national health insurance [in Canada has] been to relax further any market constraints on how physicians manipulate utilization to generate income," a view which in turn rests on the findings that average earnings of physicians, relative to average weekly wages, rose faster in the period 1957-64 than in the Medicare period 1964-71.[20] And it may also be that increasing physician supply is a weak and expensive instrumentality for coping with the problems of cost increases and the maldistribution of physician manpower.

While some suggest increasing the supply of doctors before national health insurance, other American commentators feel certain that requiring patient financial participation–through either deductibles or coinsurance–will introduce a needed and efficacious degree of cost-consciousness. Our Canadian discussants take a much less enthusiastic view of significant patient copayment. Where modest copayment was tried under Canadian Medicare–in Saskatchewan during 1968-71–the evidence appears to be that its impact was disproportionately felt by the poor and the old.[21] Moreover, there is little evidence in Canada that copayment reduced the "least medically necessary" care, and there are thus both distributional and medical grounds for questioning this policy instrument. Finally, there is the judgment by some commentators that, once in the medical system, the patient is dependent on the physician's judgments about further care and consequently that copayment is mistargeted away from the doctor, the "gatekeeper" to medical services. What copayment does do, as Robert G. Evans has pointedly said, "is reduce program costs by transferring them back to the ill rather than forward to taxpayers." In Canada, he judges, this is "politically highly unpopular, and consequently copayments as a means of cost control appears . . . a dead issue."[22]

Copayment is most clearly not a "dead" issue in the United States; indeed all of the current major proposals rely on family copayment for the great bulk of current average family health expenditures. Two considerations shape our discussion differently from Canada's. One is the effort to make copayment more equitable by varying the amounts with family income, thus trying to reduce the disproportional burden which fixed dollar copayments represent for the poor. The difficulty here, which Canadian experience does not bear upon, is that the likely supplementation of national health insurance under either the 1974 Nixon or Kennedy-Mills bills would reduce the out-of-pocket expenditures of the middle and upper income groups able to afford supplementary insurance.

Copayment under those plans would turn into a reduction of program costs through supplementation by private insurance, with the resulting distribution of actual cost sharing sharply different from the formal proposals. The second American consideration is the search for ways to limit substantially the federal program costs of national health insurance. In the political bidding of 1974 every effort has been made to show limited amounts of "new" federal expenditures, even if such arrangements represent misleading labelling of required nongovernmental expenditures as "private."[23] On the other hand, running the total personal health care bill through governmental budgets does have an impact on the opportunities for other governmental initiatives; in some respects the current Canadian emphasis on the limited impact of further ordinary medical service expenditures reflects the same perception that governmental opportunities for other programs are severely limited by the increasing share of the public budget devoted to health insurance.

ACCESS TO CARE

What are the implications for the United States of Canadian findings about the impact of national health insurance on access to medical care services? What does national health insurance mean for the utilization of medical care services generally? What, further, does the Canadian experience teach us about the distributional consequences of national health insurance, on access measured, for instance, by income class? Both of these questions are important in the current American national health insurance debate. There is the hope that lowering financial barriers will redistribute access to care much more fairly than our present arrangements and help reduce the striking inequalities in the probabilities that similar medical problems will receive equal medical attention by race, income, location, age, and connection with physicians. Both projections seem overstated when measured against Canadian experience.

We should expect relatively modest changes in the overall utilization of medical care services on the basis of Canada's experience. In both the hospital and physician sectors per capita changes in use were relatively modest in the wake of national insurance.[24] The American fears of runaway utilization from "cheap" care thus appear unrealistic, and ignore the impact of preexistent health insurance, the barriers to care which financing will not change, and the rationing which doctors will impose. Here is a case where the findings of the natural experiment–Canada–conflict with projections of sharply increased use (or crowded offices) based on estimates of the elasticity of demand for medical care in the United States (see note 25). I am not qualified to judge the full merits of this issue, but the Canadian findings, while discomforting about rising expenditures, are certainly less alarming on the issue of overall increases in actual or attempted utilization.

One's judgment of the impact of Canadian national health insurance on the distribution of access depends very much on initial expectations. All of the reported evidence I have seen suggests that national health insurance overall reallocated access to some extent from "rich" to "poor." This is true of the Beck study of Saskatchewan—measuring access by the proportion of non-users of medical care services by income class—where the findings were of substantial declines in non-use by the lowest income class and relative stability in non-use by other income classes. The Enterline *et al.* study in Quebec shows not only an increase in the use of physician care by income groups under $5000, but a decline in physician visits for income groups above $9000. Apparently similar evidence is reported by Badgley and his colleagues.[26] But the evidence is not that such redistribution took place everywhere nor that national health insurance eradicated differences in access by income class. Disparities in access remain, as our Canadian papers show, and permit observers to emphasize that the problem of access remains partially unsolved in the wake of national health insurance. As Castonguay suggests in his emphasis on the problems remaining, "achieving access to care is not strictly a financial problem; physical and psycho-social barriers are also of significant importance."

The other side, however, is that we should note the direction of redistribution in favor of the less advantaged. A recent critique of American Medicare by Karen Davis argues that equal program benefits lead to unequal and greater benefits for the higher-income aged and that income-conditioned programs like Medicaid partially redress the balance. Because our Medicare has significant cost-sharing, we should approach this interpretation with caution. It may well be that America's better-off aged are less deterred by cost-sharing, that they use more expensive services, and are much more likely to buy supplementary insurance for deductibles and coinsurance. If that is the case, and if Medicaid reduces those out-of-pocket expenditures for the poorest, one should expect that the poorest and the richest would use disproportionately larger shares of the Medicare budget.[27] But, the Canadian case suggests that where out-of-pocket costs are almost zero, equal benefits are associated with increasing access for the disadvantaged.

However one evaluates the impact of national health insurance on access, there seems agreement that removing financial barriers is insufficient for producing equal access to care. One should distinguish between equal use by income class, by region, and sex from equal access measured by the likelihood of identical medical responses to similar health conditions. Canada has not, it appears, achieved equality on the first count; in contrast, there is evidence in the United States that poor Americans (under $3000/year) see doctors as or more often than their compatriots. But the probability that a given symptom will stimulate care varies markedly with socioeconomic characteristics. What Canada suggests is that national health insurance contributes to greater equalization of access, but that it neither solves the problem nor eradicates concern for further amelioration. Yet we should note the increases in availability of medical care personnel where financial incapacity before national health insurance was a problem; LeClair reports that in Newfoundland the supply of medical practitioners in relation to population increased between 20 and 30 percent in the first three years of the Medicare program.[28]

The issue of access highlights an interesting difference in the focus of current American and Canadian discussions of medical care. Canadian commentators now sharply distinguish between access to good health and access to medical care services. The "New Perspective on the Health of Canadians" illustrates the distinction and emphasizes that Canadians cannot expect substantial improvements in their health status through medical care. Though this argument is made in the United States, it is often employed to discourage national health insurance itself. Yet it makes an enormous difference whether one highlights the nonmedical care determinants of health status before or after the introduction of insurance. The arguments for national health insurance are about the access to medical services and consequences of their use as much, if not more so, than about means to healthiness. Canadians take for granted now that illness no longer is associated with fears of destitution; they hardly mention that one of the most central impacts of national health insurance was the improved access to protection against financial catastrophe. Once it is accomplished and recognized that access varies with variables other than income, it may well be that American leaders too will focus on trying to influence environmental factors as the "key to better national health and reduced rates of increases in health costs."[29]

NATIONAL HEALTH INSURANCE AND QUALITY OF CARE

Quality of medical care is an elusive subject, hard to define but obviously touching matters of great importance. Even the famous Hall Commission report explained what quality meant by discussing what it depended upon. In seeking the "highest possible health standards," administrators of Canadian national health insurance had to realize that the quality of medical care depended on the "supply, availability, knowledge, skill, and dedication of professional qualified personnel, secondly, on the facilities at their disposal, and, thirdly, on the organization of the services."[30] The result, in both the United States and Canada, is that the difficulties of this subject are as often cited as the resolutions.

It may help, for purposes of discussion, to begin by distinguishing under the topic of quality cases of patient abuse from the inefficient use of medical care services. By abuse I mean either the gross deprivation of care when needed or the poor performance of medical care procedures. In either case the patient is harmed by the acts or omission of medical care providers. By inefficient use of resources I mean medical care practices which could be done more cheaply or the cost of which could finance more effective medical care interventions.

National health insurance in Canada seems to have had some positive effect on deprivation of care and little or no effect on the incidence of abusive care.[31] Further, it appears that Canada has employed traditional measures to deal with actual or possible instances of patient abuse. Peer review and malpractice litigation continued as the *ex post facto* measures and licensure–to eliminate unqualified personnel or facilities–remained a standard technique. To insure quality one inspected qualifications; the interest, as Kreever suggests, was more in the legal competence of practitioners than the actual competence.[32]

What does appear to have happened after the enactment of national health insurance is considerable controversy over unanticipated issues ("denturists" and acupuncture, for instance) and less over the widely publicized fears that national health insurance would immobilize the medical care system by overstraining its practitioners. This is but one example of the general point Kreever makes about the quality of care issue; the problems of quality were not a central issue of the pre-national health insurance debate and the resolution of problems has proceeded piecemeal rather than systematically.

It should be noticed that some Canadian commentators assimilate issues of cost control and fraud detection into the quality issue. The narrow definition of abuse is harm to the patient by medical action or inaction. Much broader is the concern with "abuses such as overservicing by physicians, overutilization by physicians, overcharging and so on," topics which Kreever mentions as "abuses of the system." Whether one regards these as quality issues or not, it is noteworthy that it is to these matters that much of the attention concerning review of professional service has been directed. It may well be that abuse of the program becomes a more salient issue for peer review than abuse of the body and spirit.[33]

In the concern for abuses of the system in Canada there seems somewhat less explicit attention to measuring the quality of caring, as opposed to curing or overcharging and overusing, in the wake of national health insurance. Kreever suggests "no evidence of significant deterioration" in the physician-patient relationship, but he uses malpractice litigation as the indicator and the United States as the comparative benchmark. Concern about patient and practitioner satisfaction–surely an issue in evaluating the quality of the program–remains important, but inordinately difficult to discuss with precision and convincing, as opposed to anecdotal, evidence.

An intermediate topic between abuse and inefficiency is what might be termed questionable patterns of practice. By that I mean patterns of care that do not constitute individual episodes of malpractice, but are risky in relation to medical benefits. Two classic examples are excessive prescriptions of drugs and the excessive incidence, according to considerable medical opinion, of surgical procedures like tonsillectomies and hysterectomies. This is of great importance to some American commentators; Canadian commentaries suggest it is hard to make this kind of "misuse" a broad public issue. But there is clearly concern among health care leaders that, as Abel-Smith pungently puts it, "so many people lose their appendices, their wombs, or their tonsils . . . without good cause."[34] The presumed connection between the supply of practitioners and the incidence of procedures has sharpened this worry in Canada.

Inefficient use of medical care resources does not necessarily mean direct detrimental consequences for patient health. Rather what is of concern are the opportunities for more effective health-enhancing activities which are foregone because of expenditures on less effective, expensive modes of care. One implication from Canadian experience is that this issue will become more significant than it is in the United States today. Whereas one might reasonably say that the factors which determine the quality of health should be separated from those which affect the quality of the medical procedures given, efficiency issues are increasingly at the center of Canadian discussion of health care quality. It is certainly significant that Canadian ministers refer to the "health field" (which includes all matters affecting health) as the object of federal interest and express concern that too many resources are being devoted to the personal health care system. The concern for hospital expenditures typifies the interest in inefficient use of medical care resources and, as in the United States, the call for more primary care is now familiar. But, if we are to pursue this topic, it may well be that different kinds of information are required than that now routinely produced for monitoring the costs or the "abuses" of the health insurance system.

This review of the implications of Canadian national health insurance–centered on cost, quality, and access–has been necessarily sketchy and tentative. Yet even this broad scope has left without discussion some fascinating topics in the Canadian experience: financing arrangements between the central government and the provincial administrative authorities, the role of private health insurance companies before, during, and after enactment, the handling of difficult benefit items like long-term psychiatric care and others. One hopes that the further investigation of these topics in North American health policy will be subject to a rapid rate of growth without inflation.

FOOTNOTES

1. There is evidence, in fact, that a variety of health care concerns–rising costs, interest in rationalization, worry about efficacy and patient satisfaction–are evident throughout Western Europe and North America irrespective of the details of medical care's public financing modes. See Somers, Anne R., The Rationalization of Health Services: A Universal Priority, *Inquiry*, Vol. VIII, 1971.

   The enumeration of health care concerns is extraordinarily extensive in both Canada and the United States. Note particularly, however, the interest in similar Canadian health insurance concerns and experience by the U.S. Congress' Committee on Ways and Means in its review of issues of national health insurance: "The material on Canada is in considerably more detail than that presented for other nations since the Canadian experience seems more relevant to U.S. policy." Committee on Ways and Means, *National*

Health Insurance Resource Book (Washington: G.P.O., 1974), p. 111.

2. There is a large literature on Canada's movement toward national health insurance. Among the more helpful brief interpretations, see Taylor, Malcolm G., The Canadian Health Insurance Program, *Public Administration Review,* January/February, 1973, No. 1; Hastings, J.E.F., Federal-provincial Insurance for Hospital and Physicians' Care in Canada, *International Journal of Health Services,* Vol. 1, No. 4, 1971. For fuller treatment, the basic source is the *Report of the Royal Commission on Health Services* (Hall Commission, Ottawa: the Queen's Printer, 1964) and supporting studies. For the physician sector more generally, see Blishen, B. R., *Doctors and Doctrines* (University of Toronto Press, Toronto, 1969).

   For similar information on the U.S., from a comparative perspective, see Anderson, Odin, *Health Care–Can There Be Equity: The United States, Sweden and England* (John Wiley and Sons, New York, 1972) and Marmor, T. R., *The Politics of Medicare,* Aldine, Chicago, 1973).

3. See for example, *National Health Expenditures in Canada, 1960-71 with Comparative Data for the United States,* Health Program Branch, Ottawa, October, 1973, and the documentation presented in this volume by Stuart Altman. For the proportion of national resources expended in health, see Altman, pp. 193-94.

4. The Canadian alarm was fully expressed in the *Task Force Reports on Costs of Health Care in Canada,* The Queen's Printer, Ottawa, 3 vols. Concern about the rate of inflation in the health care field was plain as well in the Economic Council of Canada's Seventh Annual Review: *Patterns of Growth,* September, 1970. The parallel American preoccupation with rising medical care costs was perhaps best evidenced by the production in the first Nixon Administration of a "white paper" on health which catalogued familiar diagnoses of the ills of the industry.

   These same concerns were apparent in the hearings on national health insurance before the Ways and Means Committee in October/November, 1971; 93rd Congress, 2nd Session, 11 volumes (Washington: G.P.O., 1971).

5. See for the period 1966-72, LeClair, Maurice, The Canadian Health Care System, elsewhere in this volume, Table 3; for the earlier period, see Andersen and Hull, Hospital Utilization and Cost Trends in Canada and the United States, *Medical Care,* Vol. 7, No. 6, November-December, 1969, special supplement, Table 5, p. 13; compare Altman in this volume, p. 198 and Table 5.

6. This information is consistent with that of Andersen and Hull, *op. cit.,* and R. G. Evans' chapter, Beyond the Medical Marketplace: Expenditure,

Utilization and Pricing of Insured Health Care in Canada, paper prepared for National Bureau of Economic Research Conference on the Role of Health Insurance in the Health Services Sector, Rochester, New York, May 31-June 1, 1974, hereafter cited as *N.B.E.R.* paper. For a somewhat different interpretation see M. LeClair's "The Canadian," *op. cit.,* pp. 62, 77, 79 where attention is focused on increased hospital expenditures and less attention paid to the differential contributants to that increase.

A number of conference participants worried that the denial of NHI's impact on hospital use in Canada might be misleading in view of the fact that the Canadians built up their hospital facilities in anticipation of universal hospital coverage. In that sense, NHI increased the supply of hospital beds indirectly, a point which should be distinguished from the view that the NHI program induced Canadians to use more hospital services directly.

7. Calculated from R. G. Evans, pp. 17, Table 2, and 22, Table 4.

8. Andersen and Hull, *op. cit.,* p. 9; see the similar interpretation in Evans, R. G., *N.B.E.R.* paper, pp. 15-20.

9. Evans, R. G. to Berman, R. A., letter, July 2, 1974, on the subject of major issues to be highlighted for Sun Valley conference on Canada's experience with national health insurance.

10. Evans, R. G., *N.B.E.R.* paper, *op. cit.,* p. 34.

11. For a discussion of the reliance on detailed, line-item budget review as the mechanism of budgetary control during the first decade of Canada's national hospital insurance, see Evans, *ibid.,* pp. 40-44, especially, and LeClair, pp. 57-58. For the arguments justifying less detailed budget review, see Castonguay, Claude, The Quebec Experience: Effects on Accessibility, elsewhere in this book, pp. 106-07, including an explanation of global budgeting. The incentive reimbursement policies are explained by Evans, R. G., *op. cit.,* and evaluated, pp. 35-43.

In a personal communication R. Sigmond noted that my comments applied to what might be called "green eyeshade" line-item budgeting. "Isn't it obvious," he asks, "that the 'green eyeshade' budget review won't work? Isn't that the lesson? Why knock a sound budget approach by implication?" by which Sigmond means "program budgeting" in which various elements of a hospital's program are reviewed separately. Sigmond is right about the lesson.

12. Judy and Lester Lave, *The Hospital Construction Act: An Evaluation of the Hill-Burton-Program 1948-1973,* Washington, D.C.: The American

Enterprise Institute for Public Policy Research, 1974, p. 3.

13. Evans, *N.B.E.R.* paper, *op. cit.,* p. 41. See note 26 in Evans's *N.B.E.R.* paper for view that Canadian experience with institutional alternatives parallels American experience under the U.S. Medicare program. Provinces with well-developed convalescent care systems, like Alberta, have relatively higher hospital costs per capita. Feldstein, M., An Econometric Model of the Medicare System, *Quarterly Journal of Economics,* Vol. 85, No. 1 (February, 1971) reports, according to Evans, that extended care facilities raise costs per hospital *episode*–what is saved in lower acute care stays is lost in long extended care stays.

14. LeClair, M., *op. cit.,* p. 15.

15. *Ibid.,* p. 74, and Table 13 which presents the large percentage changes in net physician earnings by year before and after the introduction of national medical care insurance.

16. See Bolton, D. M., Patterns of Practice: A New Dimension of Peer Review, *British Columbia Medical Journal,* February and March, 1972.

17. Abel-Smith, Brian, Value for Money in Health Services, *Social Security Bulletin,* July, 1974, Vol. 37, No. 7, p. 22.

18. For evidence on the practically invariant relationship between dominant methods of physician remuneration before and after the enactment of universal government health programs among western industrial democracies, see Glaser, William, *Paying the Doctor,* Johns Hopkins Press, Baltimore, 1970, and Marmor and Thomas, The Politics of Paying Physicians. . . , *International Journal of Health Services,* Vol. 1, No. 1, 1971. The actual working out of these common constraints in the Canadian case is mentioned in all of the conference papers.

19. LeClair, *op. cit.,* p. 76. The "supersaturation-spillover" approach is criticized in Evans, John R., Health Manpower Problems: The Canadian Experience, prepared for the Institute of Medicine, Washington, D.C., May 8-9, 1974, p. 15.

20. Evans, *N.B.E.R.* paper, *op. cit.,* p. 52.

21. Discussed in LeClair, pp. 48-49 and Table 7, based on Beck, R. G., The Demand for Physician Services in Saskatchewan, unpublished Ph.D. thesis, University of Alberta, 1971.

22. Evans, communication to Berman, R. A., p. 6, and LeClair, for discussion of the physician as the "gatekeeper" of medical care expenditures, p. 79.

23. This issue is clearly defined by Karen Davis in the chapter on "National Health Insurance," in Blechman, Gramlich, and Hartman, *Setting National Priorities: The 1975 Budget* (Washington, D.C.: The Brookings Institution, 1974).

24. For the hospital sector, see Evans, *N.B.E.R.* paper, *op. cit.*, Table IV, p. 22. See LeClair, Table 5, discussed on p. 43, on changes in per capita physician use, all "consistent with the view" that government medical insurance did not generate a surge of patient-initiated demand.

25. See, for instance, Newhouse, Phelps, and Schwartz, "Policy Options and the Impact of National Health Insurance," The Rand Corporation, June, 1974, a report published almost in its entirety in the *New England Journal of Medicine,* June 13, 1974.

26. Beck, R. G., Economic Class and Access to Physician Services Under Medical Care Insurance, *International Journal of Health Services,* Vol. 3, No. 3, 1973; Enterline, P.E., *et al.*, The Distribution of Medical Care Services Before and After 'Free' Care–The Quebec Experience, *New England Journal of Medicine,* Vol. 289, No. 22, November 29, 1973; Badgley, R. E., *et al.,* The Impact of Medicare in Wheatville, Saskatchewan, 1960-65, *Canadian Journal of Public Health,* Vol. 58, No. 3 (March, 1967).

27. See Karen Davis, *op. cit.*, pp. 214-217.

28. LeClair, *op. cit.*, p. 75.

29. Issue raised in connection with the conference paper by Horace Kreever, "National Health Insurance and Problems of Quality," personal communication.

30. *Hall Commission Report, op. cit.*, p. 1.

31. See LeClair, *op. cit.,* p. 43 for suggestion of how Canadian national health insurance appears to have favorably affected infant and maternal mortality through wider use of prenatal care.

32. Kreever, Horace, "National Health Insurance and Problems of Quality," paper prepared for Sun Valley Forum on National Health, August, 1974, p. 214.

33. Kreever, *op. cit.*, p. 218.

34. Abel-Smith, *op. cit.*, p. 18.

ACKNOWLEDGMENTS

A considerable number of people generously helped me in the preparation of this essay. I want to warmly thank them while absolving them of responsibilities for what I did with their assistance. Wayne Hoffman and Tom Heagy provided valuable research assistance both at the beginning and during the final revisions of the paper. Odin Anderson and Robert Kudrle helpfully commented on an early draft. William Bailey, Robert Sigmond, and Joseph Newhouse gave me the benefit of their extensive written comments on the paper presented at the Sun Valley conference itself. I want to thank all of the conference participants but particularly note the helpful assistance of John Evans, Maurice LeClair, and Robert Evans. Malcolm Taylor of Canada's York University was very kind in assisting me during the initial interviews I had in Canada. Finally, I want to thank the staff members at the Center for Health Administration Studies, University of Chicago who so efficiently and good-naturedly worked on this essay—Lynn Carter, Elaine Scheye and Evelyn Friedman.

V CONCLUSIONS

National Health Insurance in Canada: Implications for the United States Symposium Report

The Sun Valley Forum on National Health, a nonprofit institution, was established in 1971 to pursue educational activities concerning public policy questions relating to the nation's health care system. In June, 1971, the Forum addressed a major symposium to the financing of the nation's health care system; in June, 1972, the Forum turned to the organization of the nation's system for delivering medical care; the June, 1973, symposium was devoted to the subject of primary health care.

In the summer of 1974, the Forum undertook a review of the Canadian experience with national health insurance. The purpose was to ascertain what lessons the United States can learn from the Canadian experience as the United States moves toward the adoption of some form of national health program. Five expert papers were commissioned for the symposium, four of them written by Canadians. Thirty-nine persons attended the symposium, including practicing physicians, academicians, medical care specialists, economists, hospital administrators, government officials, members of the press, lawyers, and insurance and health care industry executives. One participant was from Great Britain, eight were from Canada, and the balance from the United States.

At the conclusion of the 1974 symposium, the following report was prepared on the basis of the preceding four days of discussion. All participants were given an opportunity to comment on the report if they wished, but since the subject of the report is lessons for the United States, only United States participants were called upon to endorse or dissent from the report. It should not be assumed that any participant necessarily subscribes to every conclusion appearing in the report; but except where the report indicates that a participant accepted the proffered opportunity to dissent or express a separate opinion, the report represents the sense of the United States participants in the symposium.*

RICHARD A. BERMAN
Rapporteur

*Mr. Constantine took no part in the preparation of this report.

The Canadian experience with its national health insurance system provides a useful source of instruction and guidance for the United States as it considers the adoption of some form of national health insurance program. The situations in the two countries are, of course, not identical. The United States would not exactly relive the Canadian experience even if it were to adopt the same plan of national health insurance. But the overall structure of the health care system of Canada prior to the adoption of its national health insurance program was sufficiently parallel to that of the United States today that the following general lessons from the Canadian experience can be usefully drawn by the United States.

Access to and Patterns of Care

1. Introduction of national health insurance in Canada was not intended to and did not appreciably alter the nation's basic structure for the provision of medical care.

(a) If the United States were to adopt a plan substantially the same as Canada's, there is no significant reason to expect that United States experience would be different in this respect.

2. Removal of financial barriers to medical care improved equity of access and removed the fear of financial catastrophe caused by illness. Since the adoption of national health insurance, the poor in Canada have been going to doctors earlier and more often.

(a) If the United States were to adopt a plan substantially the same as Canada's, there is no significant reason to expect that United States experience would be different in this respect.

3. Although some feared that the introduction in 1968 of national health insurance in Canada would produce an overwhelming immediate demand for services that would swamp existing hospital and physician capacities, this did not in fact develop. The system has, however, increased the total of medical services provided, yielding increase in aggregate cost and pressure for new resources.

(a) If the United States were to adopt a plan substantially the same as Canada's, there is no significant reason to expect that United States experience would be different in this respect.*

*Dr. Wilbur believes that Canada's step by step introduction of its hospital insurance plan and its medical care plan over a period of several years was the reason why the system was able to absorb the changes without swamping and believes the United States should draw the lesson indicated to move by steps and not all at once.

4. By providing medical care purchasing power for all citizens, national health insurance in Canada has in some degree made it possible for physicians to go to poor and rural areas, but has not solved the problem of providing adequate health services in such areas, particularly in the specialties.

(a) If the United States were to adopt a plan substantially the same as Canada's, there is no significant reason to expect that United States experience would be different in this respect.

(b) If it were desired to avoid this result, different features would have to be included in the United States plan.

5. Removal of financial barriers to access in Canada has not solved all problems of access for patients. Attitudinal barriers persist, and sporadic overcrowding and queuing interpose other impediments to access and produce at least a form of temporal rationing.

(a) If the United States were to adopt a plan substantially the same as Canada's, there is no significant reason to expect that United States experience would be different in this respect.

6. By providing medical care purchasing power for all citizens, national health insurance in Canada may have helped slow the movement toward specialization of health practitioners and encouraged a turn toward primary care. It has not significantly contributed toward, and may have deterred, a solution to the problem of organizing an efficient system for delivery of primary care.

(a) If the United States were to adopt a plan substantially the same as Canada's, there is no significant reason to expect that United States experience would be different in this respect.

(b) If it were desired to avoid this result, different features would have to be included in the United States plan.

Quality of care and relationships

7. The great majority of the Canadian public appear to have perceived neither a reduction nor an improvement in the quality of medical care as a result of the adoption of a national health insurance plan.

(a) If the United States were to adopt a plan substantially the same as Canada's, there is no significant reason to expect that United States experience would be different in this respect.

8. There is no evidence that national health insurance in Canada has impaired the physician-patient relationship.

(a) If the United States were to adopt a plan substantially the same as Canada's, there is no significant reason to expect that United States experience would be different in this respect.

9. Canada has sought to improve the quality of medical services through investment in educational programs for health practitioners and through correction of substandard medical facilities. But in no country have standards or techniques been developed for measuring the quality of performance of medical procedures, or their health outcomes, so that no lesson for the United States can be inferred as to the effect of the Canadian health insurance system on quality of performance or outcomes.

Costs of medical care

10. The objectives of the Canadian national health insurance system were universality of coverage, comprehensiveness of benefits, portability of benefits and public accountability; cost containment was not a major initial objective. Total national expenditures for medical care under the Canadian system are now moving upward rapidly and will continue to do so unless new control strategies are introduced and effectively pursued.

(a) If the United States were to adopt a plan substantially the same as Canada's, there is no significant reason to expect that United States experience would be different in this respect.

(b) If it were desired to avoid this result, different features would have to be included in the United States plan.

11. In addition to the rise in total expenditures for medical care in Canada, unit costs and prices for health services have also risen. In addition to general inflation, forces driving medical costs upward include: union pressures for wage increases of non-physician health personnel, introduction of expensive new medical technology, absence of standards by which to judge what is to be considered an adequate level of medical care, and the lack of effective incentives to contain costs. In Canada, introduction of national health insurance reduced resistance to these pressures and to that extent contributed to the increases in aggregate cost. Price increases for medical care in Canada have moved upward in a generally parallel way to medical costs in the United States, where over 90 percent of hospital expenditures are already paid for by health insurance.

(a) If the United States were to adopt a plan substantially the same as Canada's, there is no significant reason to expect that United States experience would be different in this respect.

(b) If it were desired to avoid this result, different features would have to be included in the United States plan.

12. The Canadian experience demonstrates again that for medical services, market processes of supply and demand do not work in their usual way; within very wide limits, the level of medical services used is primarily determined not by the user but by the supplier, particularly the physician. Users can apparently consume virtually unlimited medical service and, in an open-ended reimbursable financing system, physicians have no incentive to contain the level of services provided unless special controls and sanctions are built in to discourage a continuing upward movement in total utilization.

(a) If the United States were to adopt a plan substantially the same as Canada's, there is no significant reason to expect that United States experience would be different in this respect.

13. In Canada, the supply of physicians has been sharply increased in recent years as a result of governmentally financed expansion of the medical schools and net immigration. This increase may have inhibited the rate of increase in, but it has not led to a lowering of medical fee structures through competition nor has it significantly altered imbalances in the geographic distribution of physicians. The increase in supply has, as indicated in Paragraph 12, increased the aggregate level of utilization and expenditures for medical services.

(a) If the United States were to adopt a plan substantially the same as Canada's, there is no significant reason to expect that United States experience would be different in this respect.

14. Canadian expenditures for hospital care have risen sharply in recent years but the increase is mainly attributable to the sharp increase in hospital beds produced by earlier government programs. Increases in hospital expenditures are attributable to the rise in costs *per diem* per patient; there have been no significant changes in the patterns of admission of patients into hospitals consequent upon the national health insurance plan.

(a) If the United States were to adopt a plan substantially the same as Canada's, there is no significant reason to expect that United States experience would be different in this respect.

15. Standardized physician fee schedules have been developed in each

Canadian province and are recognized as an essential element of the Canadian system. There are, however, no significant constraints upon the physician's ability to multiply units of care. Fixed fee schedules may have inhibited sharper escalation of physicians' incomes but they have not led either to a leveling off of physicians' incomes or to a significant containment of total medical services expenditures.

(a) If the United States were to adopt a plan substantially the same as Canada's, there is no significant reason to expect that United States experience would be different in this respect.

(b) If it were desired to avoid this result, different features would have to be included in the United States plan.

16. Some Canadian provinces experimented for a short time with modest copayment and deductible requirements. That experience indicated that such provisions to some extent redistributed the costs from taxpayers to the ill, and to some extent operated as a barrier to receipt of services by the poor, but had relatively little effect upon general levels of utilization of medical services and no ascertainable substantial effect in restraining total medical care expenditures.*

(a) If the United States were to adopt a plan substantially the same as Canada's, there is no significant reason to expect that United States experience would be different in this respect.

(b) If it were desired to avoid this result, different features would have to be built in to the United States plan.

17. Canadian experience indicates that professional peer review of physicians' charges has worked satisfactorily to detect and control excessive utilization and billing and fraudulent or inappropriate claims, but has not been effective in containing the multiplication of units of care under the fee-for-service system.

(a) If the United States were to adopt a plan substantially the same as Canada's, there is no significant reason to expect that United States experience would be different in this respect.

18. Since the beginning of its national health insurance Canada has used line budget review systems. These have not effectively restrained hospital expenditures and Canada is therefore now turning to an attempt to limit

*Mr. Altman believes the Canadian experience in this respect was too limited in scale and time to draw definitive conclusions on this point either for Canada or for the United States.

hospital expenditures by "global budgeting"–that is, by setting only a total budget for a hospital, leaving more expenditure flexibility for hospital administrators, more latitude for discretionary use of hospital resources and, hopefully, more incentive for economies. If it had been politically possible, it would have been better to build in this and other administrative controls when the system was first adopted, since it has proved difficult to change the system to introduce new controls once it is in place.

(a) If the United States were to adopt a plan substantially the same as Canada's original plan, there is no significant reason to expect that United States experience would be different in this respect.

(b) If it were desired to avoid this result, different features would have to be included in the United States plan.

19. The marketplace normally uses price as the rationing allocator of a good or service among users. The national health insurance system in Canada removed price as the rationer of medical services but instituted no alternative process of rationing except crowding and queuing. The result, taken together with unit cost rises, has been a marked and unanticipated increase in total expenditures. With administrative controls on cost ineffective so far, Canadian governmental authorities are now turning to the strategies of limiting the supply of physicians and hospital beds, converting and consolidating hospital services and seeking to find ways to assess whether professional procedures prescribed were in fact necessary. It is hoped that such restrictions on supply may not imply a lower level of medical services if combined with "physician extenders," or other manpower substitution arrangements.

(a) If the United States were to adopt a plan substantially the same as Canada's, there is no significant reason to expect that United States experience would be different in this respect.

(b) If it were desired to avoid this result, different features would have to be included in the United States plan.

Administration and operation

Though some informed persons have contended that a national health insurance program, with public administration, can provide a powerful administrative mechanism for controlling costs and improving the economy of the health care system, the Canadian experience cannot be cited as an illustration. But it is also true that it cannot be shown that the introduction of national health insurance in Canada has been a major cause for the sharp increase it has experienced in unit medical costs.

21. A key factor in the successful establishment and deployment of the Canadian national health insurance system was the strength, depth and continuity of trained civil service agencies and personnel in place at the federal and provincial levels of Canadian government. If such personnel had not been available or readily developable, there would have been major difficulties installing and operating the system.

(a) If the United States were to adopt a plan substantially the same as Canada's, there is no significant reason to expect that United States experience would be different in this respect. Since the United States does not have the same depth in the health care component of its civil service at federal, state, and local levels, the United States could expect a less satisfactory experience in this respect than Canada if it adopted substantially the same plan.*

(b) To meet this aspect of the problem, different features would have to be included in the United States plan.

22. A major factor in the smoothness with which publicly administered health insurance was introduced into the Canadian provinces was the development of a basic area of understanding between governmental units at all levels and the physicians and institutional health care providers affected by the insurance plan. Where such a joint understanding was lacking, there were traumatic disturbances, including at least one physicians' strike.

(a) If the United States were to adopt a plan substantially the same as Canada's, there is no significant reason to expect that United States experience would be different in this respect; matters would go well if such a joint understanding were present, and badly if there were not.

23. In Canada it has proved administratively possible to carry out a universal health insurance program that relies on separately defined roles for central government, for provincial and other levels of government and for a variety of different providers of health care, including for-profit and not-for-profit persons and organizations.

(a) If the United States were to adopt a plan substantially the same as Canada's, there is no significant reason to expect that United States experience would be different in this respect.

---

*Messrs. Caper and Glasser believe that experience with Medicare, Medicaid and other governmental health programs have equipped the health component of the Social Security Administration and state health authorities to administer effectively a plan like Canada's, and, if there is any implication to the contrary in Paragraph 21(a), dissent therefrom.

24. From its initiation, the Canadian national health care system has been decentralized to the provincial level, but still further decentralization has been found necessary to permit a larger portion of the planning and administration of health services to be brought closer to the level of those affected, to reconcile competing interests in the allocation of resources, and to provide the opportunity for participation of the public and providers in the establishment of policies and priorities.

(a) If the United States were to adopt a plan substantially the same as Canada's, there is no significant reason to expect that United States experience would be different in this respect.

25. The Canadian national health insurance system has demonstrated its capacity to generate large amounts of uniformly reported information which can be compiled into a data base on medical care problems previously unavailable. For want of advance planning and provision, however, these data are not in a form that is relevant to managerial decision-making and to assessment of the efficiency of health care operations.

(a) If the United States were to adopt a plan substantially the same as Canada's, there is no significant reason to expect that United States experience would be different in this respect.

(b) If it were desired to avoid this result, different features would have to be included in the United States plan. Advanced steps in this direction have recently been taken in the United States.

26. The Canadian national health insurance system developed no substantial experience with the use of nonprofit or for-profit private insurance carriers since, with few and brief exceptions, the Canadians decided against the use of such carriers as a part of their national insurance system.

General Comments

27. There appears to be substantial unanimity today in Canada as to the necessity and desirability of national health insurance.

28. The Canadian national health insurance system has not been, and was not originally contemplated to be, a panacea. Apart from problems of efficiency and expenditure control, the system has either left substantially unsolved, or led to the creation of, at least the following problems relating to medical care:

- Geographic maldistribution of medical resources continues;

- Over-specialization and imbalance in physicians' training and practice continue;

- Pressures have arisen to increase coverage of health insurance plans beyond physicians' services so as to include, for example, reimbursements for dental care, as well as other less established areas of care such as chiropractics and acupuncture;
- Institution of the national insurance plans has tended to solidify the existing medical care system and fee-for-service payment. There is no longer any pecuniary incentive for anyone to develop community health centers (HMOs), or for patients to use them;
- With public expectations raised by the creation of the national health system in Canada, patients continue to demand more personalized service.

A closing comment: medical care vs. health

The Symposium reported here was addressed to the medical care systems of Canada and the United States. But no medical care system, however financed or administered, can achieve health. The fundamental problems of health result not from lack of curative services and facilities but from social, biological, environmental and life style factors. Many of the major causes of illness, death and suffering are preventable or deferrable, but they call for environmental, cultural and behavioral changes that lie largely outside the present medical care systems of both countries. Yet both Canada, with a national health insurance plan, and the United States, with no such plan, devote over 90 percent of their health expenditures to efforts to cure illness and less than 10 percent to the prevention of illness and the maintenance of health. That allocation of attention and resources is palpably unsound.

This vital point has been given recent recognition in the working paper, *A New Perspective on the Health of Canadians,* published in 1974 by the Canadian Ministry of National Health and Welfare.

VI APPENDIX

THE SUN VALLEY FORUM ON NATIONAL HEALTH, INC.

The Sun Valley Forum on National Health is a nonprofit educational organization incorporated in 1970 under the laws of Idaho. The purpose of the Forum is to work toward the improvement of the health of Americans and of the health care delivery system. The Forum seeks this objective through educational activities–the sponsorship of symposia, conferences and lectures and the preparation and publication of books, papers and reports. Governed by a board of directors of medical professionals and lay leaders, the Forum endeavors to carry out its programs at the highest possible level of quality and excellence.

Activities of the Forum center in Sun Valley, a facility well suited and equipped for sustained serious discussion. The Forum's symposia bring together leaders and experts to meet, to share ideas, and to review expert papers on aspects of the nation's health problems. Symposium participants include professionals in all health related fields as well as other persons associated with or interested in health affairs, such as representatives of consumers, businessmen, public officials and educators.

Since its founding in 1970 the Forum has held four such symposia. These were major undertakings, each lasting six days, involving about 30 participants, concentrating on a group of specially commissioned working papers, and each producing a final report of the symposium.

Activities of the Sun Valley Forum on National Health are supported by grants from individuals, corporations, foundations and the Department of Health, Education and Welfare's National Center for Health Services Research and Development.

The views presented in this book are those of the authors and symposium participants and not necessarily those of the officers, directors, or staff members of The Sun Valley Forum on National Health, Inc.

FORUM BOARD OF DIRECTORS

Franklin D. Murphy, M.D.
Chairman of the Board and Chief Executive Officer, Times-Mirror Company; former Chancellor, University of California at Los Angeles

Gerard Piel
President and Publisher, *Scientific American*

Charles L. Schultze
Senior Fellow, The Brookings Institution; former Director, U.S. Bureau of the Budget

Mitchell Spellman, M.D.
Dean, Charles R. Drew Postgraduate Medical School

Robert G. Lindee (Executive Director)
Vice-President, The Henry J. Kaiser Family Foundation, Palo Alto, California

David B. Lincoln (Secretary)
Elam, Burke, Jeppesen, Evans and Boyd, Sun Valley, Idaho

James E. Phelps (Treasurer)
Senior Vice-President, First Security Bank of Idaho, Boise, Idaho

Carl P. Burke (General Counsel)
Boise, Idaho

Mrs. Judy Spates Housel (Assistant Secretary)
Sun Valley, Idaho

INDEX